The
Aquarium
Fish
Handbook

The Aquarium Fish Handbook

The complete reference
from anemonefish to
zamora woodcats

Dick Mills and Derek Lambert

CHARTWELL
BOOKS

A QUARTO BOOK

This edition published in 2014 by
CHARTWELL BOOKS
an imprint of Book Sales
a division of Quarto Publishing Group USA Inc.
276 Fifth Avenue Suite 206
New York, New York 10001
USA

Copyright © 2004 Quarto Inc.

ISBN 978-0-7858-3179-2

QUAR.FBB

Conceived, designed, and produced by
Quarto Publishing plc
The Old Brewery
6 Blundell Street
London N7 9BH

Project Editor: **Kate Tuckett**
Senior Art Editor: **Penny Cobb**
Designer: **Paul Griffin**
Photographer: **Paul Forrester, Colin Bowling**
Copy Editor: **Anne Plume**
Proofreader: **Sue Viccars**
Indexer: **Pamela Ellis**

Art Director: **Moira Clinch**
Publisher: **Piers Spence**

Manufactured by Universal Graphic, Singapore
Printed by Midas Printing International Ltd, China

9 8 7 6 5 4 3 2 1

Contents

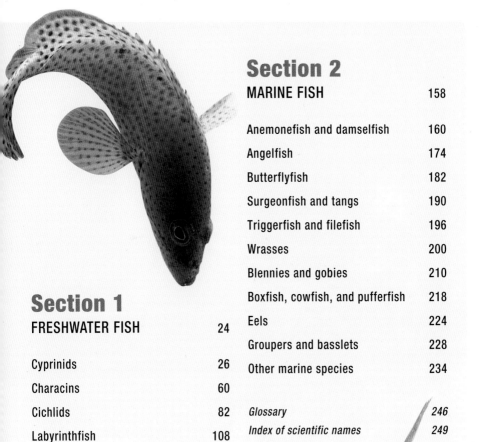

Introduction

Fishkeeping is an incredible opportunity to enter an entirely different world. One can keep fish from almost any area of the globe—from jungle streams to coral reefs, from those that have been cultivated by man for thousands of years to the latest "discovery." Because fish are from an environment quite different to our own, the risk of them causing any disruption to the human way of life is minimal. They will bring a host of benefits into the household—vivid colors,

Black-tailed humbug, see page 170.

soothing scenes—and most species need only a small amount of regular care. The total time spent on maintaining the aquarium and caring for the fish is far less than the time you will spend gazing at it for enjoyment. With today's reliable and readily available equipment there is no need to fear the technical complexities. The variety of fish available to the aquarist is also larger than ever before. This supply tends to arrive at the dealer's outlet in good condition, as modern air transport systems make the journey quicker, and

Spotted climbing perch, see page 110.

dealers understand more about how to avoid stressing the fish during transit. Conservationists want to ensure that fish species do not become extinct in the wild, and for this reason some species may cease to be available until methods for rearing them on a commercial scale are developed. Aquarists should be patient, support fish conservation efforts, and focus their attention upon the hundreds of species already being bred. Keeping an aquarium is a rewarding hobby. You will learn how fish live and feed, how they react to each other, and how they reproduce. You could be the person to unlock the secret of a species that has proved impossible to breed in captivity and thereby help save it from extinction.

Spotted prawn goby, see page 214.

A well-designed aquarium will provide an environment in which your fish will feel safe and at ease.

Fish Physiology

Throughout this work, continual reference has been made to the visual attraction of fish in all their shapes, sizes, and colors. While all these collectively may be of fascinating interest to us, to the fish they have a much more important purpose, for each, in its turn, provides the fish with its way of existence. With aquarium fish there are physiological factors that are necessarily different to those found in terrestrial animals. The most important differences allow the fish to breathe, control its bodily fluid levels, and maintain its position; other abilities such as coloration for species identification, camouflage, or defense ploys may also be found in terrestrial animals.

Gills and other Oxygen-extracting Organs

Fish require oxygen, and to get it into their bloodstream they must extract it from its dissolved state in the surrounding water. Water is drawn in through the mouth and passed over a set of gill membranes, before being expelled past the gill cover (operculum) at the sides of the head. As the passing water comes into contact with the gill membranes, oxygen is transfused into the tiny blood vessels and is then conducted around the fish's body by the heart.

Where natural waters are likely to be oxygen-deficient, the fish native to that habitat have developed an auxiliary breathing organ. This consists of a labyrinth-like construction of tissue, located just behind the gills, in which atmospheric air can be stored and oxygen extracted from it.

Osmotic Regulation

Wherever two fluids of differing strengths are separated by a membrane there is an automatic tendency for the water from the weaker fluid to pass through the membrane to dilute the stronger. In a fish, this can be quite a problem. For example, in a freshwater species the internal body fluids are stronger than the water surrounding the fish; water then passes through the fish's skin (the membrane) and would cause the fish's body to

The freshwater Siamese fighter must excrete copious amounts of water that continuously pass into its body. The marine clownfish replaces lost water by literally "drinking like a fish."

swell up. To counteract this, the freshwater fish has to excrete as much water as possible. For marine fish, the problem is reversed with water constantly being lost from the fish's body into the surrounding water. In order to maintain correct body fluid levels, the marine fish has to literally "drink like a fish," excreting little water but ensuring it does excrete salts.

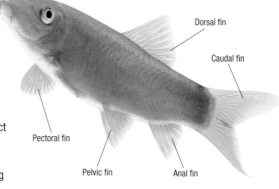

Dorsal fin

Caudal fin

Pectoral fin

Pelvic fin

Anal fin

Fins

Usually there are seven fins on a fish (some may have eight, others only five)—the dorsal, anal, caudal, pectoral, and pelvic fins. Some fins are singular and are arranged in the vertical plane, while other fins are paired, allowing for more flexible movement. Two of the single fins, the dorsal and anal, help to stabilize the fish from rolling from side to side. The third, the caudal fin, is generally used to supply propulsion, although some marine species, such as triggerfish and seahorses, use their dorsal fins instead.

The paired fins can be used for abrupt changes of movement and direction, acting as brakes or hydroplanes. The pelvic fins may be developed into bony processes, as in freshwater angelfish for example, or long filaments equipped with taste cells, as in gouramies. There are examples of fish whose fins do not comply with these general rules. For example catfish have an extra fin behind the dorsal fin, rainbowfish have two distinct dorsal fins, and triggerfish have no pelvic fins.

Body

The body shape of any fish provides an indication of the lifestyle it leads. Slender, torpedo-shaped bodies with crescent-shaped caudal fins are just right for speedy swimming, either in short sharp dashes or for more prolonged periods. A disc shape, usually compressed laterally, makes it easy for the fish to slip in among aquatic plant stems or reed beds; because of the larger surface area presented to the water by their bodies, these fish are generally found in slow-moving or stationary waters. Vertically compressed fish such as marine rays are naturally best suited to the bottom area where their body color patterns blend into the substrate.

Scales

Fish rely on their skin covering to help them effortlessly slip through the water. Scales are thin bone-like plates that cover the skin of most fish and are laid in an overlapping fashion from the snout to the tail. There are two main types of scales—ctenoid, which have tiny teeth along their rear edge, and cycloid, which are smooth-edged. The

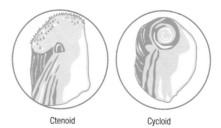

Ctenoid

Cycloid

purpose of scales is twofold; they give the body a very smooth exterior and they also protect the vital internal organs from physical damage and deter parasites from burrowing into the skin.

Senses

Like human beings, fish have the five senses of sight, hearing, taste, touch, and smell, although their senses of taste and smell are far superior to ours. Because of their permanent immersion in water, fish do not need eyelids to protect their eyes.

Generally, nocturnal species have larger eyes (for efficient light-gathering) than daytime-active species. Although sight is important, it is of little use where the water is dark and muddy, so the fish has to use other methods for both

The reef squirrelfish has large eyes, which are an advantage in its nocturnal quest for food.

navigation and location of food. The blind cave fish (*Astyanax sp.*) is a prime example. Over the years, living in underground caves, the fish has lost the use of—or rather, the need for—eyes and these have become atrophied, the fish navigating its way around the water and finding food by other means.

Taste buds are often found at the ends of pelvic fins or in pits over the body (especially the head) and in the barbels surrounding the mouth. Unlike human beings, in fish the nostrils are exclusively used for smelling and

play no part in the breathing process.

Because water is such a dense medium, the tiniest vibration is rapidly transmitted and herein lies the secret of how fish navigate safely and accurately. Along the flanks of the fish you may be able to see a line of pierced scales. These openings are the outer end of a nervous system that receives and translates vibrations and changes in water.

It may be difficult to assess exactly how a fish hears as, strictly speaking, the perception of sound is basically translating received vibrations. While some fish perceive sound through a set of bones connected to the swim bladder, it is also likely that the fish "hears" via the lateral line system too.

Color

The color of a fish serves several purposes—species recognition, camouflage as a means of defense, and as a warning deterrent. The typical "metallic" luster of a fish is created by deposits of guanin, a waste product, immediately beneath the scales. Depending upon the angle at which these scales are laid down, different reflected colors can be seen.

The stonefish relies on camouflage to hide its presence.

The pufferfish inflates to almost twice its normal body size to deter predators.

Defense

One popular defense that many fish have at their disposal is an arsenal of prickly spines. Triggerfish use these spines to lock themselves into a small crevice to prevent capture. Some marine species have other methods of defense—pufferfish inflate their bodies, lionfish have venom in the hollow spines of their fins, and stingrays have large, sharp dorsal spines.

Color patterns are another widely used means of defense. Any number of cryptic patterns will disguise the fish's true body shape. Many fish are "over-colored" to advertise that their flesh is poisonous. False "eyes" are positioned at the wrong end of the body to draw attention away from the real vital organ.

Reproduction

Fish reproduction in the aquarium comprises two distinct methods—egglaying and livebearing. In either case an egg is fertilized by male sperm, but it is how this happens that categorizes fish reproduction for the hobbyist.

• **Egg Scattering:** Eggs are expelled into the water by the female and fertilized by the male's milt (sperm), which is released into the water at around the same time. The fertilized eggs then hang in plants or are swept away by water currents to hatch, being totally disregarded by the parents.

• **Egg Depositing:** Some marine species deposit eggs in protective "egg cases," which become attached to submerged obstacles by tendrils. Others are caregivers, much like the freshwater cichlids.

• **Nesting:** In some freshwater anabantids, the male fish creates a bubble nest, made of saliva bubbles or plant material. This nest floats on the water's surface and the male coaxes a female beneath the nest into which the fertilized eggs are placed following a spawning embrace.

• **Mouthbrooding:** After the eggs are fertilized, one partner takes the whole batch of eggs into its throat cavity to hatch. After the fry leave the parent's throat they may continue to treat it as a safe haven. Mouthbrooding is found in freshwater cichlids, anabantoids, and in marine groups such as jawfish and cardinalfish.

• **Livebearing:** Livebearing female fish have their eggs fertilized internally. This is achieved in different ways depending on the species or family, although most use some sort of fin modification in the male to achieve this. It may only be a case of the anal fin developing a notch in it when he becomes sexually mature. Some of the rays will then form a channel down which sperm can move into the female.

Fry may or may not be passed nutrition from their mother during development. Guppies don't feed their babies during development but platies and swordtails do. Gestation takes from about 30 days in poecillids up to twelve weeks in stingrays.

Basic Aquarium Needs

No matter where fish come from—fresh- or saltwater, tropical or temperate climates—they all have the same basic need for space, suitable water conditions, warmth, lighting, decoration, feeding, and maintenance.

Space

Fish need living space. Depending upon the species, this may mean room to swim in a constantly active manner, an area in which to stake out a territory, or simply room to get away from other fish.

A rough guide as to how many fish any aquarium will hold is to allocate a set water surface area to a set "length" of fish (don't include the caudal fin in this measurement). Below are some useful guidelines:

CALCULATING THE NUMBER OF FISH YOUR AQUARIUM WILL HOLD

TROPICAL FRESHWATER
1 in (2.5cm) body length of fish per 12 sq. in (75sq. cm) of water surface.

COLDWATER FRESHWATER
1 in (2.5cm) body length of fish per 30 sq. in (190sq. cm) of water surface.

TROPICAL MARINE
1 in (2.5cm) body length of fish per 48 sq. in (300sq. cm) of water surface.

Taking a "standard" size aquarium, 36 x 12 in (90 x 30cm), which offers a water surface area of 432 sq. in (2,700sq. cm), the following total "body length" of fish can be kept:

TROPICAL MARINE	COLDWATER	TROPICAL FRESHWATER
$\frac{432}{12}$ = 36 in (90cm) of fish	$\frac{432}{50}$ = 14 in (36cm) of fish	$\frac{432}{48}$ = 9 in (22.5cm) of fish

Water Conditions

All species should be given excellent and well-maintained water conditions. Generally, freshwater fish, whether tropical or coldwater, can be maintained in correctly treated municipal tap water but will do best, especially when breeding is attempted, when given those water conditions that approximate to their place of origination—this may be conditions in the wild or those at their commercial hatching station.

Obviously, marine fish will need to be kept in saltwater. While some fishkeepers may be lucky enough to live near to the sea (and can guarantee a source of clean sea water), most hobbyists keep their marine species in synthetic salt water made up from commercially available "salt mixes." The degree of "saltiness" is monitored by checking the specific gravity (S.G.) of the aquarium water. It should be maintained at the correct level and water of the same S.G. used to "top up" the aquarium after water changes. "Topping up" evaporation losses is done using "fresh" water, as no salts will have been lost, and adding more saltwater will upset the S.G.

The problem with keeping fish in static water is that it is not exposed to the self-cleaning procedures, as in a river or the sea, and even in these natural areas the fish has the ability to swim away to cleaner areas. The main problem is ammonia-based compounds that build up in the water as a result of the fish's excretions, and the decay of food and plant debris. However, an efficient filtration system, which should embody mechanical (straining out visible suspended matter), chemical (absorbing organics from the water), and biological (converting ammonia-based compounds into less harmful nitrate) functions, will ensure water deterioration is kept to a minimum.

INSTALLING A BIOLOGICAL FILTER
Once the base plate of the biological filter is fitted into the base tank, attach an uplift tube to the base plate.

A good depth of substrate (at least 2 in [5cm]) provides a home for nitrifying bacteria.

When breeding is to be attempted, the question of water quality is often of prime importance and sometimes changes have to be made to trigger spawning activity. Fish may have to be subjected to temperature changes (up or down, depending on the species) or more specific water conditions may have to be created. This requires measurement of the water's acidity or alkalinity (pH), and its softness or hardness. All necessary adjustments, especially to temperature and pH, must be made gradually, over a period of time and in small increments.

Heating

Both freshwater and marine tropical species will require the water to be maintained at a steady temperature, usually around 75°F (24°C). Heating is not necessary in coldwater fishkeeping except in special circumstances— for instance, to increase the rate of growth in young goldfish or, with garden ponds, to maintain an opening in any ice that would otherwise cover the pond.

Heating the aquarium is achieved by using submersible, thermostatically controlled heating elements. Also available are microchip controlled devices that provide audible and visual alarms should the set temperatures be exceeded and that can keep a log of maximum and minimum temperatures.

The size of the aquarium heater should be chosen to suit the size of the aquarium. Roughly 10 watts of electricity per 1.3 gallons (5 liters) of water should be adequate for an aquarium in the average living room. In large aquariums (over $35\frac{1}{2}$ in/90cm in

External liquid crystal thermometers provide at-a-glance monitoring.

length) the wattage required can be shared between two heating units, one placed at either end of the aquarium, to ensure an even distribution of heat. Using an oversize heater in a small aquarium means that it will operate in frequent short bursts, but the real danger is of rapidly overheating the aquarium should the thermostat fall into the permanently "on" position.

Lighting

Light enables freshwater aquatic plants to photosynthesize, and in the process to remove carbon dioxide from the water and add a little surplus oxygen. Algae fulfill the same role in marine systems. Also, many corals have symbiotic algae living within them that also require light.

The tropical "day" is typically around 12 hours of daylight and most aquariums function well when provided with between 12 and 14 hours of light. You may need to experiment with the strength of the light (as opposed to the time period) in order to produce luxuriant plant growth. Doubling the amount of light (achieved either by fitting another lamp or an additional reflector to the existing lamp) will improve matters but you must ensure that you

Mount heating units clear of the substrate to allow good water circulation.

then have enough plants to make use of the extra light energy.

It is the norm for fluorescent lamps to be used for aquarium lighting. These give an even light and operate at a cooler temperature than tungsten lamps, which have a shortened life in the enclosed space of the aquarium hood. There are several types of fluorescent lamps available to provide the exact "hue" of lighting required.

If an aquarium has a water depth greater than the usual 15 to $17\frac{1}{2}$ in (38 to 45cm), the use of pendant metal halide or mercury vapor lamps may be preferred. In this instance, the regular aquarium hood has to be dispensed with and the lamp fitting hung immediately above the water's surface.

Shelter and Decoration

Despite the fact that we want to be able to see our fish clearly, a bare aquarium is not a particularly aesthetic sight and the fish will not display their true colors or feel at ease within it. Generally, freshwater aquariums are furnished with a layer of substrate material in which aquatic plants can root. (The substrate can also function as a biological filter if so

Powder blue surgeon, see page 193.

desired.) The presence of plants serves several purposes in the aquarium—as decoration, as natural water cleansers, as shelter, as spawning sites for the fish, and, in some cases, as food.

Marine aquariums can be decorated with the skeletons of dead corals or with living rock and living corals, too. The choice of fish may have to be modified to exclude species that would prey on live invertebrates in this instance.

Many species of fish appreciate the opportunity to "get away from it all." Rocky retreats form an important part of their needs. Make sure that all rock work is firmly anchored and that it does not form a trap behind which a fish could become imprisoned. It is best to use rocks that are impervious and that will not dissolve so that the water quality is not affected.

Plants

Sand and gravel

Feeding

All fish require food, but not all fish eat the same foods or feed in the same way. Most tropical freshwater fish are omnivores, although there are some that are more herbivorous. Coldwater freshwater fish are also omnivores. Tropical marine fish can be more selective in their eating habits, some preferring algae and green materials, others preying on smaller fish and invertebrates.

By looking at the position of the mouth, a fish's method of feeding becomes clear: an upward tilting mouth indicates a fish that takes its food from the water's surface; a

Flakes   Ant eggs

terminally-situated mouth at the tip of the snout on a horizontal line through the center of the body usually belongs to a mid-water swimmer that catches its food as it falls through the water. A downturned mouth, accompanied by a flat-bottomed profile, often has barbels (fleshy "whiskers") associated with it: this is an ideal arrangement for locating and collecting food from the riverbed and shows that it is a bottom-dwelling species. Many species of bottom-dwelling fish may be nocturnal by nature and require feeding at night.

Foods can come in various forms—flake, pellet, granular, tablet, powder, or liquid—and made in different formulae according to a fish's natural preferences and age.

Naturally, fish in the wild do not receive the same diet but catch their own foods, much of which is available in freeze-dried or frozen forms. Some live foods can be cultured or collected by the hobbyist and fed to aquarium fish. The occupants of the rain-barrel—mosquito, midge, and gnat larvae—are all relished by aquarium fish. Garden worms may be collected and other types—whiteworm, grindalworm, microworm, etc.—may be cultured for feeding to young fry.

Waterborne crustacea such as Daphnia and Cyclops can provide extra food for fish, but there is a risk that if these are collected

The position of a fish's mouth is often the best indicator of its feeding habits.

from the wild they may introduce disease into the aquarium. There is a similar risk with Tubifex worms, which come from polluted muddy riverbanks. As frozen or freeze-dried forms of these foods are available, it is not worth risking the health of your fish to use suspect "live" forms.

Overfeeding kills more fish than anything else: not from producing overweight fish but from polluting the water with uneaten food. It is best to feed "little and often," making sure that the fish eat what is given within a few minutes at most.

Copperband butterflyfish, see page 188.

Maintenance

One of the attractions of fishkeeping is that it can be considered a "low maintenance" interest.

A daily check would obviously include a "fish count"—do this at feeding times when all the fish should gather together. Investigate any missing fish; however, bear in mind that nocturnal species usually hide away during "tank light." Once the aquarium is established there is no need to check water temperatures—an occasional touch on the glass with the hand is usually enough to confirm that everything is fine.

Bicolor chromis, see page 167.

Weekly tasks may involve siphoning off any accumulated mulm or detritus that has collected on the substrate. If an undergravel biological filter is used, an occasional raking over of the substrate (and the use of a gravel washer) will ensure that the oxygenating water flow through the substrate is unimpeded. Remove algae from the front glass but leave any growth on the side and rear walls of the aquarium for the benefit of any herbivores. Prune back any excessive plant growth and use by re-rooting any cuttings to provide new plants. Keep cover glasses scrupulously clean so that all the available light energy reaches the aquarium.

Regular partial water changes, coupled with filtration, keep the levels of dissolved (possibly toxic) material to a minimum. When siphoning out the desired proportion of old aquarium water, take it from the substrate level to remove detritus at the same time. For marine aquariums, it is best to prepare replacement synthetic saltwater ahead of water changes.

Availability and Choice

The next time you are kept waiting for a flight at an overcrowded airport, think about the fact that at any one time there are probably more fish flying around the skies than people, such is the volume of trade. It follows, therefore, that there is an enormous selection available at your local dealers, just waiting for you to choose from. The basic guidelines are that fish should be chosen for their compatibility to each other, their foods, and the aquarium set-up.

Cuban hogfish, see page 202.

Size

It should be fairly obvious, for economic reasons, that all imported fish (of whatever species) destined for the aquarium will be juveniles—you get more to a transportation box that way. However, it might not be so obvious to the beginner that fish, depending upon the species, grow at different rates. So, from a selection of young specimens that are all the same size, in a few months time there could be an enormous variation. When selecting a fish, always try to find out its adult size or the size that it is likely to attain under captive conditions.

Compatibility

The largest and fastest-developing fish from a group of mixed juvenile specimens could become aggressive and look upon some of the remainder as potential food. Work on the principle that big fish always eat little ones. The sheer bulk of a large fish can upset smaller fish; for example, the larger fish will get to the food first and eat most of it. Small fish may also be intimidated about showing themselves when there is a large, dominant species in the tank. Sometimes it's not just size but natural instinct that turns a fish into a social liability. It is not always confined to specific fish; some fish, particularly some varieties of marines, simply cannot tolerate another fish that might have the same body shape or coloration as their own. Part of the problem has to be lack of "space" in captivity when compared to the areas that the same fish would enjoy in nature.

You will learn how the physical features of the fish, particularly the position of the mouth, dictate at what water depths the fish normally swims, i.e.,

Suckermouth catfish, see page 129.

where food is most plentiful. Use this information to select a cross section of fish from the three strata of water levels—top, middle, and bottom—so that your aquarium represents the whole underwater scene.

Choosing your Fish
Always buy carefully and, if possible, do some research on your intended purchases beforehand. Reject any fish you cannot care for in terms of space or food; never buy a fish that is showing signs of stress (folded down fins is a good guide in freshwater fish), or that has spots, pimples, cuts, sores, wounds, split (or missing) fins, is bloated or too thin, cannot swim effortlessly, or maintain its position in the water. With marine fish it is also prudent to ask to see the fish feeding.

Never buy fish the first time you see them in a dealer's tanks. Buying the newest arrival may keep you ahead of your fishkeeping friends but it is better to wait until the dealer has quarantined the fish and it has settled down first; after all, it may suddenly show signs of disease or exhibit some anti-social behavior in the first few days in your care.

Try to shop at a local dealer. He will most certainly be keeping fish in the same water conditions as you are, and should know all the pitfalls about doing so. Buying fish from suppliers outside your locale is a bit of a gamble unless you know about the water conditions. By regularly using a local dealer, he will get to know your previous purchases and be in a better position to advise you.

Graceful black angelfish and pearl gourami are displayed to good effect against a stunning blue backdrop.

Health Problems

The last thing any would-be fishkeeper wants to think about is health risks to the fish but, unfortunately, fish are susceptible to outbreaks.

Preventing Disease

The first defense is to obtain healthy fish and then try to keep them that way. Never buy fish from a dealer's tank in which other fish are obviously sick, dying, or dead. If you can, quarantine new stock for two to three weeks before adding them to your collection.

The second defense is to know your fish and what constitutes their normal behavior. There is always a reason for unnatural behavior and these signs are the earliest warning you will get. If you do spot any irregularities check up on the fish's environment first. If you've been lazy about water changes, overfed the fish, or neglected the aquarium, correct these things first. There is an adage that states, "Look after the water and the fish will look after themselves."

Recognizing Disease

It is not always easy to diagnose diseases correctly, particularly where the problem may be internal with few external, visible symptoms. In these cases, once symptoms do become visible it may be too late to treat.

Sometimes the disease may be a secondary effect with the real reason for the problem hard to find or unsuspected. Usually the more common ailments seen on the fish can be treated successfully, with only a few requiring expert attention or the use of antibiotics. However, the first step is to recognize the symptoms of the disease.

Visible spots, an increased breathing rate, and "flicking" against firm objects in the aquarium are all signs of a parasitic attack. Viruses are harder to diagnose but may cause a bloated body, inability to swim or position properly, and white feces trailing from the vent. Most viral infections, particularly in marine fish, may be regarded as secondary infections which can often be traced back to poor aquarium conditions.

Diseases

• White Spot (*Ichthyophthiriasis*): This illness is easy to identify as the fish's body and fins are covered with tiny white spots. The responsible parasite has a three-part cyclic life cycle: living on the fish, encysting at the substrate, and free-swimming as it searches for a new host. It is only during its free-swimming phase that it can be treated. Treating the whole aquarium with a remedy is effective. The marine fish equivalent is called *Cryptocaryon*.

• Velvet: Similar to the symptoms of White Spot but with much smaller dots. The tiny spots give a dusty covering effect. Both freshwater and marine fish are affected and the parasites are similar species of *Oodinium* and *Amyloodimium*. Both respond to treatments available at aquatic dealers.

• Fungus (*Saprolegnia*): The body of the fish may break out into tufts of "cotton wool-like" growths. Remedies are effective.

• Mouth "Fungus": This usually only reacts favorably to antibiotics.

• Skin and Gill Flukes: Affected fish scratch themselves against rocks or the bottom substrate, as though to dislodge the parasite

Healthy cardinal and glowlight tetra shoal spectactularly in an established aquarium.

of skin flukes (*Gyrodactylus*); excess mucus may be produced. Fish with gill flukes (*Dactylogyrus*) have difficulty breathing and will hang at the water's surface, panting, with wide, inflamed gills. Remedies are effective but the fish should be removed to a hospital tank while their main home is disinfected.

• **Fin Rot:** The tissues between the fin rays degenerate. This ailment is not a disease in itself but often sets in as a secondary effect, when a fin gets torn or as a result of dirty aquarium water conditions. The real remedy (or prevention) is to maintain clean water conditions at all times.

• **Dropsy:** The scales stand out from the body due to an internal build up of fluid. There is no reliable cure and the fish is best euthanized.

• **Lymphocystis:** This is a seasonal ailment often striking when coldwater fish are emerging from winter conditions into spring. The cauliflower-like growths may look unpleasant but often fade away of their own

accord. A similar condition occurs in marine fish, and is thought to be caused by dietary deficiencies.

• **Tuberculosis:** The fish loses color and gradually gets thinner due to an internal ailment that is usually too advanced once the signs are visible. The victim is best euthanized.

• **Carcinoma:** A tumor whose accelerated growth impinges on the vital organs of a fish, causing deformity and, eventually, death.

Treating Disease

Usually, contagious diseases are best treated in the tank, with the whole population of the tank being treated. For freshwater collections (tropical and coldwater) this is usually unproblematic, but with marine fish you must only treat the fish. The reason for this is that many remedies are lethal to certain invertebrates. It is vital to use any remedy in strict accordance with the manufacturer's instructions. Dosing the aquarium correctly relies on how much water your aquarium holds, and your aeration and filtration system. Once the remedy has done its job, the water must be cleared of it. If the treatment does not appear to be working, return the water to normal conditions before trying a new remedy.

The use of antibiotics varies as regulations differ between countries. All are obtainable only through a veterinarian and can be administered by him or, where the antibiotic is contained within a fish food, by the fishkeeper.

Sometimes a single fish may be struck down, or maybe you spot the disease at its earliest appearance on one particular fish. Often with parasitic attacks, a short-term bath in saltwater (for freshwater species) and freshwater (for saltwater species) may effect a rapid cure, but always remove the fish from the bath as soon as it appears to become distressed.

How to use this book

A list of the species covered on the following spreads is given on the introductory spread to each section. A key to the symbols used to provide more details about each species can be found opposite, and in the back of this book there is a handy pull-out version that can be used while flicking through the directory. Within each aquarium group, the fish species are ordered alphabetically, first according to their biological family affiliation, then by species within each family.

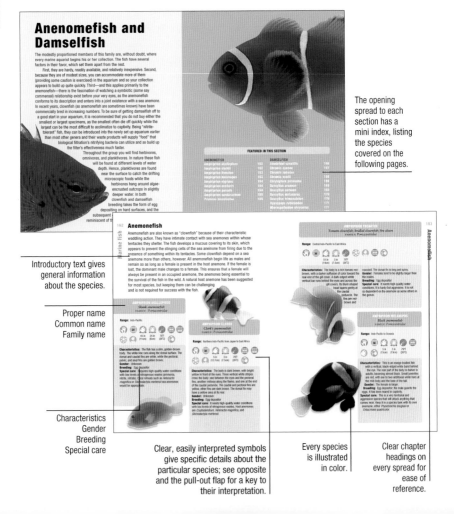

The opening spread to each section has a mini index, listing the species covered on the following pages.

Introductory text gives general information about the species.

Proper name
Common name
Family name

Characteristics
Gender
Breeding
Special care

Clear, easily interpreted symbols give specific details about the particular species; see opposite and the pull-out flap for a key to their interpretation.

Every species is illustrated in color.

Clear chapter headings on every spread for ease of reference.

Ease of keeping

1 to 10—1 = easiest

1 to **4**—the easiest species to care for.
5 to **8**—extra care needed—intermediate numbers indicate that the species requires special care (diet, water conditions, temperature adjustments, incompatibility etc.) beyond those required for normal community collections.
9 to **10**—most difficult—you should carefully consider your reasons for wanting to keep any species with this high rating. Some species cannot be easily acclimatized to aquarium life, and some may be endangered through over-collection.

Tank size

minimum volume

Can vary according to the size and particular habits of your fish. The minimum volume of water required is given in gallons/liters or it could just be cubic feet/meters.

Size

in the wild   in captivity

In the wild indicates adult size (in inches and centimeters) of species in nature.
In captivity indicates the size species may attain in captivity under ideal conditions, i.e., plenty of room, correct feeding, and optimum water conditions.

The sizes given are for mature fish, but for very sound commercial reasons, the majority of aquarium-suitable species are caught (and transported) as juveniles. Increasingly more and more species are being captive-bred, but are still marketed as juveniles. The size attained in captivity is dependent upon the fishkeeper's skills and, of course, the conditions under which the species are kept. Therefore, definite figures on size in captivity are not possible and the information provided is for guidance only, so that you can estimate the total number of species your aquarium may support.

Temperature

minimum to maximum

Indicates the optimum water temperature for your tank.

Strata

top   middle   bottom

Indicates the water level favored by each species.

Compatability

single   community   safe with   safe with
specimen   fish   small fish   invertebrates

Single specimen usually means only one representative of any such species within a community collection. Some fish won't tolerate a different species if it is of a similar shape or color.
Community fish may be kept in a mixed collection with due regard to any extremes of physical size between species being kept together.
Safe with small fish indicates large fish that are peaceful toward smaller tankmates.
Safe with invertebrates means that the fish isn't likely to eat the invertebrates. Note that keeping fish and invertebrates together presents an additional problem; the copper-based remedies used to treat fish diseases successfully are lethal to invertebrates.

Feeding

herbivore   omnivore   predator

Herbivore prefers mainly vegetable matter in diet.
Omnivore means all foods taken. Any preferences are noted in the text.
Predator means a carnivorous diet, which often includes other fish.

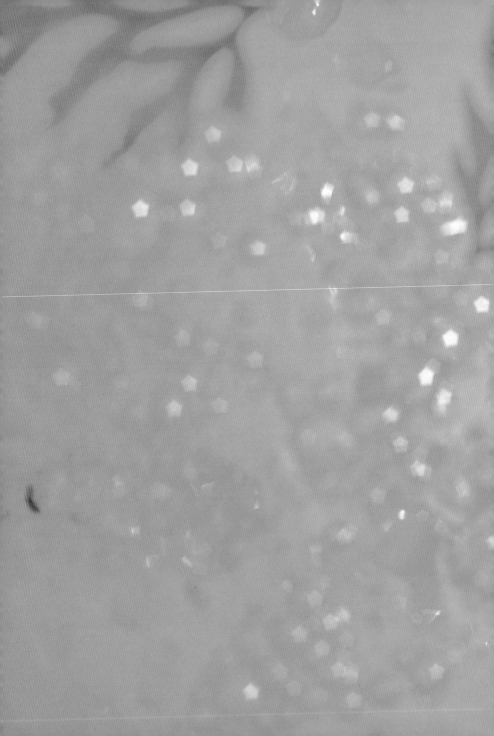

FRESHWATER FISH

While the major groups of popular freshwater aquarium fishes are represented, the experienced fishkeeper will be aware that some species are conspicuous by their absence, for example killifishes. They are spectacularly beautiful and have a most interesting method of breeding. Unfortunately, they are not available worldwide, their care is somewhat specialized, and the majority of aquatic dealers do not stock them. However, thanks to the growth of specialist societies, obtaining stocks is becoming easier. Monthly aquarium journals will be able to direct you to a source of these fish. It is for these reasons that killifish have been omitted. Another consideration is whether or not to encourage the keeping of endangered species; those whose "in-captivity" care is known to be problematical or species that have been "color-injected." Where such conflicts occur, information is provided.

Cyprinids

Fish within the Cyprinidae family make excellent aquarium subjects for three main reasons. First, there are over 1,500 species to choose from; second, they are very adaptable; and, third, they range in size from around 1 in (2.5cm) up to 1 ft (30cm), meaning that there is a family member to suit any fishkeeper.

Unlike some other fish species, cyprinids do not have teeth in their mouths, but this is balanced by the presence of pharyngeal teeth in the throat, which help grind up food as it passes to the stomach. Close examination of the arrangement of these teeth enables ichthyologists to identify, or distinguish between, the various species.

Within aquarium circles, three main tropical groups stand out in the family—barbs, danios, and rasboras. While cyprinids are members of the Cyprinidae family, this family is one of the larger order of Cypriniformes. Another family within this order is the Cobitidae family. This popular group of fish is commonly known as loaches. They are included in this chapter for ease of reference.

The popularity of cyprinids is not limited to tropical species. The family also boasts several genera that are classed as coldwater fish—in the context of this book this means those fish that do not require heated aquarium water. The favorite among coldwater cyprinids is, of course, the goldfish, *Carassius auratus*, together with its many varieties. Cyprinids are called "opportunistic spawners"—ripe adults come together to spawn using egg-scattering methods and for the most part do not exercise any parental care—although the spawning method of *Rasbora heteromorpha* differs from the norm as it deposits its eggs beneath plant leaves.

Cyprinids are generally easy to keep, being hardy, resistant to disease, and very accommodating in their housing and feeding needs. Apart from a varied diet, all they require is a clean, suitably furnished aquarium (usually with plants, although some species do have vegetarian tendencies). For breeding, it is normal practice to use a separate breeding aquarium, set up with spawn-saving precautions, as cyprinids have a taste for their own eggs.

FEATURED IN THIS SECTION

Barbs

The name "barb" is derived from the scientific name *barbus*, which is Latin for "bearded," a reference to the small barbels, or fleshy whiskers, often found around the mouth area. The popularity of barbs is quite justifiable as they offer the fishkeeper a range of fish suitable for all sizes of aquarium. Most barbs are deep-bodied, although there are some more sleekly built species found in related groups other than *barbus*. The majority of barbs suitable for the aquarium are modest in size. All are omnivorous, have a hardy constitution, and have a compatible disposition toward other tank inhabitants.

BARBUS ARULIUS
Arulius barb
FAMILY: *Cyprinidae*

Range: Southern India

| 1 | 36 | | | 5 in (12cm) | 4 in (10cm) | 70–77°F (21–25°C) | | | | |

Characteristics: This active shoaling fish has three ill-defined, vertical black bands that reach halfway down the flanks of its blue-gray body; the beginnings of a fourth band appears at the base of its dorsal fin. The top half of the body is green-yellow, accentuated by attractive iridescences.
Gender: The male has long extensions on its dorsal fin; these are not as pronounced in the female.
Breeding: This fish needs soft, acidic water to reproduce well in captivity. It will eat its own eggs after spawning is complete. Expect 100 fry from a single spawning.
Special care: The arulius barb is happy in a planted aquarium, where it may nibble soft-leaved plants. Smaller fish may not feel comfortable in its presence, due to its constant movement around the tank.

BARBUS CONCHONIUS
Rosy barb
FAMILY: *Cyprinidae*

Range: Southern India

6 in	3 in	70–77°F
(15cm)	(7.5cm)	(21–25°C)

Characteristics: This long-established favorite takes its popular name from the copper-red metallic sheen on the flanks of the male. In recent years, a new long-finned strain has been developed.

Gender: The dorsal, anal, and pelvic fins of the male are black; these markings are less pronounced on the female, and she can be further identified by a plumper body shape when viewed from above.

Breeding: This species is ideal for fishkeepers attempting aquarium breeding for the first time, as it is very prolific; however, precautions must be taken to prevent parents from eating the eggs.

Special care: It is most content in a well-planted tank with some top shading from floating plants.

BARBUS EUGRAMMUS
Zebra barb; striped barb
FAMILY: *Cyprinidae*

Range: Malaysia, Sumatra, and Borneo

6 in	4⅛ in	70–77°F
(15cm)	(10.5cm)	(21–25°C)

Characteristics: This is an active, fast-swimming fish. It has an elongated body with a high dorsal fin and a deep, boat-shaped belly. Its pale golden-yellow body is crossed horizontally by a number of even, dark stripes.

Gender: The male is identified from the female by its slimmer body with more pronounced stripes; the female is plumper and has a higher arched back.

Breeding: An easy egg-scatterer; it produces broods of several hundred.

Special care: A middle- and lower-level swimmer, the zebra barb is peaceful and coexists well with a community of fishes mixed in size. It is omnivorous, and will thrive in most types of water.

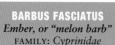

BARBUS FASCIATUS
Ember, or "melon barb"
FAMILY: *Cyprinidae*

Range: India, Malaysia, and Indonesia

6 in   4 in   70–77 °F
(15cm) (10cm) (21–25 °C)

Characteristics: This fish has an elongated body, and a pronounced convex curve to its ventral contour. The body color is pale golden brown, which shades down to silver or pink.
Gender: The male's dorsal fin is black with a red edge, while the pelvic fins are reddish, and the anal fin black. The female is much less intensely colored. When mature, male fish show an intense pink-red coloration, with the black bars becoming almost merged together by an overall dusting of black.
Breeding: Note that if trying to breed this species, precautions need to be taken against egg eating.
Special care: This is a peaceful fish, and is suitable for a community collection of fish of mixed size. It requires a well-planted aquarium, and will accept most types of water.

BARBUS FILAMENTOSUS
Filament barb; black-spot barb
FAMILY: *Cyprinidae*

Range: Southern India, Sri Lanka

6 in   6 in   70–77°F
(15cm) (15cm) (21–25°C)

Characteristics: This barb is fairly elongated in shape. The juvenile has three bars running down the yellowish-brown flanks, beginning at the front of the dorsal fin and ending at the caudal peduncle. The dorsal fin shows some red, and the caudal fin has a red patch in each fin lobe, together with a darker outer area and a white tip. When adult, the dark bars disappear (with the exception of a patch just above the anal fin) and the body deepens considerably, taking on a silvery greenish-yellow color.
Gender: The male's dorsal fin has filaments that extend from the first few rays; these are absent in the female.
Breeding: This fish is a prolific breeder, but care does need to be taken to prevent egg eating.
Special care: A hardy fish that can tolerate lower than normal aquarium temperatures.

BARBUS GELIUS
Gelius barb; golden dwarf barb
FAMILY: *Cyprinidae*

Range: India, Bengal

1   18

1½ in   1½ in   65–72°F
(4cm)   (4cm)   (18–22°C)

Characteristics: This fish has a high back and a deep belly, coupled with a slender caudal peduncle. The basic body color is golden brown on the upper parts, shading to silver below. The color is more intense when the fish is in good condition. A few irregular, smudged black patches appear on the body.
Gender: The female is paler in color, and plumper than the male.

Breeding: Egg scatterer; use only mature adults for breeding.
Special care: This species is an active, gregarious fish and should be kept in a small shoal. It makes an excellent subject for a species tank or a community of small fish.

BARBUS LATERISTRIGA
Spanner barb; "T" barb
FAMILY: *Cyprinidae*

Range: Thailand, Indonesia, and Malaysia

1   48

7 in   6¼ in   70–77°F
(18cm)   (16cm)   (21–25°C)

Characteristics: The body color is light golden brown, with silvery metallic iridescences. Two black vertical bars cross the body, with another black line running horizontally to connect them; this continues across the caudal peduncle into the central rays of the caudal fin. The top and bottom edges of the caudal fin are black, as are the leading areas of the dorsal and pelvic fins. With the onset of maturity, the body color deepens, and the dramatic patterning becomes obscured and less distinct.
Gender: The female is plumper.
Breeding: This fish is an egg scatterer, and care should be taken that the parents do not eat the eggs.
Special care: A hardy fish that can be kept with a community of fish of varying size.

BARBUS NIGROFASCIATUS
Black ruby barb; purple-headed barb
FAMILY: *Cyprinidae*

Range: Sri Lanka

2½ in   2½ in   70–77°F
(6.25cm) (6.25cm) (21–25°C)

Characteristics: A stocky fish with a basic body color of golden yellow with three vertical black bars. The scales have dark forward edges and silver rear edges. The dorsal, pelvic, anal, and caudal fins are cloudy black.

Gender: When in breeding condition, the male's body turns red, and the head becomes purple. The fins are jet black, and are held erect during proud displays to the female. The female can be further distinguished by her plumper body.

Breeding: An egg scatterer; each female will produce 50–70 eggs.

Special care: Although hardy, this fish is prone to white spot disease. It recovers easily after using readily available remedies.

BARBUS "ODESSA"
Odessa barb
FAMILY: *Cyprinidae*

Range: Asia

2½ in   2½ in   59–77°F
(6.25cm) (6.25cm) (15–25°C)

Characteristics: This fish has an elongated body, but its body depth falls between that of the deeper-bellied barbs and the slimmer species. Its body coloration is a pale greenish-brown, with clearly defined scales. It has two dark blotches on the flanks, one behind the gill cover, and the other ahead of the caudal peduncle.

Gender: The male develops a broad red band along the body and some dark speckling in the dorsal fin. The female is duller in coloration, with a plumper body.

Breeding: This fish breeds well in captivity, but the parents will eat the eggs.

Special care: Easy to manage; this fish is best kept in a well-planted community aquarium. It is tolerant of most types of water.

BARBUS OLIGOLEPIS
Checker barb
FAMILY: *Cyprinidae*

Range: Indonesia, Sumatra

2 in (5cm) 2 in (5cm) 70–77 °F (21–25 °C)

Characteristics: The common name of this golden yellow-brown fish derives from the checkerboard pattern of its scales: each one has a dark edge and a dark front area. The area beneath the dark line along the flanks is sometimes less checkered.

Gender: The fins are reddish-orange, with a more yellowish hue on the female, and edged with black on the male.

Breeding: An egg scatterer; the parents must be prevented from eating their eggs.

Special care: This fish looks best in a well-planted aquarium with open swimming spaces, where it will cruise the middle and lower levels in shoals. Although the males often display to each other, they are not violent.

BARBUS PENTAZONA
Five-banded barb
FAMILY: *Cyprinidae*

Range: Borneo, Malaysia, and Sumatra

2 in (5cm) 2 in (5cm) 70–77°F (21–25°C)

Characteristics: This fish has a more elongated shape than other vertically striped barbs. Its body color is a yellowy golden brown. Five dark bands cross the body, the first passing through the eye. The fins have a reddish tint at the base. There are two pairs of barbels at the mouth. A number of subspecies are known, with slight differences in color.

Gender: The female is plumper, and paler in color than the male.

Breeding: An egg scatterer that will eat its own eggs.

Special care: A middle- and lower-level swimmer, this fish mixes well with a community of different species. It likes plenty of lush plants for use as hiding places in the aquarium.

BARBUS SCHUBERTI
Schuberti barb
FAMILY: *Cyprinidae*

Range: China, Hong Kong, and Vietnam

1	36	N/a	3 in (7.5cm)	64–75°F (18–24°C)

Characteristics: An elongated, plump-sided fish with a yellow body color, dark green metallic areas around the top half of the body, and some dark speckles on the dorsal surface. Larger blotches run along the top lateral line, and a dark vertical blotch crosses the tip of the narrow caudal peduncle. The eyes are reddish, and the fins are red, streaked with yellow; the base of the caudal fin and the two lobes also have bright red areas.

Gender: The females are plumper than the males.

Breeding: This barb is a prolific breeder, and it is easy to breed them in captivity.

Special care: A middle- to lower-level swimmer; it is easily kept in a mixed community of fish.

BARBUS SCHWANENFELDI
Tinfoil barb
FAMILY: *Cyprinidae*

Range: Borneo, Sumatra, and Thailand

1	60	17¾ in (45cm)	12 in (30cm)	66–77°F (19–25°C)

Characteristics: The diamond-shaped body has a high dorsal profile and a moderately deep belly. The greenish-brown tinge of the dorsal surface shades down to silver flanks with well-defined scales. It has a small head with dark, gold-rimmed eyes. The triangular dorsal fin is black with a red base; the pelvic and anal fins are bright red-orange. The large, deeply forked caudal is red with black edges at the top and bottom.

Gender: The females are plumper than the males when mature.

Breeding: An egg scatterer producing thousands of eggs.

Special care: This barb prefers soft water and a spacious aquarium. It loves eating vegetation, so aquarium plants are not suitable. Although peaceful, this barb may be too active for smaller fish in its tank.

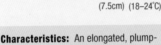

BARBUS SEMIFASCIOLATUS
Golden barb
FAMILY: *Cyprinidae*

Range: China, Hong Kong, and Vietnam

4
36

4 in   3 in   64–75°F
(10cm)   (7.5cm) (18–24°C)

Characteristics: Its overall yellowish hue contrasts with a subtle silvery sheen on the ventral surface. Some fish—especially juveniles—have dark vertical streaks distributed randomly, but these tend to fade with age. The golden barb's similarity to *B. schuberti* makes the two color morphs difficult to differentiate. Both these fish are probably man-made cultivars, with the wild fish being called green, or half-striped, barbs.
Gender: The female is plumper than the male.

Breeding: This is a prolific egg scatterer, and the adults will eat their eggs.
Special care: This fish is content in most types of water and with some plant cover.

BARBUS TETRAZONA
Tiger barb
FAMILY: *Cyprinidae*

Range: Sumatra, Indonesia, and Borneo

1
24

2¾ in   2½ in   70–77°F
(7cm)   (6.5cm)   (21–25°C)

Characteristics: The body of this fish is crossed by four vertical dark bands, suggesting tiger stripes: one band through the eyes, one on each side of the dorsal fin, and one at the extreme rear end of the caudal peduncle.
Gender: The snout of the male is bright red. The female is less intensely marked.
Breeding: Prolific egg scatterer
Special care: When kept with slower-moving, long-finned fish it will develop a tendency toward fin nipping. This can be avoided by keeping the barb in sufficient numbers so that it does not annoy other species.

BARBUS TETRAZONA
Red tiger barb
FAMILY: *Cyprinidae*

Range: Man-made cultivar

2¾ in (7cm) 2½ in (6.5cm) 70–77°F (21–25°C)

Characteristics: This barb has been developed using selective aquarium-breeding techniques; its body has a red hue, with very few of the original bands showing. Breeders have produced "albino" variants, where the dark vertical bands are replaced with white. However, in most cases the albino claim cannot be justified because the eyes remain pigmented.

Gender: The female is plumper.

Breeding: See *Barbus tetrazona* (p.35)

Special care: See *Barbus tetrazona* (p.35)

BARBUS TETRAZONA
Green tiger barb
FAMILY: *Cyprinidae*

Range: Man-made cultivar

2¾ in (7cm) 2½ in (6.5cm) 70–77°F (21–25°C)

Characteristics: An aquarium-developed strain of *B. tetrazona*, the green tiger barb is sometimes known as the "moss-banded barb." The coloring of the fins remains the same, but the overall coloring and pattern differ from fish to fish.

Gender: The female is distinguished by her plumper profile when she is in breeding condition.

Breeding: See *Barbus tetrazona* (p.35)

Special care: See *Barbus tetrazona* (p.35)

BARBUS TICTO
Ticto barb; two-spot barb; tic-tac-toe barb
FAMILY: *Cyprinidae*

Range: Sri Lanka, India

4 in (10cm) 3 in (7.5cm) 59–77°F (15–25°C)

Characteristics: The ticto barb has a pale silver-brown body with well-defined scales outlined by dark edges. Two small black patches appear on the flanks, one behind the gill cover and another at the front of the caudal peduncle. The upper part of the eyes is red; barbels are absent.
Gender: The male's red dorsal fin is flecked with black, and there is a reddish tinge to the pelvic fins; the other fins are colorless. The female's fins are paler in color, and she has a plumper body.

Breeding: A typical egg scatterer. Take care to prevent the parents from eating their eggs.
Special care: This fish prefers a water temperature that is slightly less than tropical.

BARBUS TITTEYA
Cherry barb
FAMILY: *Cyprinidae*

Range: Sri Lanka

3 in (7.5cm) 2 in (5cm) 73–78°F (23–26°C)

Characteristics: The body shape is slimmer than most barbs. In color the body is a reddish-brown, with a longitudinal band stretching from the snout to the end of the caudal peduncle; this may be repeated partially on the row of scales directly underneath. The fins match the body color.

Gender: In males the red is intensified, particularly when they are in breeding condition.
Breeding: A prolific egg scatterer. The fry are prone to velvet disease.
Special care: Due to its tendency toward shyness, the cherry barb is suitable for the smaller aquarium; it prefers being kept with fish of a similar size.

Danios and Minnows

The fish in this popular group have two things to offer the fishkeeper: active movement in the aquarium, and a willingness to breed. Their slim bodies, flattened dorsal surfaces, and slightly upturned mouths indicate that they inhabit the upper levels of the water. Like all cyprinids, they do have a tendency to eat their own eggs immediately after spawning. There are several methods of preventing this from happening in the aquarium. You can use physical barriers, such as a layer of marbles on the tank base, or a suspended netting cage that separates the parents from their eggs. Many danios can be spawned as a group, rather than just one pair at a time.

DANIO AEQUIPINNATUS
Giant danio
FAMILY: *Cyprinidae*

Range: Southwestern India, Sri Lanka

| 1 | 36 | | | | | | |

4 in
(10cm)

4 in
(10cm)

70–77°F
(21–25°C)

Characteristics: This really is the "big boy" of the group. Its pale blue body color is overlaid with an attractive selection of yellow lines and dots; the ventral area is a delicate shade of pink.
Gender: Females are rounder in the body; their yellow lines turn upward at the front of the caudal fin.
Breeding: An egg scatterer that will eat its own eggs after spawning has taken place.
Special care: A very active fish that needs plenty of swimming space. Keep in a shoal with other lively fish of a similar size.

DANIO ALBOLINEATUS
Pearl danio
FAMILY: *Cyprinidae*

Range: Burma, Thailand, and Sumatra

2¼ in (5.5cm)	2 in (5cm)	70–77°F (21–25°C)

Characteristics: The very active pearl danio has an elongated gray-green body with some iridescences. Under side-lighting, pearl danios have a beautiful pearl blue-violet hue, with a red-gold line running along the rear half of the body; the caudal peduncle is violet, and the gill cover shimmers metallic blue. Two pairs of barbels are present. The fins are mostly translucent green, but with a red tinge at the base.

Gender: The female can be distinguished by her deeper body.
Breeding: A typical egg scatterer
Special care: This fish prefers a long aquarium with plenty of swimming space, and a power filter to generate water movement. Pearl danios are excellent jumpers, so fit a secure lid.

DANIO KERRI
Blue danio
FAMILY: *Cyprinidae*

Range: The islands in the Bay of Bengal and western Thailand

2 in (5cm)	2 in (5cm)	73–77°F (23–25°C)

Characteristics: This fish usually appears an iridescent gray-blue, but turns to a lighter pastel-blue shade when spawning and when placed in sidelit conditions. It is distinguished by two gold lines that run back from the gold-rimmed eyes all the way to the caudal peduncle.

Gender: The males are slimmer, with a greater depth of color.
Breeding: A typical egg scatterer that will eat its own eggs.
Special care: This fish will live peacefully with a community of fish of modest size.

DANIO NIGROFASCIATUS
Spotted danio
FAMILY: *Cyprinidae*

Range: Burma

1¾ in   1¾ in   73–79°F
(4.5cm)   (4.5cm)   (23–26°C)

Characteristics: The spotted danio is similar to the better-known zebra danio, but it is smaller and the colors are less intensely bright. The body is gray above, and silver below; these two shades are divided by a silver stripe that runs from behind the eye into the caudal fin. Above and below this are bright blue stripes (the one above being thinner than the one below). The lower flanks are peppered with blue spots, often found in lines.
Gender: The males are slimmer.

Breeding: An egg scatterer that will eat its own eggs.
Special care: This is a peaceful, schooling fish, ideal for a small fish community. This fish is less boisterous than some other danios.

DANIO RERIO
Leopard danio
FAMILY: *Cyprinidae*

Range: India

1¾ in   1¾ in   70–77°F
(4.5cm)   (4.5cm)   (21–25°C)

Characteristics: This fish was originally called *Brachydanio frankei* but is now known to be a color morph of the zebra danio. It is streamlined, the dorsal surface being only slightly convex. The body color is golden, and covered in darker leopard spots.
Gender: The female's body is much deeper in front of the anal fin and tends to be more silvery; she may also lose much of the spotty patterning.
Breeding: A typical egg scatterer that will also eat its own eggs.
Special care: It likes plenty of open water to swim in, and appreciates good filtration, which creates some water movement.

DANIO RERIO
Zebra danio
FAMILY: *Cyprinidae*

Range: Eastern India

2 in   2 in   65–77°F
(5cm)   (5cm)   (18–25°C)

Characteristics: This fish has a torpedo-shaped body, silver to golden in color and covered in bright blue lines. The anal and caudal fins are also striped. The dorsal fin is set well back on the body, and the mouth has two pairs of barbels. A long-finned and veil-tailed strain is also available.
Gender: The male is slimmer and smaller, with a more golden background color.

Breeding: An easy egg scatterer; this fish appreciates dense clumps of plants in which to lodge its eggs.
Special care: As this fish is so active it is happiest kept in a shoal with plenty of swimming room.

TANICHTHYS ALBONUBES
White cloud mountain minnow
FAMILY: *Cyprinidae*

Range: Southern China

2 in   1¾ in   65–73°F
(5cm)   (4.5cm)   (18–23°C)

Characteristics: From an even brown shade on the top areas, the coloration gently blends down into white near the underside. The body color is offset by faint blue, red, and gold lines that run from the eyes to the caudal peduncle, terminating in a red-edged dark patch. The dorsal, pelvic, and anal fins are shaded red, yellow, or white. With its dark-edged scales, this fish looks particularly stunning under sidelighting and when placed in direct sunlight.
Gender: The female is plumper.
Breeding: An egg scatterer; it likes clumps of plants for spawning.
Special care: This fish is very hardy with regard to temperature and can be kept in an unheated tank.

Rasboras

The species now known as Rasbora only became a member of its modern-day genus after reclassifications by Pieter Bleeker in 1859, after he first altered it to Leuciscus (in 1839). As a companion group of slimmer cyprinids, rasboras offer a little extra in the way of color to the silvery danios, and although they can be speedy swimmers (especially when you try to catch them), they are usually a little more sedate in their movements around the aquarium. Although many of the body shapes may be toward the slim side, there are several deeper-bodied fish, and most of the genera occupy the middle and upper levels of the aquarium. Most reproduce in the familiar egg-scattering manner, although the Harlequin (*T. heteromorpha*) will actually deposit eggs on the underside of broad-leaved aquarium plants. Like the family as a whole, the size of fish within the Rasbora genus varies widely, from less than 1 in (2.5cm) to over 3 ft (90cm). They may be distinguished from apparent near-related cyprinids by the absence of barbels.

BORARAS MACULATA
Spotted rasbora
FAMILY: *Cyprinidae*

Range: Southeast Asia

| 1 | 24 | 1¼ in (3cm) | 1¼ in (3cm) | 73–79°F (23–26°C) | | | | |

Characteristics: This is a diminutive species with a brown, pinkish-red body. Three dark spots mark the flanks, one behind the gill cover, one at the base of the anal fin, and another behind the caudal peduncle. The fins are slightly reddish, and the first few rays of the dorsal are black and pink, colors also seen on the anal fin. It has large eyes in a small head.

Gender: The male is slimmer.

Breeding: Egg scatterer

Special care: Keep this fish with other small species.

RASBORA BORAPETENSIS
Red-tailed rasbora
FAMILY: *Cyprinidae*

Range: Southeast Asia, Thailand, and western Malaysia

2¼ in   2 in   72–79°F
(5.5cm)   (5cm)   (22–26°C)

Characteristics: The slim body of this fish has an overall pale greenish-yellow hue. A thin gold band above a dark band runs from gill cover to the caudal peduncle. There is a dark line along the base of the anal fin. The caudal base is red, and the dorsal is tinged with red, but all other fins are clear. It has an upturned mouth.
Gender: The male is slimmer than the female.
Breeding: A very prolific breeder and egg eater.
Special care: This is a schooling species that requires well-aerated water.

RASBORA ELEGANS
Elegant rasbora
FAMILY: *Cyprinidae*

Range: Borneo, Malaysia, and Sumatra

6 in   5 in   72–77°F
(15cm)   (12.5cm)   (22–25°C)

Characteristics: This rasbora has a streamlined, elongated body with a slight curvature to the dorsal and ventral profiles. The greenish-brown dorsal surface runs into silvery sides; with sidelighting, a light violet sheen appears. It has large, dark-edged scales with a dark front area, a blue-black blotch below the dorsal fin, and another at the end of the caudal peduncle. A blue-black line runs along the ventral surface at the base of the anal fin. Most fins are yellow, with a dark-tipped caudal fin.
Gender: The female can be distinguished by her plumpness.
Breeding: Prolific egg scatterer
Special care: It is a peaceful species needing plenty of swimming space.

RASBORA KALACHROMA
Clown rasbora; iridescent rasbora
FAMILY: *Cyprinidae*

Range: Borneo, Sumatra

1   36

3⅜ ft   3½ in   77–82°F
(1m)   (9cm)   (25–28°C)

Characteristics: The elongated stocky body has a pink-violet hue with well-defined iridescent scales. There is a large, blue-black blotch between the dorsal fin and the anal fin, and a smaller blue-black spot midway between the dorsal fin and the rear edge of the gill cover. The fins are yellowish, tinged with red. The anal and pelvic fins are black, the extremities tipped with white. It has large red and gold eyes in a small head.
Gender: The males are slimmer, and more intensely colored.
Breeding: An egg scatterer
Special care: This is a particularly fragile and warmth-loving species.

RASBORA PAUCIPERFORATA
Red-striped rasbora; glowlight rasbora
FAMILY: *Cyprinidae*

Range: Malaysia, Sumatra

1   24

2½ in   2¼ in   70–77°F
(6.5cm)   (5.5cm)   (21–25°C)

Characteristics: This rasbora has a slim, elongated body with slightly convex curves. A red stripe with a narrow blue-black line under it runs from the snout to the slightly tapered caudal peduncle. It has large eyes that are red above and gold below. A silvery sac containing the internal organs is visible.
Gender: The females are plumper.
Breeding: An egg scatterer. Spawning is best encouraged by keeping large enough numbers together in the shoal.
Special care: A well-planted aquarium is needed for this timid shoaling fish. Keep this species with fish of a similar size.

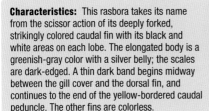

RASBORA TRILINEATA
Scissortail; spot-tail rasbora
FAMILY: *Cyprinidae*

Range: Borneo, Malaysia, and Sumatra

3½ in (9cm) | 3 in (8cm) | 73–77°F (23–25°C)

Characteristics: This rasbora takes its name from the scissor action of its deeply forked, strikingly colored caudal fin with its black and white areas on each lobe. The elongated body is a greenish-gray color with a silver belly; the scales are dark-edged. A thin dark band begins midway between the gill cover and the dorsal fin, and continues to the end of the yellow-bordered caudal peduncle. The other fins are colorless.

Gender: The female is plumper.
Breeding: An egg scatterer
Special care: This lively community fish needs a spacious aquarium.

TRIGONOSTIGMA HETEROMORPHA
Harlequin
FAMILY: *Cyprinidae*

Range: Thailand, Malaysia, and Sumatra

1¼ in (3cm) | 1¼ in (3cm) | 73–79°F (23–26°C)

Characteristics: Below the dorsal fin is a blue-black triangular patch tapering to the end of the caudal peduncle. The deep body tapers rapidly to a narrow caudal peduncle. The head is slightly snouty with a pronounced notch. The upper olive-green body shades down through pinkish-violet to silver. The dorsal fin, and the top and bottom edges of the caudal, are red-orange.

Gender: The female has a plumper body.
Breeding: After a courtship dancing display by the males, the eggs are laid and fertilized on the underside of a broad-leaved plant.
Special care: This is a shoaling fish that needs a well-planted aquarium with a dark substrate.

Flying Foxes

Here is a contrast in styles: the flying fox is a very smart fish with its white, yellow, and black horizontal stripes. It is often seen perching on horizontal surfaces in midwater, before darting off to grab a snack. The lesser-colored Siamese flying fox is a less exciting specimen, spending much of its time on the floor of the aquarium. Flying foxes will sometimes harass other species they consider to be intruders into their swimming space.

EPALZEORHYNCHUS KALLOPTERUS
Flying fox
FAMILY: *Cyprinidae*

Range: Northern India, Indonesia, Thailand, Sumatra, and Borneo

6 in	5½ in	75–79°F
(15cm)	(14cm)	(24–26°C)

Characteristics: The top of this torpedo-shaped fish is brown-green, separated by a bright yellow band from the dark main band that runs the length of the body; below this is the white ventral region. All the fins have white tips, and the dorsal fin has a black base. The fish is characterized by a down-turned mouth with two pairs of barbels.
Gender: Unknown
Breeding: This variety has not been bred in an aquarium.
Special care: This fish tends to quarrel with members of its own species, so caution should be taken as to the number of fish that are kept together.

EPALZEORHYNCHUS SIAMENSIS
Siamese flying fox
FAMILY: *Cyprinidae*

Range: Malaysia, Thailand

5½ in	5½ in	75–79°F
(14cm)	(14cm)	(24–26°C)

Characteristics: This fish has the same body shape as the flying fox, but its coloring differs, as the vivid yellow band above the broad dark band is absent. Also the band is shorter, beginning behind the eyes and not reaching into the caudal fin. The dorsal fin is long-based, and all fins are colorless. The down-turned mouth has one pair of barbels.
Gender: Unknown
Breeding: Unknown
Special care: This fish is quarrelsome with its own species, but it can be placed in a mixed community.

Sharks

It may come as a disappointment to those expecting some bloodthirsty behavior in the aquarium that the species in this section are not related to the marine "Jaws," either scientifically or behaviorally. The reason for the popular name "shark" is based on the fact that the species has a triangular dorsal fin reminiscent of the marine fish. The most colorful has to be the red-tailed black shark, whose name says it all. The other species—and especially the red-finned and ruby sharks—have their own appeal. The large black shark is quite peaceful, content to rummage around the aquarium browsing on algae; but like the larger barbs, it stirs up the water currents with its movements. The silver and Apollo sharks are active shoaling fishes, and will grow to splendid proportions if you give them the room to do so.

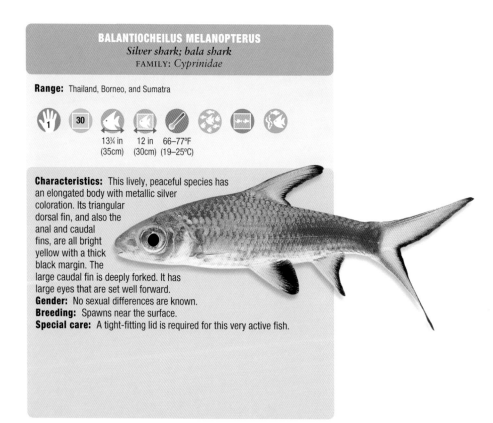

BALANTIOCHEILUS MELANOPTERUS
Silver shark; bala shark
FAMILY: *Cyprinidae*

Range: Thailand, Borneo, and Sumatra

| 1 | 30 | | | | | | |

13¾ in (35cm) 12 in (30cm) 66–77°F (19–25°C)

Characteristics: This lively, peaceful species has an elongated body with metallic silver coloration. Its triangular dorsal fin, and also the anal and caudal fins, are all bright yellow with a thick black margin. The large caudal fin is deeply forked. It has large eyes that are set well forward.
Gender: No sexual differences are known.
Breeding: Spawns near the surface.
Special care: A tight-fitting lid is required for this very active fish.

LABEO BICOLOR
Red-tailed black shark
FAMILY: *Cyprinidae*

Range: Thailand

 1 36

6 in
(15cm) 6 in
(15cm) 72–79°F
(22–26°C)

Characteristics: This shark has a jet-black body, with a flattened ventral contour. It has a bright red caudal fin, and a high triangular dorsal fin. The dorsal, pelvic, and anal fins are all black, but the pectoral fins may be yellowish-orange; in less robust fish, the black may fade to gray. The down-turned mouth has a fringed top lip and a horny bottom lip, and two pairs of barbels.

Gender: The females tend to be deeper-bodied.
Breeding: An egg scatterer in fine-leaved plants.
Special care: This shark becomes increasingly territorial with age, and can be intolerant toward its own species.

LABEO ERYTHRURUS
Red-finned shark
FAMILY: *Cyprinidae*

Range: Thailand

 1 36

6 in
(15cm) 6 in
(15cm) 72–79°F
(22–26°C)

Characteristics: This fish has a pale brown, elongated body and red fins. There is a small dark patch at the rear end of the caudal peduncle. Its down-turned, fringe-lipped mouth has two pairs of barbels. Although this fish appears peaceful, it may demonstrate anti-social behavior.
Gender: Unknown

Breeding: No breeding information available
Special care: It can be put in a community aquarium with a collection of fish of mixed sizes, but it would be wise to choose tankmates who can look after themselves.

LABEO FRENATUS
Ruby shark
FAMILY: *Cyprinidae*

Range: Thailand

6 in
(15cm)

6 in
(15cm)

72–79°F
(22–26°C)

Characteristics: The slim gray body has dark-edged scales. A dark stripe runs from the snout to the center of the eyes. The fins are red, but the outer edges of the dorsal, pelvic, and anal fins have black-and-white markings. The caudal fin is deeply forked.

There are two pairs of barbels on the down-turned mouth.
Gender: The males are slimmer than the females, and have a black-streaked anal fin.
Breeding: Unknown
Special care: Community fish

LEPTOBARBUS HOEVENI
Maroon shark
FAMILY: *Cyprinidae*

Range: Borneo, Laos, Sumatra, and Thailand

20 in
(50cm)

16 in
(40cm)

73-79°F
(23-26°C)

Characteristics: This shark has an elongated body with silvery flanks and a greenish tinge to the area above the lateral line; the large scales each have a dark front area. Young fish have a black band running from the head to the end of the caudal peduncle, which fades with age. The anal and pelvic fins are bright red, and the caudal fin is green with a red tip; the dorsal is a yellowish color. It has a large mouth with two pairs of small barbels.

Gender: No sexual differences have been noted.
Breeding: Unknown
Special care: A peaceful and very active fish that needs a large, spacious aquarium with other large fish.

Loaches

Loaches fall into two distinct body shapes: from a slightly modified orthodox "fish shape," to other species that might almost be described as "swimming worms." Loaches spend most of their time on the bottom of the aquarium, and are often better kept in some number, rather than as solitary specimens. Many are nocturnal by nature, preferring to hide away among plants and rocks by day, only emerging as darkness falls or when a tempting piece of food drops within reach.

They prefer subdued lighting, and this can be achieved by having a covering of floating plants on the water's surface. The substrate can be of a soft, sandy composition as it is not uncommon for these fish to burrow into the substrate. Loaches often make loud clicking noises, particularly when feeding; this is produced by violently expelling water through the gills, which are then snapped shut.

Little is known of their reproductive processes, but artificial means are reported to have been used to condition some loaches into spawning in an egg-scattering manner.

ACANTHOPSIS CHOIRORHYNCHUS
Horsefaced loach
FAMILY: *Cyprinidae*

Range: Southeast Asia, Burma, Java, Sumatra, and Thailand

8¾ in   8 in   75–86ºF
(22cm)   (20cm)   (24–30ºC)

Characteristics: These are spindly fish with a long snout in a tapering head, with small, high-set eyes. The pale yellow-brown body has equally spaced dark spots from behind the gill cover to the end of the caudal peduncle along the center line. These are matched by small dark blotches along the dorsal surface, with a row of very small dark speckles between. Some variation in coloration is likely between specimens.
Gender: Unknown
Breeding: Unknown
Special care: A soft sandy substrate is needed for this burrowing fish. Place specimen plants in individual pots. The water should be well-aerated with water currents.

BOTIA LOHACHATA
Pakistani loach; reticulated loach
FAMILY: *Cyprinidae*

Range: Northeastern India, Bangladesh, and Pakistan

5 in (13cm)	3 in (7.5cm)	75–86°F (24–30°C)

Characteristics: It has an elongated, light yellow body with an arched dorsal contour, a flat ventral surface, and a broad caudal peduncle. The body has dark "Y-shaped" markings that are separated by light-centered, dark blotches. The markings extend over the head, through the eyes, and down to the tip of the snout. There are four pairs of barbels. The colorless fins have dark markings and the caudal is deeply forked. It can make a loud clicking noise by sharply snapping its gills open and shut.

Gender: Unknown

Breeding: Unknown

Special care: It sometimes pesters other fishes.

BOTIA MACRACANTHA
Clown loach; tiger botia
FAMILY: *Cyprinidae*

Range: Borneo, Indonesia, and Sumatra

12 in (30cm)	10 in (25cm)	77–86°F (25–30°C)

Characteristics: This fish's scales are very small, so it appears to be scale-less. Its elongated body has an arched dorsal surface and a flattened ventral surface. Three black bands cross its body: the first crosses the eyes, the second is ahead of the dorsal fin, and the third crosses behind the dorsal and extends into the anal fin. The head is tapered, and has a down-turned mouth carrying four pairs of barbels. There is an erectile spine in front of each eye.

Gender: Unknown

Breeding: Little is known

Special care: It needs plenty of plants and tangled roots. It is advisable to keep a group, as solitary specimens do not thrive.

BOTIA MODESTA
Orange-finned loach
FAMILY: *Cyprinidae*

Range: Malaysia, Thailand, and Vietnam

 1   36

6 in (15cm)   4 in (10cm)   79–96°F (26–30°C)

Characteristics: This timid nocturnal species has an elongated, dark bluish-gray body, with an arched dorsal surface and generally flattened ventral surface. Small scales provide a slight metallic sheen. The fins are bright red-orange. There is a spine just ahead of the small eyes. It has a tapered snout, and a down-turned mouth with four pairs of barbels. It emits clicking noises.
Gender: Unknown
Breeding: Unknown
Special care: This is a timid, nocturnal species. Keep it in a community environment with fish of similar temperament.

BOTIA MORLETI
Skunk loach; Hora's loach
FAMILY: *Cyprinidae*

Range: Northern India, Thailand

2   30

8 in (20cm)   6 in (15cm)   75–79°F (24–26°C)

Characteristics: It has an elongated, golden-gray body, with a moderately arched dorsal contour, and a flat silvery ventral surface. A dark stripe runs from the tip of the snout, along the dorsal ridge, and down the rear end of the fairly deep caudal peduncle. Some faint dark vertical streaks may be visible on the flanks. The scales are very small and the skin has a dull finish. Three pairs of barbels are present. The fins are almost transparent, but slightly greenish yellow. It swims jerkily.
Gender: Unknown
Breeding: Unknown
Special care: This species is nocturnal, so it needs places to hide.

BOTIA ROSTRATA
Ladder loach
FAMILY: *Cyprinidae*

Range: Asia, Burma, and India

 1   24

2⅜ in (6cm)   2⅜ in (6cm)   72–76°F (22–25°C)

Characteristics: The cream-colored body of this fish is crossed by slightly oblique dark bands, some connected by a horizontal bar. The two lobes of the caudal fin are marked with three to four dark stripes that continue the body patterning. The dorsal fin has a dark band along the edge nearest to the body surface, and another toward its tip. A dark central band runs from the snout rearward, over the head.

It has attracted several synonyms according to much aquatic literature.
Gender: Unknown
Breeding: Unknown
Special care: It needs a well-planted aquarium, with some areas of open substrate.

BOTIA SIDTHIMUNKI
Dwarf chained loach
FAMILY: *Cyprinidae*

Range: Thailand, Cambodia

2⅜ in (6cm) 2⅜ in (6cm) 79–82°F (26–28°C)

Characteristics: This is a peaceful, shoaling fish. In color the body is a light metallic gold, overlaid with a dark "chain-link" pattern on the top half, which in mature specimens may reach further down. In shape, the body is fairly cylindrical, with a very slightly arched dorsal surface, and a flattened ventral surface, silvery-white below the chain marking midway down the flanks. The head is small and the eyes are gold-rimmed. There are three pairs of barbels. The fins are clear, but the caudal may have a dark patterning in each lobe.

Gender: Unknown

Breeding: Unknown

Special care: This active species will venture into midwater areas. It needs a well-planted aquarium.

BOTIA STRIATA
Zebra loach
FAMILY: *Cobitidae*

Range: Southern India

4 in (10cm) 4 in (10cm) 73–79°F (23–26°C)

Characteristics: One look at this loach and you can see where its common name has come from. The body is golden yellow, adorned with pairs of vertical brown lines all along it; those on the head tend to point forward, while those behind are slightly tilted backward. All the fins have broken brown bands in them to a greater or lesser extent.

Gender: Unknown

Breeding: Unknown

Special care: This fish likes some caves and plant cover in the aquarium. It is best kept in a small group as part of a community.

COBITIS TAENIATA
Spiny loach
FAMILY: *Cyprinidae*

Range: Throughout Europe

4 in (10cm) 3½ in (8cm) 57–64°F (14–18°C)

Characteristics: This species has a long, laterally compressed body with a spotted dorsal surface that continues down to the mid-line. A row of dark blotches separates it from the silvery-white ventral area. The dorsal and caudal fins are patterned with dark dots. The eyes are set up high on the small head; they have a double erectile spine beneath them. There are six barbels present around the mouth.

Gender: The male is smaller.

Breeding: This is an egg scatterer.

Special care: It needs very clean water. It is more active at night, and it appreciates a planted aquarium with some rocky furnishing.

MISGURNUS ANGUILLICAUDATUS
Japanese weatherloach; dojo
FAMILY: *Cyprinidae*

Range: Northeast Asia, central China

| 1 | 36 | 10 in (25cm) | 8 in (20cm) | 70°F (21°C) | | | | |

Characteristics: This species has an eel-like, brownish yellow body with dark specklings that extend into the rounded fins. The dorsal fin and pelvic fins are set halfway back on the body. The head is small, and the eyes are set well forward. The down-turned mouth has five pairs of barbels.
Gender: Unknown

Breeding: An egg scatterer that is not often bred in the aquarium.
Special care: It becomes very active when there is low barometric pressure. It utilizes atmospheric air breathed at the water's surface. It needs plenty of places to hide in, and it tolerates cooler temperatures. It is a peaceful, nocturnal fish, suitable for a community of mixed-size fish.

PANGIO KUHLI
Coolie loach
FAMILY: *Cyprinidae*

Range: Southeast Asia, Borneo, Java, Malaysia, and Thailand

| 1 | 48 | 4½ in (11cm) | 3½ in (8cm) | 75–86°F (24–30°C) | | | |

Characteristics: This species has a worm-like, yellowish light brown body with a pink ventral surface. Dark brown-black bands, interrupted by a yellow line or small area, cross the body vertically, stopping short of the ventral surface. The very small eyes are hidden in a dark band, and there is a sharp spine above each eye; four pairs of barbels are present. The dorsal fin is situated some way back along the body, just behind the pelvic fins. The rounded caudal fin has a dark area at its base.
Gender: Unknown
Breeding: Egg scatterer
Special care: This peaceful, gregarious fish swims among tangled plant roots; this habit makes it very difficult to catch.

Coldwater Cyprinids

Keeping coldwater species is not very different from caring for tropicals, but there are a few things to keep in mind. Tank size will determine the number of fish you can keep, and it is not a good idea to crowd your tank. The coldwater aquarium does not require heating, but may become overheated during the summer, so put it in a shady location. If temperatures do become high, some form of cooling will probably be necessary. Aeration and efficient filtration systems are almost mandatory to provide well-oxygenated, moving water, and to remove the dangers inherent in decomposing waste products.

Carassius auratus have been kept in captivity longer than any other fish, and retains an enormous following due to the wide range of varieties. Differences in color are achieved by breeding specific scale types. Nacreous and matte forms let more of the natural pigmentation show through, instead of the usual gold finish.

Goldfish are also a successful pond fish, but not all varieties are suitable for outdoor cultivation, where frost damage and/or other adverse pond-water qualities can affect them. Due to their changed physical forms, away from their natural shape, many of the more "exotically designed" fish cannot physically cope with pond life. Their delicate fins may get congested through contact with water conditions that are less than ideal. Water conditions can be kept under much closer control in the aquarium, and the wonderful flowing fins and specially bred body shapes can be seen more easily through the glass.

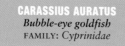

CARASSIUS AURATUS
Bubble-eye goldfish
FAMILY: *Cyprinidae*

Range: Man-made cultivar

5   36   varies   40–77°F (4–25°C)

Characteristics: This twin-tailed variety is instantly recognizable. Each eye is almost surrounded by a fluid-filled sac. The body is egg-shaped, and it does not have a dorsal fin. Body coloration can be variable, but it is usually metallic red-orange.
Gender: The males develop white tubercules on the gills and leading rays of the pectoral fins.

Breeding: This fish is an egg scatterer during the summer.
Special care: Because of the vulnerability of the eye sacs to physical damage, it is best to keep this strain in its own aquarium with no rocky furnishings or other boisterous fish.

CARASSIUS AURATUS
Calico moor
FAMILY: *Cyprinidae*

Range: Man-made cultivar

varies   40–77°F
(4–25°C)

Characteristics: This fish combines the calico pigments (red-gold, white, and black) with the flowing fins of the fantail, and the "pop" eyes of the moor. The caudal, dorsal, and anal fins are long and flowing, and the paired fins well formed.

Gender: The males develop white tubercules on the gill covers and leading rays of the pectoral fins.
Breeding: Egg scatterer during the summer.
Special care: Feed a pelleted or flake food made especially for fancy goldfish.

CARASSIUS AURATUS
Comet
FAMILY: *Cyprinidae*

Range: Man-made cultivar

varies   40–77°F
(4–25°C)

Characteristics: The comet has an elongated body, with equally curved dorsal and ventral contours. It is not as deep or as heavily built as the common goldfish. The color of this fish depends on the strain, but red-orange and lemon-yellow tend to be the most common. The main feature of this variety is the large, deeply forked caudal fin: this can be almost as long as the body itself.
Gender: The males develop white tubercules on the gill covers and leading rays of the pectoral fins.
Breeding: Egg scatterer during the summer.
Special care: It requires plenty of swimming room, and can swim exceptionally fast for short periods of time. It can be kept in a pond.

CARASSIUS AURATUS
Common goldfish
FAMILY: *Cyprinidae*

Range: Man-made cultivar

varies   40–77°F
(4–25°C)

Characteristics: It has a stocky body with equally convex dorsal and ventral contours. The body is a brilliant metallic orange-red or yellow, and this vivid color extends into the fins. The dorsal fin has a long base, the anal and caudal fins are not divided, and the caudal fin is moderately forked. Young fish are dark in color when hatched, and change to adult coloration at around one year of age—although not every fish changes color.
Gender: Males develop white tubercules on the gill covers and leading rays of the pectoral fins.
Breeding: Egg scatterer during the summer.
Special care: This fish is very hardy.

CARASSIUS AURATUS
Fantail
FAMILY: *Cyprinidae*

Range: Man-made cultivar

varies   40–77°F
(4–25°C)

Characteristics: The fantail has a relatively short body, with a deep, short caudal peduncle. Its body coloration is variable, depending on the scale formation and pigmentation. The dorsal fin is held high, and in good specimens it should be around half the body depth. It has double anal and caudal fins.

Gender: The males develop white tubercules on the gill covers and leading rays of the pectoral fins.

Breeding: Egg scatterer during the summer.

Special care: The fantail can be kept in an outdoor pond all year round, providing the water is deep enough to ensure a warm layer at the bottom where it can lie dormant.

CARASSIUS AURATUS
Lionhead
FAMILY: *Cyprinidae*

Range: Man-made cultivar

varies   40–77°F
(4–25°C)

Characteristics: The short, egg-shaped body of the lionhead does not have a dorsal fin. In some respects the lionhead is similar to the red-cap oranda, as both varieties have a raspberry-like growth on the head. The caudal fin should be held stiffly, and not allowed to drop.

Gender: Males develop white tubercules on the gill covers and leading rays of the pectoral fins.

Breeding: Egg scatterer during the summer.

Special care: The lionhead is best kept in the indoor aquarium, where its colorful features can be easily seen.

CARASSIUS AURATUS
Moor
FAMILY: *Cyprinidae*

Range: Man-made cultivar

4　**36**　varies　40–77°F
(4–25°C)

Characteristics: At one time purists insisted that the moor was always completely black, without any hint of color showing through. However, today other colors are becoming more acceptable. One unusual feature about this particular variety is its eyes: they may be normal, but in some strains they are developed as "telescopic" eyes that protrude from the head.
Gender: Males develop white tubercules on the gill covers and leading rays of the pectoral fins.
Breeding: This is an egg scatterer during the summer.
Special care: Generally not suitable for an outdoor pond.

CARASSIUS AURATUS
Pearlscale
FAMILY: *Cyprinidae*

Range: Man-made cultivar

4　**36**　varies　40–77°F
(4–25°C)

Characteristics: The scales on this fish have a pearl-like appearance; this is due to each scale having a domed, or raised, center. These fish are usually metallic or calico in color, and in most other respects, the strain appears to conform to the usual rounded body shape and "double" anal and caudal fins of the twin-tailed group of goldfish.
Gender: Males develop white tubercules on the gill covers and leading rays of the pectoral fins.
Breeding: This is an egg scatterer during the summer.
Special care: This fish should be kept in an aquarium with a central swimming area that has no sharp rocky decorations on which the scales might become damaged.

CARASSIUS AURATUS
Red-cap oranda
FAMILY: *Cyprinidae*

Range: Man-made cultivar

4   **36**   varies   40–77ºF (4–25ºC)

Characteristics: The red-cap oranda has a short, deep body, with a short, slightly down-turned caudal peduncle. The strain shown has a white body with a red coloration restricted to the raspberry-like growth on the head, known as the "wen." The dorsal fin is held high, and the anal and caudal fins are double.

Gender: Males develop white tubercules on the gill covers and leading rays of the pectoral fins.

Breeding: Egg scatterer during the summer.

Special care: Like many of the goldfish strains with more fully developed fins, the oranda needs very clean water conditions to prevent fin damage and deterioration.

CARASSIUS AURATUS
Shubunkin
FAMILY: *Cyprinidae*

Range: Man-made cultivar

1   **36**   varies   40–77ºF (4–25ºC)

Characteristics: This is similar to the common goldfish in body shape. Its coloration should include a combination of black, red, purple, blue, and brown, all appearing beneath nacreous or matte scales. The London shubunkin has the same finnage as the common goldfish, and the Bristol shubunkin has a large caudal fin with rounded lobes: this should be carried without any drooping.

Gender: Males develop white tubercules on the gill covers and leading rays of the pectoral fins.

Breeding: Egg scatterer during the summer.

Special care: This variety is suitable for an aquarium or pond.

Characins

With almost 1,200 species, characins rival the Cyprinidae family in numbers. In the wild, characins are split between Central and South America and Africa. The number of fish is truly astounding, with millions being exported each year—mostly from the Amazon region. The family contains many popular fish. Among the tetras, for example, are found the brilliant neons and cardinals, distant relatives of the notorious piranha, which brings us to one of the main characteristics of this family—teeth. They have extremely sharp teeth, even though not all characins are meat-eaters or predatory. For instance, in the wild, the pacu is a fruit-eater, devouring the juicy berries that fall into the water. Another feature of many fish in this family is the presence of an extra fin known as the adipose, between the dorsal fin and the tail. Males have tiny hooks on the anal fin to assist spawning; they also sport more intense coloration, slimmer bodies, and more exaggerated finnage.

Body sizes vary in the wild, from 1 in (2.5cm) of the South American neon tetra to 12 in (30cm) of the African longnosed distichodus. Shapes are equally diverse: hatchetfish are flat-backed and deep-bodied, while pencilfish are as slim as their name suggests. Piranhas are muscular, producing good speed, with teeth forward in the jaw to facilitate flesh tearing. Other characins are not as carnivorous, but happily eat aquarium plants.

Many characins are natural schoolers, but differences in mouth position affect feeding habits: hatchetfish have upturned mouths, well suited to catching insects. Most of the popular tetras have mouths suited for midwater feeding while *Distichodus* has a flattened body, with a downturned mouth suited to low levels.

Most characins spawn by means of egg scattering among plants. An exception is the splashing tetra, which lays its eggs out of water to protect them from predators. Although the eggs remain safe, they must be kept moist—constant splashing is required by the male swimming below.

FEATURED IN THIS SECTION

ANOSTOMUS ANOSTOMUS
Striped anostomus
FAMILY: *Anostomidae*

Range: Orinoco and Amazon river systems, Guyana, and Suriname

7 in   5½ in   72–82°F
(18cm)   (14cm)   (22–28°C)

Characteristics: This torpedo-shaped fish loves to lurk among underwater roots, where its camouflaging lines mimic those of the roots. Three dark, broad, jagged-edged bands run along the yellow-gold body. The dorsal and caudal fins have red blotches.
Gender: Larger, plumper fish are likely to be female.
Breeding: Egg scatterer

Special care: It needs plenty of green matter in its diet. Keep in small shoals to avoid quarreling between individual fish. Occasionally it may harass slower-moving fishes, such as angels or discus, whose slime-covered skin appears to hold some attraction.

ANOSTOMUS TERNETZI
Ternetz's anostomus
FAMILY: *Anostomidae*

Range: Brazil

6¼ in   4⅛ in   75–82°F
(16cm)   (10.5cm)   (24–28°C)

Characteristics: This torpedo-shaped fish has a yellow-gold body coloration, with three broad, dark bands running along the body. The upturned mouth has a distinct degree of red. The fins are colorless, with the exception of the caudal fin. This has two small yellow areas at its base, which match the body color. The small adipose fin is marked with red.
Gender: Larger, plumper fish are likely to be female.
Breeding: Egg scatterer
Special care: It is best suited to an aquarium generously planted with tough-leaved vegetation.

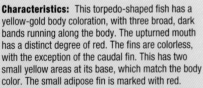

LEPORINUS OCTOFASCIATUM
Eight-banded leporinus
FAMILY: *Anostomidae*

Range: Amazonia, from Guyana to the Plate River

8½ in   6 in   73–79°F
(22cm)   (15cm)   (23–26°C)

Characteristics: The body shape of the eight-banded leporinus is elongated and cylindrical. The body coloration is a very pale blend of white and yellow. Eight dark bands encircle the body, although the actual number may vary, since some can give the appearance of being split to form double bandings. The pelvic, adipose, and anal fins have some black color. As with many members of the genus, the color patterns may become less intense or distinct with maturity.
Gender: Unknown
Breeding: Unknown
Special care: This fish requires a spacious aquarium provided with large plastic replica plants or tough-leaved natural plants.

APHYOCHARAX ANISITSI
Bloodfin; Argentine bloodfin; red-finned characin; red-finned tetra
FAMILY: *Characidae*

Range: Argentina, Paraguay

2½ in
(6.5cm)

2½ in
(6.5cm)

65–82°F
(18–28°C)

Characteristics: The body coloration consists of an olive-green dorsal surface and silvery flanks. As the common name suggests, the main coloration is present in the fins. The pelvic, anal, and lower half of the caudal fins are blood red, with only a little red in the dorsal fin.

Gender: The male may be identified by tiny hooks on the anal fin; these can become entangled in a net.
Breeding: It is an egg scatterer, and precautions should be taken to prevent egg eating.
Special care: Keep this species in a shoal in a well-planted aquarium.

ASTYANAX FASCIATUS MEXICANUS
Blind cave fish
FAMILY: *Characidae*

Range: Cave systems from Texas to Panama

3½ in
(9cm)

3½ in
(9cm)

68–77°F
(20–25°C)

Characteristics: The outstanding physical characteristic is the absence of eyes. This fish navigates using its lateral line system to avoid bumping into obstacles. The body shape follows the usual tetra pattern, although the dorsal profile has a slightly higher arch. The body coloration is plain pink with a silvery sheen. The fins resemble the body color.

Gender: The male is slimmer.
Breeding: Egg scatterer
Special care: The requirement for light is optional, and is only necessary to view the fish and to make the aquarium plants grow.

BRACHYCHALCINUS ORBICULARIS
Silver dollar tetra; disk tetra
FAMILY: *Characidae*

Range: Guyana down to the Rio Paraguay

1   48

4¾ in   4 in   65–75°F
(12cm)   (10cm)   (18–24°C)

Characteristics: The body shape is not typical of a characin, but could be described as a cross between the more heavily built piranha and the smaller, more orthodox, tetra.
Gender: Unknown
Breeding: It scatters its eggs in fine-leaved plants.

Special care: This active species needs room to swim at mid-tank level. Plastic or tough-leaved plants are appropriate, as it will eat soft-leaved plants. Provide some vegetable matter in its normal diet.

CHALCEUS MACROLEPIDOTUS
Pink-tailed chalceus
FAMILY: *Characidae*

Range: Amazonia, Guyana

4   72

10 in   8 in   71–79°F
(25cm)   (20cm)   (22–26°C)

Characteristics: The elongated body shape is stocky and somewhat cylindrical. The body coloration is olive green dorsally, with silver-green flanks. There is a blotch just behind the gill cover. The scales are very large and well defined. The deeply forked caudal fin, as the popular name implies, is colored bright pink.
Gender: Unknown
Breeding: Unknown
Special care: This large, active, hungry species needs plenty of room. Although it is suitable for a community of larger-sized fish, its tankmates should be chosen carefully for their ability to fend for themselves.

GYMNOCORYMBUS TERNETZI
Black widow
FAMILY: *Characidae*

Range: Mato Grosso (Brazil)

1   24

2½ in   2 in   68–79°F
(6.5cm)   (5cm)   (20–26°C)

Characteristics: The body shape is oval; the front two-thirds is colored silver; the rear is black with occasional iridescences. Three vertical dark bars cross the body, and the anal fin runs from below the dorsal fin to the caudal peduncle. The dorsal and anal fins are black, the adipose fin is black-edged, though its black coloration fades with age. A long-finned strain has been developed.
Gender: The male is slimmer, with a more pointed dorsal fin and a broader front part of the anal fin. The body of the female is plumper.
Breeding: Egg scatterer
Special care: This fish should be kept in shoals, and it prefers floating foods.

HASEMANIA NANA
Silvertip tetra
FAMILY: *Characidae*

Range: Brazil

2 in
(5cm)

2 in
(5cm)

73–82°F
(23–28°C)

Characteristics: The outline of this fish is slimmer than is usually expected for a tetra. The basic body color is golden brown, but varies from pale silver in females to a rich coppery brown in sexually mature males. A broadening black line, topped by a lighter gold area, begins just behind the dorsal fin and runs into the caudal fin. As its common name suggests, all of its fins are tipped with white.

Gender: The females are plumper than the males, particularly at spawning times.

Breeding: This fish is a typical egg scatterer.

Special care: It requires a well-planted aquarium that includes some bushy plants.

HEMIGRAMMUS CAUDOVITTATUS
Buenos Aires tetra
FAMILY: *Characidae*

Range: Plate River region of Argentina, Paraguay, and Brazil

3 in
(7.5cm)

3 in
(7.5cm)

60–77°F
(15–25°C)

Characteristics: The slim body has a silvery background with a vertical bar partially crossing the body behind the operculum, with another small dark blotch to the rear of this. A horizontal blue line along the body ends in the central section of the red caudal fin; at the caudal peduncle it is obscured by a black line. All fins are yellow to reddish in color; the top half of the eye is red.

Gender: The female is plumper, the male is colored with more red.

Breeding: Egg scatterer

Special care: Provide tougher-leaved vegetation in a generally well-planted aquarium.

HEMIGRAMMUS ERYTHROZONUS
Glowlight tetra
FAMILY: *Characidae*

Range: Guyana

1½ in
(4cm)

1½ in
(4cm)

75–82°F
(24–28°C)

Characteristics: Its elongated oval body is strikingly divided by a glowing red-gold line. This starts on the snout, takes in the red top half of the eye, and continues along the almost transparent body to end in a small red area at the base of the caudal fin. The dorsal and anal fins have some red at their bases and, like the pelvic fins, have milky-white tips.

Gender: The male is slimmer.

Breeding: Egg scatterer in fine-leaved plants.

Special care: These small, peaceful shoaling fish look best in a well-planted aquarium.

HEMIGRAMMUS OCELLIFER
Beacon fish; head and tail-light fish; motorist fish
FAMILY: *Characidae*

Range: Amazonia, Bolivia, and Guyana

1¾ in   1¾ in   75–82°F
(4.5cm)   (4.5cm)   (24–28°C)

Characteristics: The body outline follows the general tetra pattern. The main background is silvery gray. There is a small, green spot just behind the gill cover, the top half of the eye is bright red, and there is a gold spot above a red-bordered black blotch at the base of the caudal fin. The caudal fin has a hint of red in its upper section, and the anal and pelvic fins are white-tipped.
Gender: The male is slimmer.
Breeding: This is an easy egg scatterer.
Special care: This fish does best in a well-planted aquarium.

HEMMIGRAMMUS PULCHER
Pretty tetra
FAMILY: *Characidae*

Range: Peru, Brazil

1¾ in   1¾ in   73–80°F
(4.5cm)   (4.5cm)   (23–27°C)

Characteristics: The body outline is deeper than many tetras, with the back and head a dark gray-green color shading down through a brief purple-copper phase to the silver lower half. The eyes are reddish-purple above and bluish-green below. Directly behind the gill cover is a purplish-red mark; the lower area of the caudal peduncle is dark with a gold line above. All the fins are pinkish-purple in color.
Gender: The male is smaller, and has a pointed swim bladder.
Breeding: This fish is an egg scatterer that may be choosy about its mate.
Special care: It needs a well-planted aquarium.

HEMIGRAMMUS RHODOSTOMUS
Rummy-nosed tetra
FAMILY: *Characidae*

Range: Lower Amazon

2 in (5cm)	2 in (5cm)	75–82°F (24–28°C)

Characteristics: The most obvious features of this slim-bodied fish are its red head, and its strikingly patterned black-and-white caudal fin. With several similar-looking species available, the task of making a positive identification is difficult; however, since all require the same conditions, this does not present a problem for the average aquarist.
Gender: The male is slimmer.
Breeding: This fish scatters its eggs in fine-leaved plants.

Special care: A delicate species that requires a well-planted aquarium and soft acidic water. It is only suitable for a community of small, non-boisterous fishes, and is probably best kept in a separate species aquarium.

HYPHESSOBRYCON CALLISTUS
Blackfin flame tetra
FAMILY: *Characidae*

Range: Brazil, Paraguay

1½ in (4cm)	1 in (2.5cm)	71–82°F (22–28°C)

Characteristics: The body is red-orange, with this coloration extending to the caudal fin. The dorsal fin is black, edged in white at the rear. The pelvic and anal fins are reddish, with white on their distal edges, and the anal fin is smudged with black posteriorly. A black patch lies behind the gill cover at about the level of the lateral line.
Gender: Males have a pointed swim bladder.
Breeding: Pairs scatter eggs together in fine-leaved plants.
Special care: Keep in a shoal. If it is not well fed, this species may attack weaker members of its own school and can nip the fins of other fish.

HYPHESSOBRYCON ERYTHROSTIGMA
Bleeding heart tetra
FAMILY: *Characidae*

Range: Colombia, northern South America

| | 3 in (7.5cm) | 2¾ in (7cm) | 73–82°F (23–28°C) | |

Characteristics: The body is both high-backed, and deep. The general coloration is pinkish-silver, but the most striking feature is the glowing pink spot located on the flanks. A vertical black bar crosses the red-topped eyes. The anal fin is long-based and tinged blue-white with a black edge. The caudal fin is bluish-pink.
Gender: The male has a large, sickle-shaped dorsal fin.
Breeding: This fish scatters its eggs in plants, although this rarely happens in captivity.
Special care: This fish is quite nervous, and tends to dart around when introduced to new surroundings. A well-planted, spacious aquarium provides a sense of security.

HYPHESSOBRYCON FLAMMEUS
Flame tetra
FAMILY: *Characidae*

Range: Rio de Janeiro state, Brazil

| | 1½ in (4cm) | 1½ in (4cm) | 73–82°F (23–28°C) | |

Characteristics: The body shape of this fish is typical of the tetra group. The body is pinkish-brown with a silvery area, crossed by two dark bars just behind the gill cover. The lower rear half of the body is much more reddish. The eyes are blue. The pelvic, anal, and caudal fins are red, edged with black; the dorsal fin may be black with some white streaks, and an adipose fin is present.
Gender: Spawning males have intensified coloration, and the female shows an increasing girth.
Breeding: Egg scatterer
Special care: None required

HYPHESSOBRYCON HERBERTAXELRODI
Black neon
FAMILY: *Characidae*

Range: Mato Grosso (Brazil)

1   24   1½ in (4cm)   1½ in (4cm)   73–80 °F (23–27 °C)

Characteristics: This fish is not as deep-bodied as most tetras. A bright, light greenish-blue line along the flanks, from the top of the red-topped eyes to the top of the caudal peduncle, separates the olive green dorsal surface from a black area, which gradually pales to a silvery belly. The black area extends into the center rays of the caudal fin, where it is bordered by two light patches.
Gender: Females have generally deeper bodies and become plump when they are in spawning condition.
Breeding: Egg scatterer
Special care: Provide a dark substrate in a well-planted aquarium.

HYPHESSOBRYCON PULCHRIPINNIS
Lemon tetra
FAMILY: *Characidae*

Range: Central Brazil

1   24   2 in (5cm)   2 in (5cm)   73–82°F (23–28°C)

Characteristics: The body shape is typical of the group, with a high profile tapering evenly down to the caudal peduncle. The body coloration is a translucent greenish yellow, and its silvery internal organs and backbone are visible. The top half of the eye is bright red. All fins have an element of black with a strong yellow in them, particularly the front of the dorsal and anal fins. An albino form also exists.
Gender: The males are more brightly colored, and slimmer.
Breeding: Egg scatterer in plants.
Special care: A shoal of lemon tetras looks very impressive when kept in a well-planted aquarium with a dark substrate.

HYPHESSOBRYCON ROSACEUS
Rosy tetra
FAMILY: *Characidae*

Range: Guyana

1¼ in   1¼ in   73–79°F
(3cm)   (3cm)   (23–26°C)

Characteristics: At first sight this species could be nicknamed the "Poor Man's Bleeding Heart Tetra," since the coloring is fairly similar. However, the shape of its smaller-proportioned body is not as deep, and it lacks the glowing spot. The dorsal fin is marked with red, streaked with black, and has a white tip.
Gender: The male's dorsal fin is a well-developed sickle shape and can reach back over the adipose fin in mature specimens.
Breeding: An egg scatterer that needs soft, acidic water for the eggs to hatch.
Special care: To bring out the colors, use a dark substrate and a generously planted aquarium.

HYPHESSOBRYCON SERPAE
Serpae tetra
FAMILY: *characidae*

Range: Guyana, Amazon area

2½ in   2½ in   73–77°F
(5cm)   (5cm)   (23–25°C)

Characteristics: The body outline of this fish follows the typical tetra shape. The overall coloration is blood red, with a dark shoulder spot becoming paler on the belly. The pectoral, pelvic, and caudal fins are red, and the anal fin is red with a black margin. The dorsal fin is mostly black, with red at its base and front, and a whitish tip.
Gender: The female is plumper and lighter colored.
Breeding: Egg scatterer
Special care: It thrives in a well-planted aquarium with a dark substrate. It is likely to nip the fins of other fish.

INPAICHTHYS KERRI
Blue emperor
FAMILY: *Characidae*

Range: Upper Amazon

1½ in   1½ in   73–77°F
(4cm)   (4cm)   (23–25°C)

Characteristics: The male and the female are quite distinctive, the former being pale blue above with a less distinct dark mid-lateral stripe from the tip of the snout to the caudal peduncle. The female's stripe is darker, and the upper portion of her body is pale yellowish-green. The fins of both sexes are colorless.
Gender: The male has a beautiful blue sheen that will fade if conditions are less than perfect.
Breeding: Egg scatterer
Special care: It needs soft, acidic water, lots of growing plants, and plenty of swimming space.

MEGALAMPHODUS MEGALOPTERUS
Black phantom tetra
FAMILY: *Characidae*

Range: Central Brazil

1¼ in   1¼ in   73–79°F
(3cm)   (3cm)   (23–26°C)

Characteristics: The body coloration is a transparent silvery gray. A black teardrop-shaped mark appears on the fish's shoulder and is outlined by a surrounding bright area; the fins are black.

Gender: The female's adipose, pelvic, and anal fins contain some red, while the male's fins are less brightly marked. The dorsal fin of the male may become larger with age.

Breeding: Light-sensitive eggs are scattered in plants.

Special care: It likes a generously planted aquarium, with smaller, non-boisterous fishes. It needs soft, acidic water for its well-being in general, and especially if breeding is to be attempted.

MEGALAMPHODUS SWEGLESI
Red phantom tetra
FAMILY: *Characidae*

Range: Columbia

1¼ in   1¼ in   73–79°F
(3cm)   (3cm)   (23–26°C)

Characteristics: The body and fins are a transparent crimson, and the dorsal fin has a black blotch. There is also a dark shoulder blotch, and the pelvic and anal fins are often tipped with white. Due to the transparency of the body, the silvery sac containing the internal organs is often easily seen.

Gender: The female has a white tip to the dorsal fin.

Breeding: This is an egg scatterer; use a darkened tank.

Special care: It is a delicate fish that needs soft, acidic water. It can be kept with non-boisterous small fishes, or in a separate, well-planted species aquarium.

MOENKHAUSIA PITTIERI
Diamond tetra
FAMILY: *Characidae*

Range: Lake Valencia, Venezuela

2½ in (6cm)   2½ in (6cm)   75–82°F (24–28°C)

Characteristics: This fish has a body shape typical of the tetra group, with the dorsal and ventral profiles curving equally. When caught in sidelighting, its dark gray-blue body coloration reveals an iridescent sparkling on the flanks. The top part of the gold-rimmed eyes is bright red. The dorsal fin is sickle-shaped, the pelvic fins are rather long, and the caudal fin is deeply forked. All the fins are bluish, and have white edges.
Gender: The males have a larger dorsal fin.
Breeding: Egg scatterer
Special care: Provide a well-planted aquarium, with dark substrate and decorated with bogwood.

MOENKHAUSIA SANCTAEFILOMENAE
Yellow-banded tetra
FAMILY: *Characidae*

Range: Paraguay, western Brazil, eastern Peru, and eastern Bolivia

2¾ in (7cm)   2¾ in (7cm)   75–82°F (24–28°C)

Characteristics: The silver-colored scales cover the body surface, reflecting light and producing an attractive diamond pattern. The upper half of the eye is bright red. The fins are colorless. The caudal peduncle is bright yellow at its narrowest point, and black posteriorly, with some dark pigment spreading to the caudal fin.

Gender: The female is plumper.
Breeding: These fish use soft, acidic water and fine-leaved plants. Remove the adults as soon as they have finished spawning.
Special care: None required

NEMATOBRYCON PALMERI
Emperor tetra
FAMILY: *Characidae*

Range: Colombia

2½ in (6cm) | 2½ in (6cm) | 73–79°F (23–26°C)

Characteristics: The body is a light brownish-green, with a broad, blue-black band running along its whole length: this tapers to a thin line through the center of the caudal fin. The ventral surface is silvery.
Gender: The males have blue eyes, while females have green. The male's dorsal fin extends well back over the body, and there are extended rays from the tip of each caudal lobe as well as from the center.

Breeding: This fish scatters small numbers of eggs in plants daily.
Special care: A peaceful fish, this all-level swimmer looks best in a well-planted aquarium with a dark substrate and subdued lighting.

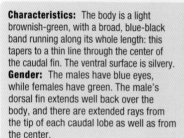

PARACHEIRODON AXELRODI
Cardinal tetra
FAMILY: *Characidae*

Range: Venezuela, Brazil, and Colombia

1¾ in (4.5cm) | 1¾ in (4.5cm) | 73–80°F (23–27°C)

Characteristics: The dorsal surface of this fish's slim body is dark greenish-brown underlined by an electric blue stripe running from its snout through the top half of each eye and on the base of the adipose fin. Below this the body is scarlet, fading to white on the belly.
Gender: The female is plumper.
Breeding: Egg scatterer
Special care: A shoaling species that appreciates a shady aquarium with clear areas of water into which it can venture. Avoid excessive water currents and bright lighting. Although it can tolerate most water conditions satisfactorily, soft, acidic water encourages the best colors.

PARACHEIRODON INNESI
Neon tetra
FAMILY: *Characidae*

Range: Peru

1½ in 1½ in 70–79°F
(4cm) (4cm) (21–26°C)

Characteristics: The dorsal surface is a dark green-brown surmounting an electric blue-green stripe running from the snout through the top half of each eye to the base of the adipose fin. Below this line the rear half of the body is bright red, and the forward part is silver.
Gender: The female is plumper and the blue-green line often appears bent.
Breeding: These fish are not difficult to breed; they follow the standard egg-scattering procedure among plants.
Special care: It likes a well-planted aquarium with a dark substrate.

PHENACOGRAMMUS INTERRUPTUS
Congo tetra
FAMILY: *Characidae*

Range: Democratic Republic of Congo

4 in 4 in 73–79ºF
(10cm) (10cm) (23–26ºC)

Characteristics: A beautiful fish originally collected in Africa, but now being bred in commercial fish farms around the world. It has an elongated body, in color blue-green above, with a golden stripe across the dorsal area, and a blue stripe below this, shading to white on the ventral surface. Seen in daylight or with the benefit of sidelighting, this is a truly beautiful fish. The center of the caudal fin has filaments, as does the dorsal fin.
Gender: The males have longer dorsal and caudal filaments, and are also more brightly colored.
Breeding: Egg scatterer in plants.
Special care: None is required: this is a hardy, peaceful community fish that can adapt to a wide range of conditions.

PRIONOBRAMA FILIGERA
Glass bloodfin; translucent bloodfin
FAMILY: *Characidae*

Range: Argentina, Brazil

2⅜ in 2⅜ in 71–86°F
(6cm) (6cm) (22–30°C)

Characteristics: This elongated fish is fairly streamlined; it has a blue-gray translucent body coloration. The long-based anal fin has a much longer first ray that is often white, as is the first ray of the pelvic fin. The caudal fin is deep red.
Gender: The female only has red at the base of the caudal fin.

Breeding: This is an egg scatterer; use soft, acidic water and fine-leaved plants.
Special care: This active fish prefers a well-planted aquarium, with some water currents and floating plants under which a shoal may gather.

PRISTELLA MAXILLARIS
X-ray fish
FAMILY: *Characidae*

Range: Venezuela, Guyana, and Brazil

1   24   1¾ in 1¾ in 75–82°F
          (4.5cm) (4.5cm) (24–28°C)

Characteristics: The body shape of this fish follows the common tetra pattern, with the body translucent so that the backbone and internal organs are visible. A dark spot lies on the shoulder just behind the gill cover. The dorsal and anal fins are tri-colored, with yellow, black, and white bands progressing away from the body.
Gender: The females are plump and the males have brighter colors.
Breeding: An egg scatterer. You may need to try several different male/female pairings before a successful spawning is achieved.
Special care: This fish uses all levels of a well-planted aquarium.

THAYERIA BOEHLKEI
Penguin fish
FAMILY: *Characidae*

Range: Brazil, Peru

1   24   2½ in 2½ in 71–82°F
          (6cm) (6cm) (22–28°C)

Characteristics: This fish displays a distinctive behavior trait: it assumes a "tail-standing" posture, remaining at the same oblique angle even when resting. A fairly wide, dark band runs from the gill cover along the body, and continues down into the lower lobe of the caudal fin. The bright yellow areas immediately above and below this dark band accentuate it even more.
Gender: The female is plumper.
Breeding: It is a prolific egg scatterer that lays large numbers of eggs.
Special care: Provide generous vegetation and some water currents in the aquarium.

THAYERIA OBLIGUUS
Penguin fish
FAMILY: *Characidae*

Range: Brazil

1   24   3 in   3 in   71–82°F
          (7.5cm) (7.5cm) (22–28°C)

Characteristics: The body is elongated and olive green above, fading to silver on the belly; a gold line runs from just behind the gill cover along the body, and continues to the end of the caudal peduncle. From the rear of the dorsal fin, a blurred dark band runs across the body and continues down into the lower lobe of the caudal fin, where it is bordered by white.

Gender: The females are noticeably fatter at spawning times.
Breeding: This is a typical egg scatterer.
Special care: It needs a well-planted aquarium, and some water currents should be provided.

DISTICHODUS LUSSOSO
Long-nosed distichodus
FAMILY: *Citharinidae*

Range: Angola, Cameroon

16 in (40cm)   13 in (33cm)   71–79°F (22–26°C)

Characteristics: This peaceful fish has a heavily built, elongated body that is compressed laterally, and a low, slowly rising dorsal profile. The body coloration is a greenish golden brown. Several equally spaced dark bands run transversely across the body, but do not quite reach the belly. The head is relatively small compared to the rest of the body, with a pointed snout and a silver lower jaw.
Gender: Unknown
Breeding: Unknown
Special care: It needs a huge aquarium furnished with rocks and roots. Plants will be eaten.

DISTICHODUS SEXFASCIATUS
Six-barred distichodus
FAMILY: *Citharinidae*

Range: Angola

12 in (30cm)   10 in (25cm)   71–79°F (22–26°C)

Characteristics: This fish is elongated, laterally compressed, and heavily built. In juveniles the body coloration consists of reddish-gold flanks, down which six transverse dark bands extend just to the ventral surface. All of the fins are bright reddish-yellow except for the adipose fin that is black, and which also has a red outer edge. In adults this coloration changes to plain gray.
Gender: Unknown
Breeding: Egg scatterer
Special care: It will eat plants, so it needs a rocky environment; any other furnishings should be nibble-proof (plastic or tough-leaved plants).

CARNEGIELLA STRIGATA
Marbled hatchetfish
FAMILY: *Gasteropelecidae*

Range: Peru

2½ in (6.5cm)   1¾ in (4.5cm)   75–82°F (24–28°C)

Characteristics: The body shape is very deep and keel-like. Its coloration is light greenish-yellow above a gold-topped, dark line running from the eyes to the caudal peduncle. Several dark, irregularly shaped bands run downward and forward across the lower body, almost parallel with the anal edge. Another dark line follows the ventral edge, ending beneath the eyes. The pectoral fins are exceptionally well developed, and can flap up and down like wings.
Gender: The female is fuller.
Breeding: It scatters eggs among fine-leafed plants.
Special care: It prefers a well-planted, spacious aquarium with a firmly secured lid and some shade, which floating plants can provide.

GASTEROPELECUS STERNICLA
Silver hatchetfish
FAMILY: *Gasteropelecidae*

Range: Guyana, Suriname, and Brazil

2½ in (6.5cm) 2½ in (6.5cm) 73–80°F (23–27°C)

Characteristics: The body shape follows the family pattern. Its coloration is plain silver, with a thin dark line on the flanks along the rear half of the body. The head is very small, the eyes are set well forward, and the mouth is upturned. The dorsal fin is set well back on the body, and the anal fin is fairly long-based. The pectoral fins are large, and wing-like.

Gender: Males look slimmer when viewed from above.
Breeding: Unknown in captivity
Special care: Keep well covered in a planted aquarium. Soft, slightly acidic water with little current or disturbance suits it best.

HEMIODOPSIS GRACILIS
Slender hemiodopsis
FAMILY: *Hemiodontidae*

Range: Brazil, Guyana

7 in (18cm) 6 in (15cm) 73–80°F (23–27°C)

Characteristics: The body is very streamlined, cylindrical in shape, and equipped with a deeply forked caudal fin; the body coloration is silver, marked with a dark spot midway along each flank, which extends as a dark line into the lower lobe of the caudal fin. In mature specimens the lower edge of the caudal fin may be red.
Gender: The female is plumper.
Breeding: Unknown in captivity
Special care: An active fish that needs well-oxygenated water. Because it is so energetic, it is also an expert jumper, and the aquarium should have a tight-fitting hood.

HEMIODOPSIS THAYERIA
Slender hemiodopsis
FAMILY: *Hemiodontidae*

Range: South America

6 in (15cm) 4 in (10cm) 73–80°F (23–27°C)

Characteristics: This species is very similar to *H. gracilis* in body shape and coloration, but this fish's body has a continuous thin black line along its entire length which splits into two at the end of the caudal peduncle to extend into both upper and lower lobes of the caudal fin.
Gender: The female is plumper.
Breeding: Unknown in captivity
Special care: With fish of this size, its continuous activity may cause more sedate fish some disturbance; it is probably best to keep this genus in a shoal of its own kind, and give it all the room it clearly needs and deserves.

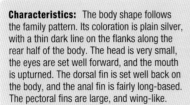

COPEINA GUTTATA
Red-spotted copeina
FAMILY: *Lebiasinidae*

Range: Amazon Basin

3 | 36

6 in (15cm) | 4¾ in (12cm) | 73–82 °F (23–28 °C)

Characteristics: This elongated fish has a body coloration of an iridescent green-brown dorsal surface with purple-violet blue flanks and a pinkish-white ventral surface. Each large scale has a red dot. The fins are yellowish, and the anal and pelvic fins often have reddish-orange edges.

Gender: The dorsal fin may be marked with black, especially in the female. The lower lobe of the male's caudal fin is smaller than the top lobe.

Breeding: The male guards and fans the fertilized eggs, which are laid in a depression in the substrate.

Special care: It needs a well-planted tank, where it cruises the upper and middle levels.

COPELLA ARNOLDI
Jumping tetra; splash tetra
FAMILY: *Lebiasinidae*

Range: Guyana

5 | 24

4 in (10cm) | 3½ in (8cm) | 71–82°F (22–28°C)

Characteristics: This slender fish has a body color that varies from tan to olive; it also has a horizontal black bar through each eye.

Gender: In the male, the outer margins of the two elements of the caudal fin are tinted red-orange, the color sometimes extending to the caudal peduncle.

Breeding: The pair jump out of the water and lay their eggs on a leaf. The male then keeps them damp by splashing them. They hatch on the third day; the fry need small live foods.

Special care: These fish are happy in a normal community aquarium with some plant cover—although make sure you have a tight-fitting lid.

NANNOSTOMUS BECKFORDI
Golden pencilfish; red pencilfish
FAMILY: *Lebiasinidaee*

Range: Brazil, Guyana

1 | 24

2½ in (6.5cm) | 2½ in (6.5cm) | 75–79°F (24–26°C)

Characteristics: The body is shaped like a pencil, and is a light green-brown above, and silver on the belly. A wide dark band runs the length of the body, ending at the base of the caudal fin between two red patches. There is a gold line above the dark band, with a hint of red above that.

Gender: The males are slimmer and have white-tipped fins.

Breeding: It scatters eggs on low-growing plants. Use soft, acidic water.

Special care: A good community fish, happy in the company of non-boisterous fish; it prefers a well-planted aquarium.

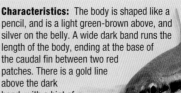

NANNOSTOMUS HARRISONI
Harrison's pencilfish
FAMILY: *Lebiasinidae*

Range: Guyana

2⅜ in (6cm)   2⅜ in (6cm)   75–82°F (24–28°C)

Characteristics: This peaceful shoaling species has a pencil-shaped body that is a light greenish-brown above, shading through greenish-gold to a dark horizontal band running from the snout to the base of the caudal fin, where it terminates as a dark blotch bordered by gold-edged red areas.
Gender: The males have a broader anal fin.

Breeding: It is an egg scatterer in plants.
Special care: This species is comfortable with other non-boisterous fish, especially in a generously planted aquarium.

NANNOSTOMUS MARGINATUS
Dwarf pencilfish
FAMILY: *Lebiasinidae*

Range: Brazil, Guyana, and Suriname

1¼ in (3cm)   1 in (2.5cm)   75–79°F (24–26°C)

Characteristics: The body is yellowish-green, paling to white in the mid-lateral region. A bold black stripe runs from the snout, through the eyes, to the end of the caudal fin. A less distinct line parallels it above, also extending to the caudal fin. There is a third, stippled, black line from the belly to the insertion of the anal fin. The dorsal fin bears a brilliant red splotch and black edging. The pelvic and anal fins are bright red, but the pectoral fins are colorless.
Gender: The males are slimmer.
Breeding: It is a typical egg scatterer.
Special care: It needs a well-planted aquarium with some floating vegetation and water movement.

NANNOSTOMUS MARYLINAE
Marylin's pencilfish
FAMILY: *Lebiasinidae*

Range: Brazil

2 in (5cm)   1½ in (4cm)   75–79°F (24–26°C)

Characteristics: In color it is olive green along the dorsal surface, and a black stripe runs from the eyes to the caudal peduncle, flanked above and below by white stripes; the fins are colorless.
Gender: The male is slimmer.
Breeding: It scatters small numbers of eggs daily.
Special care: This species does best in a small shoal, where individual males will establish small territories. It requires soft, acidic water and subdued lighting. It does not tolerate variations in water quality, and therefore is probably a better choice for the aquarist with some experience.

NANNOSTOMUS UNIFASCIATUS
One-lined pencilfish
FAMILY: *Lebiasinidae*

Range: Brazil, Columbia, and Guyana

1   24   2¾ in (7cm)   2¾ in (7cm)   77–82°F (25–28°C)

Characteristics: The body of this fish is shaped like a pencil and colored a light greenish-brown. The dorsal surface is edged by a single dark band that runs the length of the body, terminating in the first part of the caudal fin. The lower lobe of the caudal fin may be dark with some red coloration; the upper lobe often has a dark spot.

Gender: The males have a black, red, and white anal fin.
Breeding: It is a typical egg scatterer.
Special care: It is compatible with other non-boisterous fish, and needs a generously planted aquarium.

SEMAPROCHILODUS TAENIURUS
Plain-body prochilodus
FAMILY: *Prochilodontidae*

Range: Brazil to eastern Colombia

3   72   12 in (30cm)   6 in (15cm)   73–79°F (23–26°C)

Characteristics: The posterior two-thirds of the silvery body is marked with a pattern of black dots extending to the dorsal fin, and can be seen faintly on the anal fin. The caudal fin is transparent, with a series of horizontal black stripes extending across it from tip to tip; the pelvic fins are bright red when young.
Gender: The females are plumper.
Breeding: At spawning time the adults migrate upstream, even ascending strong rapids and small waterfalls. Captive spawning is unknown.
Special care: This fish requires a large, shallow, preferably well-planted aquarium, with ample filtration and water movement.

METYNNIS ARGENTEUS
Silver dollar
FAMILY: *Serrasalmidae*

Range: Brazil, Guyana

4   72   8 in (20cm)   5 in (13cm)   75–82°F (24–28°C)

Characteristics: The body shape is very deep, with a ventral region that resembles a keel. It is silvery with a small black blotch on the rear of the gill cover. There may be dark vertical bands across the body, and a dark blotch midway along the flanks, but these fade with maturity. The dorsal fin has dark speckles and, like the anal and caudal fins, is edged in red.
Gender: Males have a longer front edge to the anal fin that is also reddish.
Breeding: This fish spawns in floating plants.
Special care: Furnish the aquarium with plastic or tough-leaved plants.

MYLEUS RUBRIPINNIS
Redbook
FAMILY: *Serrasalmidae*

Range: Guyana

14 in (35cm) 5 in (13cm) 73–80°F (23–27°C)

Characteristics: This large, vegetarian relative of the piranha has a rounded, silvery body and colorless fins, except for the anal, which is bordered in black on the lower third, and tinged with red.
Gender: Unknown
Breeding: Unknown in captivity

Special care: This fish is sometimes imported with an unidentified disease condition that produces tiny, transparent blisters on the body. The condition apparently does not harm the fish. The aquarium should have plenty of water movement and aeration, as it comes from well-oxygenated waters.

SERRASALMUS NATTERERI
Red belly piranha
FAMILY: *Serrasalmidae*

Range: Guyana to La Plata region

11 in (28cm) 9⅜ in (24cm) 73–80°F (23–27°C)

Characteristics: This fish is famous for its habit of traveling in schools that can reduce an animal the size of a small pig to shreds in a few seconds. It is rather timid in the aquarium, though inclined to bite the hand that feeds it. Its body is silvery, with some darker areas on the caudal fin. From the underside of the lower jaw to the belly, the skin is tinted bright red.
Gender: Unknown
Breeding: Unknown in captivity
Special care: Provide a roomy tank with clear, clean, well-oxygenated water and a noticeable current. This species is banned in some parts of the U.S.

Cichlids

The Cichlidae family is native to Central and South America, Africa, and Asia and, with over 1,000 species, contains something for everyone. Many of these fish are territorial, particularly at spawning time, and often tear up aquarium plants when selecting a spawning site. Some are too large to be kept in a community tank, while others will happily raise young in a modest-size aquarium.

Cichlids are hearty eaters producing large quantities of waste products, so their aquarium should be fitted with an efficient filtration system and regular partial water changes should be applied. Some species, such as those from the Rift Valley lakes of Africa, are herbivorous and need a high content of vegetable matter in their diets. For good breeding results the South American species require water of a particular composition, usually soft and acidic; some, such as the discus (*Symphysodon* spp.), need to have their water conditions constantly maintained, meaning that these fantastic fish are only really suitable for the experienced fishkeeper.

The brilliantly colored African species from the Rift Valley lakes prefer hard water and require rocky outcrops as furnishings among which they can claim territories. A bright light over the tank will encourage algal growth on the rocks on which the fish will graze.

Generally, sexual differentiation (and mate selection) is best left to the fish. In some cases sex determination is difficult; males may have longer, more pointed fins. Close examination of the breeding tubes extended at spawning times by males and females may prove to be a reliable guideline.

Cichlids are egg depositors and prolific breeders. The smaller species tend to be secretive spawners. Although the females of such species become pugnacious when guarding their young, large aquariums are not always needed for a nuclear family group. Larger species are happy to select a spawning site out in the open and defend the surrounding area.

Many of the African species are mouthbrooders. The male fish has imitation egg spots on his anal fin; as the female attempts to collect these she takes his fertilizing milt into her mouth at the same time.

FEATURED IN THIS SECTION

AEQUIDENS PULCHER
Blue acara
FAMILY: *Cichlidae*

Range: Colombia, Trinidad, and Venezuela

8 in   6¼ in   65–73°F
(20cm)   (16cm)   (18–23°C)

Characteristics: This fish has a light gray, stockily built body with several dark vertical bars; these may be interconnected by a dark line running from behind the eyes, arching along the body, to the caudal peduncle. The light metallic blue center to each scale gives a sparkling effect. The fins are dark gray with light blue speckling.

Gender: The dorsal and anal fins of the male are pointed.
Breeding: This is a prolific breeder that spawns in the open on flat stones.
Special care: While generally peaceful, it may find small fish too tempting to ignore, and it does become territorial at spawning time.

AMPHILOPHUS CITRINELLUS
Midas cichlid; lemon devil
FAMILY: *Cichlidae*

Range: Southern Mexico to Nicaragua and Costa Rica

12 in   12 in   71–77°F
(30cm)   (30cm)   (22–25°C)

Characteristics: This fish's body coloration, including all its fins, can be a lemon yellow-gold, although it is usually orange, orange and white, or orange and black, with the normal form gray with black vertical bars. Its popular name is obviously inspired more from the golden connection, whereas the scientific name refers to the paler yellow shade.
Gender: Mature males often develop a pronounced forehead (the nuchal hump), and their dorsal and anal fins are more pointed than those of the female.
Breeding: Open spawner
Special care: This aggressive fish needs a spacious aquarium furnished with plastic plants and rocky decor.

AMPHILOPHUS LABIATUS
Red devil
FAMILY: *Cichlidae*

Range: Nicaragua

10 in   8 in   75–79°F
(25cm)   (20cm)   (24–26°C)

Characteristics: This is a beautiful orange and yellow fish, often with pronounced lips and nuchal hump in the male. These fish are notorious for aggressive behavior toward tankmates, including others of their own species. They are also diggers, making short work of tank decorations and plants.
Gender: The males grow larger.
Breeding: Open spawner
Special care: Keep these fish on their own in a large, well-filtered aquarium. If plants are eaten the fish will die in acidic water conditions.

APISTOGRAMMA AGASSIZII
Agassiz's dwarf cichlid
FAMILY: *Cichlidae*

Range: Brazil

3¼ in (8cm) 3 in (7.5cm) 71–77ºF (22–25ºC)

Characteristics: This dwarf cichlid has an elongated body, golden brown above with a dark stripe from snout to caudal peduncle along its greenish-blue iridescent flanks. The face has green streaks and a dark diagonal bar over the eyes. The dorsal fin has a long base and is reddish; the caudal fin comes to a central point and has a green line around its margin.

Gender: The female is smaller, light brown, and with a dark horizontal stripe and the eye bar. Her fins are more rounded.

Breeding: Cave spawner

Special care: It enjoys a well-planted aquarium with plenty of retreats. It needs plenty of live food in its diet.

APISTOGRAMMA CACATUOIDES
Cockatoo dwarf cichlid; crested dwarf cichlid
FAMILY: *Cichlidae*

Range: Amazon Basin

3½ in (9cm) 3 in (7.5cm) 75–77ºF (24–25ºC)

Characteristics: The first few rays of the male's dorsal fin are extended, much like a cockatoo's crest. The pelvic fins also have extended first rays. The fish's elongated body is greenish-brown above, becoming yellow in the ventral area. A dark band runs horizontally along the flanks, with other often incomplete lines beneath this. The caudal fin is vividly marked with red and black at its base.

Gender: The males are larger and more colorful.

Breeding: Cave spawner

Special care: It likes a well-planted aquarium with plenty of caves. The males are territorial, but given enough room and caves they will live peacefully together.

APISTOGRAMMA MACMASTERI
Macmaster's dwarf cichlid; red-tailed dwarf cichlid
FAMILY: *Cichlidae*

Range: Brazil

3⅛ in (8cm) 2¾ in (7cm) 73–86°F (23–30°C)

Characteristics: A beautiful golden-yellow fish with a bold black line running vertically through the eye. Other paler and less distinct vertical bands are present throughout the body, with a horizontal band running from snout to caudal peduncle. All the fins are pale yellow with bright red splashes of color at the top and bottom of the male's caudal fin.
Gender: The male is larger and more colorful.

Breeding: Cave spawner
Special care: It likes caves to hide and spawn in, so include plenty of natural plants in the set-up.

APISTOGRAMMA NIJSSENI
Panda dwarf cichlid; Nijssen's dwarf cichlid
FAMILY: *Cichlidae*

Range: Peru

2½ in (6.5cm) 2 in (5cm) 71–82°F (22–28°C)

Characteristics: The male's body has bluish flanks with indistinct vertical bands and a diagonal band that runs from the eyes to the gill cover. The dorsal fin is blue with a red and yellow margin, and a few of the first rays are slightly black. The caudal has a red band around its edge.
Gender: The female is bright yellow with a large dark blotch below the eye, another in the middle of her body, and finally one in her caudal peduncle. The front half of her dorsal is black, as are the pelvic fins.
Breeding: Cave spawner
Special care: The tank should be well planted, and areas should be created where the fish can retreat.

APISTOGRAMMA TRIFASCIATA
Three-striped dwarf cichlid; blue apistogramma
FAMILY: *Cichlidae*

Range: Paraguay, Brazil

2¾ in (6cm)   2 in (5cm)   78–84°F (26–29°C)

Characteristics: A golden-yellow fish with three dark bands: one runs along the dorsal ridge, another from the tip of the snout to the caudal peduncle, and the third from the base of the pectoral fin to the start of the anal fin. The dorsal fin is bluish with a red edge; the pelvic fins are blue with white edges.

Gender: The males are larger, and the third to the fifth dorsal fin rays are elongated.
Breeding: Cave spawner
Special care: This fish will thrive in a well-planted aquarium with plenty of places in which it can hide and retreat.

APISTOGRAMMA VIEJITA
Viejita dwarf cichlid
FAMILY: *Cichlidae*

Range: Colombia

3 in (7.5cm)   2¾ in (7cm)   73–86°F (23–30°C)

Characteristics: This fish's golden-brown body may have some dark flecking, and there may be red margins to the caudal fin and/or a red edge to all or part of the dorsal fin. The female intensifies her coloration from the usual drab brown into yellow with black markings when spawning and caring for the subsequent fry.
Gender: The males are larger and have an extended dorsal fin.
Breeding: Cave spawner
Special care: It requires a well-planted aquarium, with retreats and plenty of live food in its diet.

ASTRONOTUS OCELLATUS
Oscar; marbled, or velvet cichlid
FAMILY: *Cichlidae*

Range: Amazon Basin

13 in (33cm)   11 in (28cm)   71–77°F (22–25°C)

Characteristics: This cichlid has a very robust, thick body, and its features are rounded off in appearance. Its matte body is dark gray in color, with some irregular dark blotches and rust-colored markings. An eye-spot on the caudal peduncle can be seen on wild specimens. The head, generally gray with less red marking, is massive, with a very large, fleshy-lipped mouth. There are many different color forms available.
Gender: The genital papilla is pointed in the male, and blunt in the female.
Breeding: Open spawner
Special care: The aquarium should have an efficient filtration system, and regular partial water changes because of the amount of waste produced by these fish.

AULONACARA STUARTGRANTI
Malawi peacock
FAMILY: *Cichlidae*

Range: Malawi

| 5 | 48 | 13 in (33cm) | 11 in (28cm) | 75–79°F (24–26°C) | |

Characteristics: The Malawi peacock's blue-gray body is covered with a number of vertical dark stripes. The ventral area is colored silver and gold. The coloration of the female (and lesser-ranking males) is more subdued. The pelvic fins contain some yellow, and the first few rays are pale blue. The anal fin of the male carries several round yellow spots.

Gender: The male has much brighter colors.

Breeding: Mouth brooder

Special care: The water should be hard and alkaline; special Malawi salt mixes are available to create the correct conditions. Only keep this variety with other sand- and open water-dwelling Malawi cichlids.

CICHLA OCELLARIS
Peacock bass, ocellated cichlid
FAMILY: *Cichlidae*

Range: Bolivia, Brazil, Guyana, Peru, and Venezuela

| 3 | 96 | 36 in (90cm) | 36 in (90cm) | 75–80°F (24–27°C) | |

Characteristics: The body is olive, fading to golden yellow on the belly and throat. The eyes are bright red, as are the pelvic fins. The mid-lateral region is marked with three bold eye-spots, stippled black, surrounded by a lemon-yellow ring. A similar eye-spot is located on the caudal peduncle.

Gender: Mature males may be identified by a nuchal hump.

Breeding: Open spawner

Special care: Use a very large, well-aerated tank, decorated with rocks and driftwood rather than plants. Filtration should be adequate to compensate for its carnivorous appetite and messy habits.

"CICHLASOMA" FESTAE
Festae cichlid
FAMILY: *Cichlidae*

Range: Ecuador

20 in   12 in   79–82°F
(50cm)   (30cm)   (26–28°C)

Characteristics: Its elongated, heavily-built body is golden yellow-red, with a number of bluish-green, iridescent dark bands that cross the flanks vertically between the rear of the gill covers and the caudal peduncle. A bright-ringed, similarly colored dark spot appears on the upper base of the caudal fin. The fins are reddish with some blue markings.

Gender: The male festae are green without bars, and the females red-orange with heavy dark barring.
Breeding: Open spawner
Special care: This fish is aggressive, and it should be kept in a spacious aquarium with plastic plants.

"CICHLASOMA" OCTOFASCIATUM
Jack Dempsey
FAMILY: *Cichlidae*

Range: Mexico, Guatemala, and Honduras

8 in   8 in   71–77°F
(20cm) (20cm) (22–25°C)

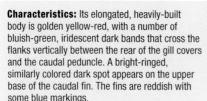

Characteristics: As a juvenile its heavily-built body is darkish brown; this turns to a darker blue-black when it is mature, with some darker barring across the dorsal surface and an often indistinct dark band along the flanks. The scales have iridescent, light metallic greenish-blue centers, with iridescent, speckling around the eyes and on the gill covers.
Gender: The female is generally paler, and her dorsal and anal fins are rounded.
Breeding: Open spawner
Special care: This territorial fish is likely to uproot plants, and may harass small fish.

"CICHLASOMA" SALVINI
Salvin's cichlid
FAMILY: *Cichlidae*

Range: Mexico, Belize, Honduras, and Guatemala

6 in   4 in   71–79°F
(15cm) (10cm) (22–26°C)

Characteristics: The body is golden yellow, with prominent dark bands running along the dorsal surface and over the lateral line from the eye to the caudal peduncle. The face bears a series of dark bands beginning just anterior to the dorsal fin and ending at the level of the eye. Below the mid-line, the body is marked in light blue and red, with the same colors being repeated in the fins.
Gender: The males have more pointed fins and brighter colors.
Breeding: Open spawner
Special care: Pairs become extremely aggressive.

CLEITHRACARA MARONII
Keyhole cichlid
FAMILY: *Cichlidae*

Range: Guyana

3   48

6 in (15cm)   3¼ in (8cm)   71–77°F (22–25°C)

Characteristics: The pale gray body has a distinctive, keyhole-shaped pattern of dark blotches on the flanks. Juvenile specimens have a dark band that runs vertically through the eye, and a single dark blotch that later develops into the keyhole pattern.
Gender: The males are larger and have longer dorsal and anal fins.

Breeding: Open spawner
Special care: This fish does best in soft, acidic water with ample filtration; it needs hiding places among rocks or driftwood. It does not damage plants, and actually appreciates vegetation in the aquarium.

CRENICICHLA LEPIDOTA
Two-spot pike cichlid
FAMILY: *Cichlidae*

Range: Brazil, Bolivia

7   60

10 in (25cm)   8 in (20cm)   73–82°F (23–28°C)

Characteristics: The elongated body can vary from silvery blue-gray, to pearly green, to slightly yellowish, with a darker dorsal surface. A dark band runs from the snout, through the eyes, to the base of the caudal fin. Immediately behind the gill cover this line may be broken by a bright-ringed dark blotch, and there is another similar eye-spot on the base of the caudal fin.
Gender: The males are larger, with more pointed dorsal and anal fins.
Breeding: Open spawner
Special care: This piscivore should only be kept with other large fish, as it will eat anything it can fit in its mouth.

CRYPTOHEROS NIGROFASCIATUS
Convict cichlid; zebra cichlid
FAMILY: *Cichlidae*

Range: Streams, rivers, and lakes of Central America

1   36

6 in (15cm)   4 in (10cm)   68–73°F (20–23°C)

Characteristics: This fish's stocky body, including the fins, is gray with numerous vertical dark bands crossing it, although they only encroach a little way into the dorsal and anal fins. Some yellow coloring and iridescent scaling may be seen in the lower body. A pinkish, leucistic form has been developed by selective aquarium breeding.

Above: The pinkish, near-albino, form of the convict cichlid.

Gender: The dorsal and anal fins have filamentous extensions in male specimens.
Breeding: Open spawner or cave spawner
Special care: This fish has a bad reputation for eating plants, and for other anti-social, disruptive tendencies.

CYPRICHROMIS LEPTOSOMA
Bright-finned slender cichlid
FAMILY: *Cichlidae*

Range: Lake Tanganyika

| 5 in | 5 in | 71–80°F |
| (13cm) | (13cm) | (22–27°C) |

Characteristics: This fish has an elongated body that is creamy gray in color with a blue sheen. The lower part of the head is yellow, and there is a small yellow saddle-shaped area on the upper part of the caudal peduncle. The base of the dorsal fin is long, with the greater depth at the rear of the fin. The anal fin is only half as long, but shares the same configuration.

Gender: The male is more colorful.

Breeding: Maternal mouth brooder

Special care: Keep this variety as a shoal in a large aquarium with rocky retreats.

DICROSSUS FILAMENTOSUS
Checkerboard cichlid
FAMILY: *Cichlidae*

Range: Brazil, Bolivia

| 3½ in | 3 in | 73–77°F |
| (9cm) | (7.5cm) | (23–25°C) |

Characteristics: The body is yellow, darker above and silvery-white below. A band runs from the snout to the end of the gill cover, then becomes a number of blotches forming a horizontal line ending at the caudal peduncle. Above and below these are greenish lines. The long-based dorsal fin and lyre-shaped caudal fin are both edged with light blue, have reddish speckles, and terminate in extended filaments.

Gender: The males have much more color and longer fins than the females.

Breeding: Open spawner

Special care: It is a shy species that needs soft, acidic water and prefers live foods.

ETROPLUS MACULATUS
Orange chromide
FAMILY: *Cichlidae*

Range: India, Sri Lanka

3½ in   3¼ in   68–79°F
(9cm)   (8cm)   (20–26°C)

Characteristics: This is a pale yellow to orange fish with rows of red dots along the flanks. Occasionally (and depending on the mood of the fish) a central black blotch may appear on the flanks, and the anal and pelvic fins become darker.
Gender: It is difficult to sex; the male may have red fringes to its fins.
Breeding: Their eggs are laid on sea-grass leaves in the wild (plastic vallis can be used in captivity).

The fry feed from the mucus on their parents' bodies in the first few months.
Special care: This fish requires a well-planted aquarium with retreats. Medium-hard alkaline water suits it well, with the addition of sea salt. Acidic water conditions will kill these fish.

ETROPLUS SURATENSIS
Green chromide; banded chromide
FAMILY: *Cichlidae*

Range: India, Sri Lanka

17¾ in   12 in   73–79°F
(45cm)   (30cm)   (23–26°C)

Characteristics: The dark olive body is paler behind the gill cover, and camouflaged with a series of dark green vertical bars. Its fins are light olive green to colorless. Bright dots cover the body from behind the gill cover to the caudal peduncle.
Gender: Males may grow larger; otherwise there are no discernible differences in appearance between males and females.

Breeding: Open spawner or cave spawner
Special care: This fish cannot be acclimatized to freshwater: it must be kept in brackish to full marine water. It will eat aquarium plants.

HEMICHROMIS BIMACULATUS
Jewel cichlid
FAMILY: *Cichlidae*

Range: Southern Guinea to Liberia

5   48

6 in   4 in   70–73°F
(15cm)   (10cm)   (21–23°C)

Characteristics: The red body has metallic blue iridescent speckling. There are two bright-ringed dark spots, one on the extreme rear edge of the gill covers and another midway along the body. The long-based dorsal fin, the shorter anal fin, and the rounded caudal fin carry the iridescent speckling.

Gender: The male has a pointed genital papilla.
Breeding: Open spawner
Special care: This is a pugnacious species best kept as a single species tank of jewel cichlids.

HERICHTHYS CYANOGUTTATUS
Texas cichlid
FAMILY: *Cichlidae*

Range: Mexico, Texas

1   72

12 in   10 in   68–75°F
(30cm)   (25cm)   (20–24°C)

Characteristics: The body is bluish-green in color with many iridescences that spread on to all the fins. There are two dark blotches, one midway along the flanks and the other on the caudal peduncle. The former is much more apparent in juvenile specimens, but the latter survives into adulthood.
Gender: Males develop a hump on the forehead with maturity. They also have more pointed dorsal and anal fins.
Breeding: Open spawner
Special care: This territorial, aggressive fish should be kept in a spacious aquarium with plastic plants. This species should ideally be kept on its own.

HEROS EFASCIATUS
Severum
FAMILY: *Cichlidae*

Range: Amazon Basin

8 in (20cm)   8 in (20cm)   73–77°F (23–25°C)

Characteristics: This variety has an oblong body shape, with a steep head profile, red-rimmed eyes, and a short caudal peduncle. The body is golden brown. Juveniles have vertical stripes crossing the body; in adults these are a series of dark blotches along the lower flanks. One dark stripe runs down from the rear of the dorsal fin across the caudal peduncle and into the anal fin; the rest of the body is covered with small red-brown dots. This is a gold or xanthic strain.

Gender: The female lacks the spots on the head and scales.

Breeding: Open spawner

Special care: It will thrive in a well-planted, roomy aquarium with plenty of rocky retreats.

HYBRID CULTIVAR
Blood-red parrot
FAMILY: *Cichlidae*

Range: Man-made cultivar

N/a   6 in (15cm)   71–77°F (22–25°C)

Characteristics: The strangely shaped head with its narrow beak has given rise to the name parrot cichlid, and the bright, red-orange coloration suggested the name blood-red parrot. Other colors are available, but may be dyed rather than natural. This fish should not be confused with the true parrot cichlid, *Hoplarchus psittacus*.

Gender: Unknown

Breeding: Breeding in captivity is possible, depending on ancestry.

Special care: As with many larger cichlids, this one has messy eating habits, so provide adequate filtration.

JULIDOCHROMIS DICKFELDI
Dickfeldi; Dickfeld's Julie
FAMILY: *Cichlidae*

Range: Lake Tanganyika

4 in | 3.2 in | 70–77°F
(10cm) | (8cm) | (21–25°C)

Characteristics: This distinctive fish has a cylindrical, pale white-brown body with three equally spaced, longitudinal dark bands, the lowest of which occupies the center line of the fish and runs from the snout to the end of the caudal peduncle. The dorsal and anal fins both have a long base with dark rays; the intermediate tissues are pale blue, a color that runs along the edges of most of the fins.

Gender: There are no visible sexual differences except, perhaps, that the female tends to be larger.
Breeding: Cave spawner
Special care: This fish can be kept in a relatively small aquarium with plenty of rockwork and caves.

JULIDOCHROMIS MARLIERI
Marlieri; Marlier's Julie
FAMILY: *Cichlidae*

Range: Lake Tanganyika

4¾ in | 4¾ in | 71–77°F
(12cm) | (12cm) | (22–25°C)

Characteristics: This fish's body is cylindrical in shape and very light cream in color; it is crossed with three dark bands, the lowest of which is on the center line. These lines are crossed vertically at regular intervals by indistinct dark bars that reach almost to the ventral surface. The eyes have a golden inner ring and are surrounded by a dark rim. The fins are dark, with cream markings.

Gender: The male is smaller, and has a nuchal hump.
Breeding: Cave spawner
Special care: Its ideal environment in captivity is a well-planted aquarium with rocky retreats.

JULIDOCHROMIS ORNATUS
Ornatus
FAMILY: *Cichlidae*

Range: Lake Tanganyika

3¼ in (8cm)	3 in (7.5cm)	70–77ºF (21–25ºC)

Characteristics: The body is white to golden yellow, overlaid with dark bands, the first from the bottom edge of the eyes to the caudal peduncle, the next beginning at the top of the eyes and extending to the rear margin of the dorsal fin, and the uppermost from the snout across the top of the head and down the back and into the bottom third of the dorsal fin. Juveniles lack the yellow coloration.
Gender: The males are larger than the females.
Breeding: Cave spawner
Special care: This fish requires hard, alkaline water, good filtration, and numerous rocks and caves.

JULIDOCHROMIS REGANI
Regani; Regan's Julie; striped Julie
FAMILY: *Cichlidae*

Range: Lake Tanganyika

6 in (15cm)	5 in (12cm)	71–77ºF (22–25ºC)

Characteristics: The light yellow-gold body has four to five dark bands that run its whole length, covering the face and terminating at the end of the caudal peduncle. The long-based dorsal fin has a yellow-gold base, followed by a black inner margin and light blue edging; the rounded caudal fin is marked in a similar way.
Gender: The male is smaller with pointed genital papilla.
Breeding: Cave spawner
Special care: Include plenty of rockwork and good filtration.

JULIDOCHROMIS TRANSCRIPTUS
Black and white Julie; transcriptus
FAMILY: *Cichlidae*

Range: Lake Tanganyika

2¾ in (7cm)	2¾ in (7cm)	70–77ºF (21–25ºC)

Characteristics: The body is yellow below the level of the eye, dark brown above, and with a double row of lighter yellow spots forming a line from the tip of the snout, through the eyes, along the flanks, and ending at the caudal peduncle. The dark brown coloration extends to the dorsal fin, which is edged in white. The caudal fin has a white margin with a thin black edge, and a second concentric inner white line.
Gender: The male's genital papilla is pointed.
Breeding: Cave spawner
Special care: This fish requires hard, alkaline water and numerous rocks, arranged to form caves.

LABEOTROPHEUS FUELLEBORNI
Fuelleborn's cichlid
FAMILY: *Cichlidae*

Range: Lake Malawi

6¼ in	4¾ in	71–77°F
(16cm)	(12cm)	(22–25°C)

Characteristics: The "red top" male is blue-gray, with numerous vertical dark bars covering the body and forehead. The dorsal fin can be varying shades of red with some dark rays and a lighter edge in the rear portion. The anal fin is red, with a few yellowish egg spots. An OB (Orange Blotch) form is known, which varies from orange with heavy blotching to pale orange with speckling.

Gender: The females come in both color forms, but lack egg spots on the anal fin.
Breeding: Maternal mouth brooder
Special care: This aggressive fish is intolerant of its own kind and even of similarly colored fish. Keep them in a large mbuna community aquarium.

LABEOTROPHEUS TREWAVASAE
Trewavasae cichlid
FAMILY: *Cichlidae*

Range: Lake Malawi

4¾ in	4 in	71–77°F
(12cm)	(10cm)	(22–25°C)

Characteristics: The body colors of this species range from almost pure white to a black-mottled variation, to blue-mauve with regular dark vertical bandings, to orange. Add to these basics the presence of an orange-red, long-based dorsal fin, and you have a whole color spectrum to choose from.
Gender: The males have a false egg spot patterning on the anal fin—but so do some females.
Breeding: Maternal mouth brooder
Special care: Keep these fish in a spacious mbuna community aquarium furnished with rocks and algal growth.

LABIDOCHROMIS CAERULEUS
Caeruleus; blue-white labido
FAMILY: *Cichlidae*

Range: Lake Malawi

4 in	4 in	71–7°F
(10cm)	(10cm)	(22–25°C)

Characteristics: The range of this fish stretches all along the west coast and produces a comparable range in coloration, from gray-blue at one end, shading to whiter then bright yellow at the other. This cichlid, with its bright yellow body and black-edged fins, rivals some marine fish for coloration.
Gender: The males are more colorful as well as being larger.

Breeding: Maternal mouth brooder
Special care: Adult males may quarrel, but juvenile fish can be kept in shoals. Keep in a mbuna community.

MELANOCHROMIS AURATUS
Auratus
FAMILY: *Cichlidae*

Range: Lake Malawi

5 in	4¼ in	71–77°F
(13cm)	(11cm)	(22–25°C)

Characteristics: Most females and all juveniles are yellow with two white-edged black bars on the upper half of the body running from the snout to the end of the caudal fin. A third white-bordered dark line runs along the middle of the yellow dorsal fin. The caudal fin has a yellow lower half and dark speckles on the upper. Mature males (and some territorial females) turn dark blue-black, with a silvery light-blue streak along the center line.
Gender: The male's anal fin has a few egg spots.
Breeding: Maternal mouth brooder
Special care: Provide a male with a harem of females. Use a spacious aquarium with plenty of rocky retreats and algal growth.

MELANOCHROMIS CHIPOKAE
Chipokae
FAMILY: *Cichlidae*

Range: Lake Malawi

4 | 48 | 6 in (15cm) | 5 in (13cm) | 71–77°F (22–25°C)

Characteristics: This fish is similar to the Auratus though with a more elongated head. Mature males lose the yellow coloring of juvenility and develop dark blue-black bodies with a broad, silvery light-blue band along the center line that ends just inside the base of the caudal fin. There is a second fainter band above it. Females retain their juvenile coloration of bright yellow body with white-bordered black bands.
Gender: The male's anal fin carries a few egg spots.
Breeding: Maternal mouth brooder

Special care: This fish needs a rocky aquarium with other mbuna.

MELANOCHROMIS JOHANNI
Johanni
FAMILY: *Cichlidae*

Range: Lake Malawi

4 | 48 | 4¾ in (12cm) | 4¾ in (12cm) | 71–77°F (22–25°C)

Characteristics: The mature male's body is elongated and slightly laterally compressed in shape; in color it is blue-black-brown with a silvery light-blue line running across the forehead, over the top of the eyes, and along the body just above the center line to end on the caudal peduncle. Approximately the same distance below the center line is another silvery blue-gray line. The females are bright orange.
Gender: The males have egg spots.
Breeding: Maternal mouth brooder
Special care: This fish needs a rocky aquarium, with other mbuna.

METRIACLIMA LOMBARDOI
Lombardoi; kennyi mbuna
FAMILY: *Cichlidae*

Range: Lake Malawi

4 | 48 | 5½ in (14cm) | 4 in (10cm) | 71–77°F (22–25°C)

Characteristics: This species is one of the very few examples where the female has the more attractive patterning. The male is bright yellow with some brown bars partially crossing the body. The fins are plain yellow with egg spots on the anal fin. The female has a pale white/blue body with a number of equally spaced, tapering blue/black vertical bands almost crossing the body, having originated midway across the width of the dorsal fin.

The fins are pale blue with darker markings.
Gender: The male has egg spots. Dominant females may develop similar color to males, but they never have the egg spots.
Breeding: Maternal mouth brooder
Special care: It is suitable for a mbuna community.

METRIACLIMA ZEBRA
Zebra
FAMILY: *Cichlidae*

Range: Lake Malawi

4   48

6 in (15cm)   5 in (13cm)   71–77°F (22–25°C)

Above: A red variant of the original zebra mbuna.

Characteristics: The zebra was instantly received with enthusiasm due to its coloration, especially by aquarists whose hard domestic tapwater often precluded them from keeping colorful fish that require soft water. Its body is light blue with numerous dark blue bands vertically crossing the body. The area below the eyes, together with the gill cover, mouth, throat, and forward part of the ventral region, is dark blue. The fins are light blue except the pelvic ones. The females are variable in color.

Gender: The males have egg spots—although so do a few females.

Breeding: Maternal mouth brooder

Special care: Use a mbuna community aquarium.

MICROGEOPHAGUS RAMIREZI
Ram; butterfly cichlid
FAMILY: *Cichlidae*

Range: Colombia, Venezuela

1   24

2¾ in (7cm)   2½ in (6.5cm)   71–79°F (22–26°C)

Characteristics: This fish has an elongated oval body shape, and a narrow caudal peduncle. The posterior two-thirds is blue with violet-blue iridescent scales, and a dark blotch below the dorsal fin. The anterior part is more yellowish, with a bar running through the red eye. The dorsal, anal, and caudal fins are reddish, and all carry iridescent blue specklings; the pelvic fins are red with a dark front edge. Gold and long-finned strains are available.

Gender: The second ray of the male's dorsal fin is black, and much extended.

Breeding: Open spawner

Special care: This fish will flourish in a well-planted aquarium with soft, acidic water.

NANOCHROMIS PARILUS
Blue Congo dwarf cichlid
FAMILY: *Cichlidae*

Range: Zaire Basin

3¼ in (8cm) 3 in (7.5cm) 71–77°F (22–25°C)

Characteristics: A pretty, elongated dwarf cichlid. This fish is a soft-looking, gray-brown color with some bluish areas toward the head and purplish areas on the belly, particularly visible on the female. The caudal fin has red patterning in it.

Gender: The male fish are generally larger and have more pointed dorsal and anal fins. The genital papilla of the female is visible virtually all the time.

Breeding: Cave spawner

Special care: This fish may be more content in a single-species aquarium.

NEOLAMPROLOGUS BRICHARDI
Fairy cichlid; Princess of Burundi; brichardi; Brichard's lamprologus
FAMILY: *Cichlidae*

Range: Lake Tanganyika

3½ in (9cm) 3½ in (9cm) 71–77°F (22–25°C)

Characteristics: This fish has a light brown, elongated body. On the rear of the gill cover is a gold-yellow spot, followed by a black patch. There are some blue facial markings below the mouth, and the eyes are brilliant blue. The fins are edged in blue-white. The base of both the dorsal and anal fins is long, with a pointed extension, and the caudal fin has a pronounced extension on each tip, making it lyre-shaped.

Gender: The male's dorsal and caudal fin extensions are longer.

Breeding: This is a cave spawner. Older siblings care for the young as well as the adults.

Special care: This peaceful fish needs a rocky environment, and medium to hard alkaline water.

NEOLAMPROLOGUS LELEUPI
Lemon cichlid
FAMILY: *Cichlidae*

Range: Lake Tanganyika

3½ in (9cm) 3½ in (9cm) 71–77°F (22–25°C)

Characteristics: The elongated body is bright yellow to orange. The mouth region may have some light brown coloring. The pupils of the eyes are dark and separated from the iris by a gold ring. All fins share the same color as the body, with only a hint of a darker shading at their rear edges.

Gender: The male is larger, with a bigger head.

Breeding: Cave spawner

Special care: This aggressive fish needs a spacious aquarium with many rocky cave-like retreats, and hard alkaline water.

PARACHROMIS DOVII
Wolf cichlid; Dow's cichlid
FAMILY: *Cichlidae*

Range: Honduras, Nicaragua, and Costa Rica

7   72   22½ in   16 in   71–82°F
          (70cm)   (40cm)   (22–28°C)

Characteristics: It is silvery blue in color, with a darker dorsal surface. A dark horizontal band made up of broken blotches runs from the gill cover to the end of the caudal peduncle, terminating in a dark blotch at the root of the caudal fin. Depending upon the mood of the fish, numerous dark narrow vertical bands can be seen crossing the sides.
Gender: The males are bluish, and the females are yellow with bands; there is also a big nuchal hump in the male.
Breeding: It is an open spawner.
Special care: Use an efficient filtration system, coupled with frequent partial water changes to keep this piscivore's environment clean.

PARACHROMIS MANAGUENSIS
Jaguar cichlid; mannie; managua cichlid
FAMILY: *Cichlidae*

Range: Honduras, Nicaragua, and Costa Rica

7   72   12 in   12 in   73–77°F
          (30cm)   (30cm)   (23–25°C)

Characteristics: It has an elongated, stocky, silvery blue-gray body covered with numerous dark irregular-shaped specklings that spread into all the fins. Depending upon the mood of the fish, a dark band, made up of almost connected blotches, may be seen along the flanks.
Gender: The males have pointed dorsal and anal fins, and are more colorful.

Breeding: Open spawner
Special care: A large aquarium is needed, with rockwork and plastic rather than real plants. This is a territorial and aggressive piscivore.

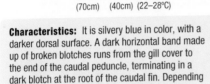

PELVICACHROMIS PULCHER
Kribensis
FAMILY: *Cichlidae*

Range: Nigeria

4 in (10cm)   4 in (10cm)   70–77°F (21–25°C)

Characteristics: The body is elongated, with approximately equal dorsal and ventral contours, although the latter may be fuller in the female. The lower half of the body is silvery pinkish-violet in the male; the belly area of the female takes on a deep purple, rich plum color. The female has gold areas above and below the eyes.

Gender: The color differences identify the male gender. The male has longer dorsal and anal fins.

Breeding: This is a cave spawner. Water pH values are known to have an effect on the proportion of the sexes within the brood.

Special care: Keep these fish in a well-planted aquarium with some caves and rocky hideaways. They are ideal for a community tank.

PSEUDOTROPHEUS ELONGATUS
Slender mbuna
FAMILY: *Cichlidae*

Range: Lake Malawi

         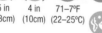

5 in (13cm)   4 in (10cm)   71–7°F (22–25°C)

Characteristics: This fish has an elongated body that is sooty-black-deep blue in color. From behind the gill covers a number of light blue bands cross the body vertically, stopping short of the ventral surface. The final blue band extends into the caudal fin, flaring out among the otherwise dark rays. All the other fins are dark.

Gender: The male's anal fin has egg spots.

Breeding: Maternal mouth brooder

Special care: This aggressive fish should be kept in a spacious aquarium with plenty of rocky furnishing and algal growth.

PTEROPHYLLUM ALTUM
Altum angelfish
FAMILY: *Cichlidae*

Range: Orinoco River

7 in (18cm)   5 in (13cm)   82–86°F (28–30°C)

Characteristics: The body of this fish is disc-like, and severely compressed laterally. Its body coloration is silver, with several dark bands crossing vertically, and entering the dorsal and anal fins. There is a distinct notch in the outline of the forehead above the snout. The dorsal and anal fins are long, and in mature specimens filaments extend from their tips. The caudal fin has top and bottom extensions.

Gender: Unknown

Breeding: This is an open spawner on vertical surfaces.

Special care: This fish needs a deep aquarium with very soft acidic water, and lots of growing plants. It is an extremely difficult and delicate fish to keep.

PTEROPHYLLUM SCALARE
Angelfish
FAMILY: *Cichlidae*

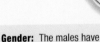

Range: Amazon and Rio Negro systems

6 in   5 in   75–82°F
(15cm) (13cm) (24–28°C)

Characteristics: The body coloration of the original wild species is silver, with several dark vertical bands crossing the body and entering the dorsal and anal fins, with occasional dark speckling between the bands. Lots of color forms have been developed. The dorsal and anal fins are tall, with filaments extending from the caudal lobes in mature specimens, and thread-like pelvic fins extending below the anal fin.

Gender: The males have pointed genital papilla.
Breeding: This is an open spawner on vertical surfaces.
Special care: Keep this fish in a well-planted aquarium with other fish too large to eat—neons will eventually be eaten!

SATANOPERCA ACUTICEPS
Sparkling geophagus
FAMILY: *Cichlidae*

Range: Amazon Basin

10 in   6 in   75–79°F
(25cm) (15cm) (24–26°C)

Characteristics: The body is light olive green with a series of dark blotches mid-laterally, beginning just behind the gill cover and ending at the caudal peduncle. Pale lines extend from the snout through the eyes, and continue beyond the gill cover as horizontal rows of bright dots that give the species its common name.
Gender: Male has longer dorsal and anal fins.
Breeding: This fish is a pit spawner, although it probably does not breed in captivity.
Special care: It feeds by taking in a mouthful of sand and extracting small invertebrates. In the aquarium use a sand substrate and feed a variety of small, meaty, or live foods.

SATANOPERCA DAEMON
Slender geophagus; three-spotted eartheater
FAMILY: *Cichlidae*

Range: Rio Negro, Amazon, and Orinoco

12 in   8 in   80–86°F
(30cm) (20cm) (27–30°C)

Characteristics: The elongated body is blue-gray with a yellowish tinge to the lower flanks; the scales have dark edges. There are two dark blotches on the flanks, the forwardmost one lying exactly midway along the body, the second between the rear parts of the dorsal and anal fin. A bright-ringed dark blotch appears on the base of the caudal fin, slightly above the horizontal line.
Gender: In the male, the dorsal and anal fins have longer rays than those of the female.
Breeding: Open spawner
Special care: Use a sand substrate, plastic plants, and well-anchored rocks. This peaceful fish is suitable for a community collection of mixed-size fish.

SATANOPERCA JURAPARI
Eartheater; demonfish
FAMILY: *Cichlidae*

Range: Brazil, Guyana

10 in	6 in	75–79°F
(25cm)	(15cm)	(24–26°C)

Characteristics: The entire body is silvery, with colorless fins. The face and dorsal surface, down to the lateral line, are decorated with olive-green lines that help to camouflage the fish in its natural habitat.
Gender: The males have pointed genital papilla.
Breeding: These are maternal and paternal mouth brooders. The eggs are first placed on a rock by the female, who subsequently takes them into her mouth for brooding after they are fertilized by the male. Both parents then share the duty of brooding the eggs in the mouth. For a time after the fry become free swimming, they may return to the parent's mouth at night or at the approach of danger.
Special care: Because of its habitual digging behavior, only the hardiest plants should be included in this fish's tank, and a sand substrate should be used.

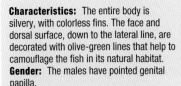

SCIAENOCHROMIS AHLI
Electric blue "haplochromis"
FAMILY: *Cichlidae*

Range: Lake Malawi

8 in	8 in	75–79°F
(20cm)	(20cm)	(24–26°C)

Characteristics: The brilliant blue body is marked by indistinct, dark blue vertical bars, and the anal and dorsal fins are edged in paler blue. The eyes are golden, and thus appear larger than they actually are.
Gender: The males are bright blue when sexually active.
Breeding: Maternal mouth brooder

Special care: This is a good choice for a community of haplochromine cichlids from Lake Malawi. Provide plenty of room, rockwork, and hard, alkaline water. In the wild this variety feeds on fish fry, but it will take any small live, frozen, and dried foods in captivity.

STEATOCRANUS TINANTI
Tinanti; slender lionhead cichlid
FAMILY: *Cichlidae*

Range: Democratic Republic of the Congo

6 in   4 in   77–80°F
(15cm)   (10cm)   (25–27°C)

Characteristics: A very slender species, with the head quite large in proportion to the rest of the body, and the swim bladder barely existent. The cryptic dark vertical bands on the cream-yellow body help to disguise its presence on the riverbed.
Gender: The male has elongated dorsal and anal fins.

Breeding: Cave spawner
Special care: It needs soft, slightly acidic water, and a roomy tank with rocks and driftwood instead of plants. It greedily accepts all types of aquarium foods.

SYMPHYSODON AEQUIFASCIATA HARALDI
Blue discus
FAMILY: *Cichlidae*

Range: South America

6 in   6 in   79–86°F
(15cm)   (15cm)   (26–30°C)

Characteristics: This splendid fish has a round body that is laterally compressed and disc-like. In color the body is brown, and crossed with dark vertical bars, over which is laid a pattern of blue wavy lines that extend into the dorsal and anal fins. These fins have a long base, almost reaching the caudal fin. The dorsal fin may have a red edge, the anal a dark inner margin covering the blue markings.

Gender: The male has a pointed genital papilla.
Breeding: This is an open spawner on vertical surfaces. The young feed on the parents' mucus for the first few weeks.
Special care: The aquarium should be spacious, and furnished with tall plants. Soft acidic water conditions are ideal.

THORICHTHYS MEEKI
Firemouth
FAMILY: *Cichlidae*

Range: Mexico, Guatemala, and Belize

6 in (15cm) **5 in** (13cm) **70–75°F** (21–24°C)

Characteristics: Its body is greenish-gray, with clearly defined scales, and there is a dark spot on the gill cover just behind the eyes. There is a mid-lateral band that is sometimes fragmented. Faint vertical bars may also be present. The fiery red coloration of the lower mouth and chest region is found in both sexes. When displaying, the gills are extended below the operculum, which is also flared out.
Gender: The males have more pointed dorsal and anal fins.
Breeding: Open spawner
Special care: It likes a well-planted tank with some caves and rockwork.

VIEJA HARTWEGI
Hartweg's cichlid
FAMILY: *Cichlidae*

Range: Southern Mexico

12 in (30cm) **12 in** (30cm) **75–80°F** (24–27°C)

Characteristics: The body coloration depends upon lighting conditions, as the pinkish-turquoise sheen is best seen when light comes from the side. The whole body is covered with small red-brown spots, and according to temperament a number of dark, vertical crossbands may be seen; but generally the usual patterning is a thin dark band along the flanks. The rear edge of the caudal fin is red.
Gender: The female is smaller and has less color.
Breeding: Open spawner
Special care: This variety is not tolerant of its own kind. It likes some hideaways among rocks and underwater roots, although it may eat aquarium plants.

TROPHEOPS TROPHEOPS
Tropheops
FAMILY: *Cichlidae*

Range: Lake Malawi

5½ in (14cm) **5½ in** (14cm) **70–77°F** (21–25°C)

Characteristics: The body is usually brownish, and crossed vertically by numerous indistinct dark bars; these may show up more clearly when the fish is under stress. The head is blunt, with a very steep forehead between the large, high-set eyes and mouth; the upper lip turns over the lower. The pelvic and anal fins have dark and light blue edges.
Gender: The male's anal fin bears a few egg spots. The females sometimes have a mottled coloration totally different to that of the males.
Breeding: Maternal mouth brooder
Special care: Use a mbuna community aquarium, with plenty of rocky retreats and algal growth.

Labyrinthfish

Strictly speaking the Anabantidae family only contains the climbing perch fish, but the family name has become almost a blanket term for labyrinthfish, to give them their popular name. A feature of the whole group is the extra breathing accessory—the labyrinth organ—which is located in the head just behind the gills. This organ consists of a mass of convoluted tissue into which moist air, gulped at the surface, is stored and from which oxygen can be extracted. This organ is of enormous benefit to the fish should the waters in which they live become depleted of oxygen through pollution. The group, whose members have their natural habitats in Southeast Asia and equatorial Africa, contains fish of modest and giant size, of peaceful and predatory dispositions. The predatory genus, *Ctenopoma*, is found in equatorial Africa but, while some of these fish are quite beautifully marked, careful consideration has to be given as to the fish that they are kept with.

The popular and numerous species of gourami belong to the Belontidae family. These fish have adapted pelvic fins that are mostly single filaments with taste buds at the end. Another family member is the Siamese fighting fish, *Betta splendens*. All specimens found in the aquatic dealers are captive bred; wild specimens do not have the bright colors or the elaborate finnage.

The kissing gourami, *Helostoma temmincki*, belongs to the Helostomidae family and the very large giant gourami, *Osphronemus goramy*, is the sole species in the Osphronemidae family. These fish can be kept as part of a community collection, as solitary specimens, or in a single-species collection. The majority are bubble-nest builders—the males construct a floating nest of bubbles and saliva, under which the female is coaxed and the eggs expelled and fertilized. Males become very territorial when guarding the eggs and it is best to remove the female after spawning to save her from attacks by the male. An exception to this reproduction method is the chocolate gourami, *Sphaerichthys osphromenoides*, which is a mouthbrooder.

CTENOPOMA ACUTIROSTRE
Spotted climbing perch
FAMILY: *Anabantidae*

Range: Zaire

8 in
(20cm)

6 in
(15cm)

73–82°F
(23–28°C)

Characteristics: It has an oval, golden-brown body covered with leopard-like spots, a pointed snout, and truncated rear. The caudal peduncle is almost non-existent. There is a dark spot at the base of the caudal fin. The mouth is situated terminally, and can extend outward to form a wide tube that engulfs prey. The dorsal and anal fins are predominantly spiny, though they become softer as they terminate; the anal and dorsal fins both have a long base, almost reaching to include the caudal fin. The golden-brown fins may have slightly darker speckling.

Gender: The female may have fewer spots.

Breeding: Bubble nest builder

Special care: This predatory fish cannot be kept with smaller fish.

CTENOPOMA MULTISPINIS
Many-spined ctenopoma
FAMILY: *Anabantidae*

Range: East and Central Africa

6¼ in
(16cm)

6 in
(15cm)

75–81°F
(24–27°C)

Characteristics: The tan body has a checkerboard pattern of dark scales. It has a colorless, spined dorsal fin, with spines on the cheeks and gill covers. It grows rather large for an anabantid, and is a messy feeder. It is greedy and aggressive.

Gender: The male has a spiny area.

Breeding: Courtship is intense. In due course, oily eggs rise to the water surface.

Special care: This fish needs a roomy tank, good filtration, and regular partial water changes.

MICROCTENOPOMA NANUM
Dwarf climbing perch
FAMILY: *Anabantidae*

Range: Cameroon to Zaire

3¼ in
(8cm)

3¼ in
(8cm)

65–75°F
(18–24°C)

Characteristics: It has a pale body marked with a series of olive vertical bars from gill cover to caudal peduncle. The bars extend on to the pale dorsal and anal fins. The tail fin is also colorless, with white along the spines. It has olive markings on the head, and a dark spot on the gill cover. A pair becomes quite aggressive at spawning time.

Gender: Males are territorial. They have longer anal and dorsal fins. Females are duller in color.

Breeding: Bubble nester

Special care: This fish prefers a planted tank with soft, slightly acidic water. It can be kept in a community tank.

BETTA SPLENDENS
Siamese fighting fish
FAMILY: *Belontiidae*

Range: Thailand, Cambodia

2½ in (6.5cm)   2½ in (6.5cm)   75—82°F (24—28°C)

Characteristics: It has a cylindrical body, the dorsal and ventral surfaces being moderately curved. The male's long, flowing dorsal has a relatively small base; the flowing anal fin has a long base, the caudal is well rounded. The pelvic fins are very long, with only a few rays. Many colors and varieties have been developed.

Gender: The females have a white "egg spot" at their anus.
Breeding: Bubble nester
Special care: The males are very aggressive toward each other, so be sure to have only one per aquarium.

COLISA FASCIATA
Banded gourami
FAMILY: *Belontiidae*

Range: India, Bengal, Assam, and Burma

4 in (10cm)   3¼ in (8cm)   72–82°F (22–28°C)

Characteristics: The pale body and colorless fins are marked in rust red and neon blue, and form a banded pattern on the flanks. The anal fin is electric blue, edged in red.
Gender: The males are more highly colored, with long, flowing finnage. The females are short-finned.
Breeding: Bubble nesters
Special care: Soft, acidic water and plenty of vegetation suit this species best. It can be included in a community aquarium with species having similar requirements.

COLISA LABIOSA
Thick-lipped gourami
FAMILY: *Belontiidae*

Range: Northern India, Burma

3¼ in (8cm)   3¼ in (8cm)   72–82°F (22–28°C)

Characteristics: This fish has a long but fairly deep golden-brown body, crossed diagonally with equally spaced bands of turquoise on the rear two-thirds. The upturned mouth has well-formed lips. The male's dorsal fin is very pointed. The anal fin is brown, with turquoise speckling in the male, with lighter edging.
Gender: The throat area in the male is turquoise, while in the female it is silver. The female is less colorful.
Breeding: Bubble nester
Special are: A large, well-planted aquarium is ideal, and a gentle flow of water is beneficial.

COLISA LALIA
Dwarf gourami
FAMILY: *Belontiidae*

Range: India, Borneo

2⅜ in 2 in 72–82°F
(6cm) (5cm) (22–28°C)

Characteristics: The body is silvery-gray with numerous bright red and blue vertical stripes. The lower head and throat are turquoise blue, with a slightly upturned mouth and red eyes. The dorsal, caudal, and anal fins are blue with red speckling; the orange pelvic fins are thread-like.
Gender: The females are less highly colored and are often plumper in the body.
Breeding: Bubble nester
Special Care: Usually quite peaceful in the community aquarium, the male can become very pugnacious when breeding.

COLISA LALIA
Red sunset gourami
FAMILY: *Belontiidae*

Range: India, Borneo

2 in 2 in 72–80°F
(5cm) (5cm) (22–27°C)

Characteristics: The color form of the wild type sunset or dwarf gourami is peaceful and non-aggressive. The body is a golden orange with a silvery head. The dorsal fin is blue, becoming golden posteriorly. The caudal fin rays and posterior part of the anal fin are orange, with colorless tissue in between. The anal fin becomes blue on its anterior edge. The whisker-like pectoral fins are white.
Gender: Females are less colorful.
Breeding: Bubble nester
Special care: It requires a roomy, well-planted tank with soft, slightly acidic water. It needs frequent water changes.

MACROPODUS OPERCULARIS
Paradise fish
FAMILY: *Belontiidae*

Range: Paddy fields of eastern Asia

4 in 3¼ in 61–78°F
(10cm) (8cm) (16–25°C)

Characteristics: It is pugnacious and aggressive. The body is a pale electric blue, darkening to nearly black on the long, flowing dorsal and anal fins. Vertical red bars begin as a diffuse patch behind the gill cover, and continue to the caudal peduncle. The caudal fin is red with light blue markings.
Gender: The males are generally larger and more brightly colored than the females.
Breeding: Bubble nester
Special care: It likes cooler waters than many other members of its family. It has a wide temperature tolerance.

TRICHOGASTER LEERI
Lace, pearl, or mosaic gourami
FAMILY: *Belontiidae*

Range: Borneo, Malaysia, and Sumatra

4¾ in (12cm) 4¼ in (11cm) 74–82°F (24–42°C)

Characteristics: This fish has a silvery body with a mosaic pattern of dark spots; a dark line runs from the snout, through the eyes to the caudal peduncle. The male's long dorsal is short-based, with long, trailing filaments in the rear portion. The anal fin has a long base. The male displays a bright orange throat, chest, pelvic fins, and the front of the anal fin.

Gender: The female has a shorter, rounder dorsal, and a silvery throat.
Breeding: Bubble nester
Special care: A peaceful fish suitable for a community of mixed-size fish.

TRICHOGASTER MICROLEPIS
Moonlight gourami
FAMILY: *Belontiidae*

Range: Cambodia, Thailand

7 in (18cm) 5½ in (14cm) 79–86°F (26–30°C)

Characteristics: The silver body has an even sheen. There is a notch in the profile of the head just above the upturned mouth. The eyes have dark pupils with reddish-gold irises. The long-based silvery anal fin runs from just behind the pelvic fins along the body to just before the caudal. Very long orange, thread-like pelvic fins.
Gender: The male has much longer dorsal and pelvic fins. The female is less colorful.
Breeding: Bubble nester
Special care: It likes a well-planted aquarium; it breeds better in soft water.

TRICHOGASTER PECTORALIS
Snakeskin gourami
FAMILY: *Belontiidae*

Range: Southeast Asia

8 in (20cm) 6 in (15cm) 73–82°F (23–28°C)

Characteristics: It has a pale green to silvery body with a pattern of dark blotches along the mid-line from the gill cover to the caudal peduncle. This is a non-aggressive species.
Gender: The female's anal fin is edged in bright yellow; the male possesses orange-red pelvic fins.
Breeding: Bubble nester
Special Care: It is peaceful toward its tankmates, even when it is spawning. It is important to provide plants or other hiding places.

TRICHOGASTER TRICHOPTERUS
Three-spot gourami
FAMILY: *Belontiidae*

Range: Southeast Asia

4¾ in (12cm)   4¼ in (11cm)   72–82°F (22–28°C)

Characteristics: This is a very hardy, peaceful, long-lived fish. The body is a delicate light powder blue, with two dark spots on the flanks, one midway, the other at the end of the caudal peduncle. The eyes form the third spot. The fins are clear, with some blue specklings.

Gender: The males have a longer dorsal fin and some orange coloring to the thread-like pelvic fins.

Breeding: Bubble nester

Special care: This fish needs a well-planted aquarium in a community of mixed-size fish. It is a prolific breeder; females may need protection from vigorously chasing males after spawning.

TRICHOPSIS VITTATUS
Croaking gourami
FAMILY: *Belontiidae*

Range: Southeast Asia, particularly Vietnam, Thailand, and Malaysia

3¼ in (8cm)   2⅜ in (6cm)   72–82°F (22–28°C)

Characteristics: This is a gentle species that croaks. The golden-brown body is relatively slim, with two or three longitudinal markings made up of reddish-brown dots or small blotches. There is reddish-brown streaking on the small head; the red-rimmed blue eyes are set well forward. The short-based dorsal fin is set well back. The anal fin is longer-based, and widens toward the rear. All fins are bluish, speckled with red.

Gender: The female is less colorful.

Breeding: Bubble nester

Special care: It likes to hide among plants. Keep it with other small species.

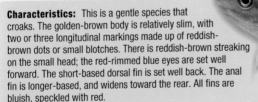

HELOSTOMA TEMMINCKI
Kissing gourami
FAMILY: *Helostomidae*

Range: Borneo, Java, Sumatra, and Thailand

3   48

10 in   8 in   72–82°F
(25cm)   (20cm)   (22–28°C)

Characteristics: The body can be either greenish-silver, with rows of tiny darker dots, or a pale rose-pink. The head is pointed, with a thick-lipped mouth. The dorsal and anal fins both have very long bases, with spines for about two-thirds of their length. The caudal fin has a straight rear edge. All fins are fairly colorless.

Gender: It is difficult to sex.
Breeding: Bubble nester
Special care: This peaceful fish is suitable for a community of larger fish. Generally, it breeds more successfully in soft water.

OSPHRONEMUS GORAMY
Gourami
FAMILY: *Osphronemidae*

Range: China, Java, Malaysia, and eastern India

3   72

24 in   20 in   68–86°F
(60cm)   (50cm)   (20–30°C)

Characteristics: Young fish have silvery bronze-gray bodies crossed by several vertical dark bars. The pointed head has eyes set well forward. The fins are bronze, the pelvic fins being filamentous and bronze-yellow. The adult fish is dull gray. It has large, fleshy, upturned lips. The dorsal and caudal fins are dark gray.
Gender: Males have more pointed fins;

the female is more heavily built.
Breeding: Bubble nester
Special care: It has a prodigious appetite for aquarium plants. It is best kept on its own, or with other large fish, in a rockily furnished aquarium of a suitable size.

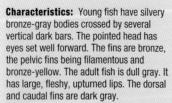

Catfish

See-through fish, fish that swim upside down, fish that walk on land, fish that use electricity to kill, and fish that emit sound are but a few of the piscine attractions to be found in this group of fish from the Americas, Africa, and Asia. The variety in size is astonishing—from midgets of 1 in (2.5cm) right up to South American giants reaching 4.5 ft (120cm).

A common feature among the majority of catfish is their bottom-dwelling habit. Another characteristic, often missed by aquarists keeping just one as a cleaner, is that many species are quite gregarious and delight in being kept in numbers of their own kind. Many are nocturnal by nature, and so their "normal" activities often go unnoticed, unless they can be fooled into coming out earlier in the evening by altering the lighting times of their aquarium.

Catfish's flat-bottomed bodies allow them to hug the bottom of the river or streambed without being swept away by water currents. They are excellent at locating food among the debris on the aquarium floor; taste cells in the barbels assist in this task, and are particularly useful in muddy water or at night, when visibility is impaired. Unlike the majority of other fish, catfish have no scales as such; their skin may be left naked or covered with overlapping bony plates called scutes. They often take in air from the surface, but, unlike anabantids, they have no auxiliary breathing organ in the head, and oxygen is extracted from gulped atmospheric air in the hind part of the gut.

Usually omnivorous (and with vigorous appetites), some species are more herbivorous and are sought after by hobbyists as a means of controlling algae. Such species have sucker-like mouths equipped with rasping teeth; in the absence of an algae-covered tank they require extra green matter in their diet, which can be lettuce, spinach, or even canned peas.

Catfish spawn in several ways: Corydoras deposit eggs on any flat surface, the eggs being carried to the site by the female between her pelvic fins. The armored catfish, *Callichthys callichthys*, builds a bubble nest in which to place the eggs beneath a plant leaf. Others spawn on flat surfaces, in pits dug in the gravel, or inside pipes; still others are mouthbrooders.

FEATURED IN THIS SECTION

ARIUS SEEMANI
American shark catfish
FAMILY: *Ariidae*

Range: From Colombia to as far north as California

5 | 72 | 13¾ in (35cm) | 12 in (30cm) | 72–79°F (22–26°C)

Characteristics: This is a marine species that can adapt to life in freshwater. It has a silvery body with charcoal-gray fins. The anal, pelvic, and pectoral fins are darker than the dorsal, adipose, and caudal fins, and are edged in white.

Gender: The female has lighter colored fins.

Breeding: Paternal mouth brooder

Special care: In nature this fish prefers insect larvae, and can be fed mosquito larvae or frozen crustaceans, along with the usual flake foods and tablets. It needs water currents and well-oxygenated water. Usually, only young specimens are imported for the aquarium. As they grow their color fades. Since adults spend their lives in the sea, a marine tank will be required after they reach maturity.

AUCHENIPTERICHTHYS THORACATUS
Midnight catfish; zamora woodcat
FAMILY: *Auchenipteridae*

Range: Upper Amazon

1 | 36 | 4¾ in (12cm) | 4 in (10cm) | 70–77°F (21–25°C)

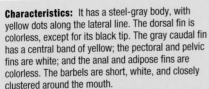

Characteristics: It has a steel-gray body, with yellow dots along the lateral line. The dorsal fin is colorless, except for its black tip. The gray caudal fin has a central band of yellow; the pectoral and pelvic fins are white; and the anal and adipose fins are colorless. The barbels are short, white, and closely clustered around the mouth.

Gender: Males have thickened dorsal and pelvic fin spines.

Breeding: The male fertilizes the female internally before the eggs are released.

Special care: This nocturnal fish is a good community subject, as long as its tankmates are too large to swallow. Provide a well-planted, roomy aquarium with driftwood. Moderately soft, slightly acidic water suits it well. Feed with a wide variety of meaty foods.

CHRYSICHTHYS ORNATUS
Ornate catfish
FAMILY: *Bagridae*

Range: Zaire, central tropical Africa

2 48

10 in (25cm) 8 in (20cm) 70–77°F (21–25°C)

Characteristics: This fish is long and heavily built, with a slightly arched dorsal surface and flattened profile. Its body is golden brown with areas of darker patterning that fade with age. The belly is silvery white. The head is flat, and the eyes are set high above the general profile. There are two barbels on the upper lip and six on the lower. All the fins are speckled with dark dots.
Gender: The male fish has long spines in the pectoral fins.

Breeding: Unknown
Special care: This is a predator that is best kept in a well-planted aquarium. Include plenty of hiding places, and only keep it with fish that are larger than itself.

BROCHIS SPLENDENS
Common brochis; green cat; short-bodied catfish
FAMILY: *Callichthyidae*

Range: Brazil, Ecuador, and Peru

1 36

3 in (7.5cm) 3 in (7.5cm) 72–82°F (22–28°C)

Characteristics: The body color is metallic green, becoming pinkish on the belly and with a dark blotch on the operculum. The body is stockily built, and covered with two rows of bony scutes; the eyes are mobile, and often move independently. There are three pairs of barbels; the fins are mostly pinkish-brown in color; and the dorsal fin has a longer base than Corydoras.
Gender: The female is plumper.

Breeding: The female carries the eggs between her pelvic fins, and deposits them on a firm surface.
Special care: This fish needs a well-planted aquarium, but with open areas of soft, sandy substrate. It will make brief dashes to the surface to take in atmospheric air; the oxygen is then extracted in its hindgut.

CALLICHTHYS CALLICHTHYS
Hassar; slender armored catfish
FAMILY: *Callichthyidae*

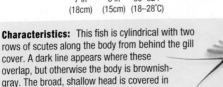

Range: Brazil

1   36

7 in   6 in   65–82°F
(18cm)   (15cm)   (18–28°C)

Characteristics: This fish is cylindrical with two rows of scutes along the body from behind the gill cover. A dark line appears where these overlap, but otherwise the body is brownish-gray. The broad, shallow head is covered in armor plating; the eyes are small. There are two pairs of long barbels.
Gender: The female is plumper; the male has longer pelvic fin spines.
Breeding: This is a bubble nester that uses floating or broad-leaved plants to build its nest; the male guards the nest until the eggs hatch.
Special care: This fish is nocturnal, so feed at night. Provide plenty of retreats for daytime use, with some floating plant cover.

The male (above, top) has stout pectoral fins, while the female (above, bottom) has a more robust body.

CORYDORAS AENEUS
Bronze corydoras
FAMILY: *Callichthyidae*

Range: South America, Trinidad

2   24

2¾ in   2¾ in   70–77°F
(7cm)   (7cm)   (21–25°C)

Characteristics: The stocky body is bronze colored and covered with two rows of bony scutes, the top row having a dark grayish-green, metallic sheen. The operculum is also a metallic green. There are three pairs of barbels, and the fins are pinkish-brown. Several wild color morphs exist, as well as an albino form. Sadly, color-injected fish are also offered for sale.

Gender: Seen from above the female is wider at the pectoral fins.
Breeding: This fish sticks its fertilized eggs on plant leaves and the aquarium glass.
Special care: It needs to be housed in a well-planted aquarium with open areas of soft, sandy substrate. Feed some sinking tablet foods.

CORYDORAS BARBATUS
Bearded corydoras; filigree cory
FAMILY: *Callichthyidae*

Range: Rio de Janeiro state, Brazil

3⅜ in   3⅜ in   65–75°F
(8.5cm)   (8.5cm)   (18–24°C)

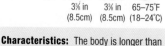

Characteristics: The body is longer than most Corydoras, and covered with two rows of bony scutes; the creamy-white coloration has a dark, reticulated patterning with a band running along the flanks to the caudal peduncle. The belly is a plain cream color. The long, shallow-sloping head has three pairs of barbels; the fins are mottled.
Gender: The male has cheek bristles.
Breeding: The female carries the eggs between her fins and deposits them on a firm surface.

Special care: This fish needs a well-planted aquarium with open areas of soft, sandy substrate.

CORYDORAS ELEGANS
Elegant corydoras
FAMILY: *Callichthyidae*

Range: Brazil

2½ in   2½ in   70–77°F
(6.5cm)   (6.5cm)   (21–25°C)

Characteristics: This is a slender cory, its body covered with two rows of bony scutes, the upper area of the upper row dark, with another band running just above where the two rows meet. The belly is cream to pink in color. The head itself is fairly short, and the eyes relatively large. There are three pairs of barbels. The dorsal fin has dark speckles.

Gender: The male is darker and slimmer.
Breeding: This fish sticks its eggs to plant leaves and the aquarium glass.
Special care: Never use a sharp substrate for Corydoras, as this can cause the barbels to wear down.

CORYDORAS HARALDSHULTZI
Harald Shultz's cory
FAMILY: *Callichthyidae*

Range: Brazil

3 in
(7.5cm)   3 in
(7.5cm)   70–77°F
(21–25°C)

Characteristics: The background color is a silvery blue-gray; the ventral surface is slightly pink, and a dark reticulated pattern covers the whole body. Toward the rear, some of the patterning along the flanks forms parallel lines. The moderately large head is also covered with numerous separate dark spots. The down-turned mouth has three pairs of barbels. Most of the fins carry the dark patterning of the body.
Gender: The male is slimmer.
Breeding: The female carries the eggs between her fins, and deposits them on a firm surface.
Special care: Provide a well-planted aquarium with open areas of soft, sandy substrate.

CORYDORAS LEUCOMELAS
Blackfin corydoras; false-spotted catfish
FAMILY: *Callichthyidae*

Range: Colombia, Peru

2⅜ in
(6cm)   2⅜ in
(6cm)   70–77°F
(21–25°C)

Characteristics: The silvery-gray body is sprinkled with black spots, except for the very pale yellowish-white belly. A vertical dark bar crosses the eyes and curves up toward the dorsal fin. A dark blotch at the base of the dorsal fin extends into the fin to color its front part, while dotted patterning on the caudal fin forms vertical banding. Three pairs of barbels adorn the mouth.
Gender: The female is larger and plumper.
Breeding: It spawns in typical Corydoras fashion, depositing the eggs on a firm surface.
Special care: No special care is required.

CORYDORAS PALEATUS
Peppered cory
FAMILY: *Callichthyidae*

Range: Brazil, Uruguay, and Argentina

2¾ in   2¾ in   68–77°F
(7cm)   (7cm)   (20–25°C)

Characteristics: The cream-colored body is overlaid with brownish-green mottling that extends into the finnage. Wild-caught fish tend to be better colored, and the males have much longer and more pointed dorsal and pelvic fins, with the hard spiny rays greatly elongated. An albino form has also been bred.

Gender: The females are plumper, with more rounded pectoral and pelvic fins.
Breeding: This species sticks adhesive eggs on the aquarium glass, or other decor.
Special care: None is required. This is a hardy, peaceful community fish. Make sure it has its fair share of food by feeding some sinking catfish pellets.

CORYDORAS PANDA
Panda cory
FAMILY: *Callichthyidae*

Range: Peru

2 in   2 in   70–77°F
(5cm)   (5cm)   (21–25°C)

Characteristics: A peaceful fish that has become very popular among hobbyists. It appears at first glance to be a slim-bodied *C. aeneus*, with the normal two rows of scutes along the flanks clearly defined. However, four dark patches—one covering each eye, one on the dorsal fin, and one on the caudal peduncle—mark this fish out, and explain its popular name of "panda." The overall body coloration is a pale golden brown.

Gender: The male is more slender.
Breeding: This is a typical Corydoras, although the eggs are deposited in plants rather than on flat surfaces.
Special care: None is required.

CORYDORAS TRILINEATUS
Three-line cory
FAMILY: *Callichthyidae*

Range: Peru, Colombia, and Ecuador

2 in   2 in   72–79°F
(5cm) (5cm) (22–26°C)

Characteristics: An extremely variable, short-snouted cory. The dorsal fin has a black blotch; the caudal fin can have from three to seven vertical bars made up of black spots on each of the fin rays; the adipose fin has a black marking; and all the other fins are clear. The body color is cream, with a zigzag black stripe running along the junction of the bony scutes from below the dorsal fin to the caudal peduncle. Above and below this is clear of patterning, while the rest of the body has black lines or spotting.

Gender: The female is fuller, and with more rounded pelvic and pectoral fins.

Breeding: This species deposits eggs on plants or the aquarium glass.

Special care: A hardy fish that is ideal for a community aquarium.

DIANEMA LONGIBARBIS
Porthole catfish
FAMILY: *Callichthyidae*

Range: Peru

4 in   4 in   71–79°F
(10cm) (10cm (22–26°C)

Characteristics: The body color is creamy gray, with dark speckling generally on the upper row of scutes, and a pinkish ventral surface. The head is long and flat, the mouth terminal rather than underslung. Two pairs of long barbels are held out in front of the fish as it swims. The fins are colorless, and the tail is forked.

Gender: The female is fuller.

Breeding: This fish builds a bubble nest in floating plants.

Special care: It thrives in a well-planted aquarium with some broad-leaved plants on which it may rest.

DIANEMA UROSTRIATA
Stripe-tailed catfish; flagtail porthole catfish
FAMILY: *Callichthyidae*

Range: Brazil

5 in   5 in   71–79°F
(13cm) (13cm) (22–26°C)

Characteristics: An active, shoaling fish, mainly nocturnal. The body is elongated and cylindrical, with some dark speckling overlaying a grayish-brown background; this becomes lighter on the belly, and silver below the head. The head is long and flattened, the mouth terminal, and the two pairs of long barbels are held out in front of the fish as it swims. The forked caudal fin has horizontal black and white stripes, which gives this species its popular name.

Gender: The female is fuller.

Breeding: This is a bubble nester.

Special care: This fish prefers a well-planted aquarium with some broad-leaved plants on which it can rest.

HOPLOSTERNUM THORACATUM
Port Hoplo; atipa
FAMILY: *Callichthyidae*

Range: Panama, northern South America to Brazil

8 in   8 in   65–82°F
(20cm) (20cm) (18–28°C)

Characteristics: The body color is variable, usually a mixture of red and brown, or black and brown. The compressed head forms a pointed snout, and two pairs of long barbels are present, usually pointing forward. The fins are rounded, with some dark speckling over a bluish tinge. The rounded caudal fin has a light-colored area across its root.

Gender: The male is slightly smaller than the female and has darker coloring.

Breeding: Paternal bubble nester

Special care: A fish that likes plenty of hideaways in a generally well-planted aquarium.

ACANTHODORAS SPINOSISSIMUS
Chocolate catfish; spiny catfish; Channel catfish; "talking" catfish
FAMILY: *Doradidae*

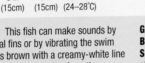

Range: Middle Amazon area

6 in   6 in   70–82°F
(15cm)   (15cm)   (24–28°C)

Characteristics: This fish can make sounds by rotating its pectoral fins or by vibrating the swim bladder. Its body is brown with a creamy-white line consisting of thorny spines running from the shoulder to the caudal peduncle. There are other rows of brown spines on each side. The anterior lower half of the body is marked with wavy, cream-colored lines. All fins are cream with dark speckling.

Gender: Unknown
Breeding: Unknown
Special care: It appreciates plenty of retreats in a generously planted aquarium. Keep only with fish that are too large to fit in its mouth.

AGAMYXIS PECTINIFRONS
White-spotted doradid
FAMILY: *Doradidae*

Range: Ecuador, Peru

5½ in   5½ in   68–79°F
(14cm)   (14cm)   (20–26°C)

Characteristics: The body shape at the head is wide, and tapers to the caudal peduncle; it is slightly compressed vertically. The body, fins, and the three pairs of barbels are black with white spots, and the mouth is large. Several horizontal rows of spines run along the body between the dorsal surface and midway down the body; there is also a sharp serration on the leading edges of the dorsal and pectoral fins.
Gender: Unknown
Breeding: Unknown
Special care: This fish is generally nocturnal, although it will be seen around the aquarium in daylight, too. It likes a well-planted tank, with plenty of hiding places to retreat to, where it will feel safe.

AMBLYDORAS HANCOCKI
Hancock's amblydoras
FAMILY: *Doradidae*

Range: Brazil, Guyana, and Colombia

5 in   5 in   73–82°F
(13cm)   (13cm)   (23–28°C)

Characteristics: The bony plates that cover this fish's body have thorny spikes. The mouth is terminal, with three pairs of long barbels. The body color is usually dark brown with irregular blotches. A line of whitish "thorns" runs along the body from below the dorsal fin to the end of the caudal peduncle; beneath it there is a striking dark line. The speckled caudal fin is set off by a dark band across its base.
Gender: The male has a spotted belly.
Breeding: Bubble nester
Special care: A well-planted aquarium, with retreats formed from roots or rocks, will suit this species.

ACANTHICUS ADONIS
Adonis
FAMILY: *Loricaridae*

Range: Brazil, Peru

| 2 | 72 | 11¾ in (30cm) | 9⅞ in (25cm) | 71–79°F (21–26°C) | |

Characteristics: A whiptail-like sucking catfish, dark brown to black in color, with fine yellow or white spots. The spotting fades with age. The dorsal fin is large and almost sail-like; at the top and bottom of the lyre-shaped caudal fin are long filaments.

Gender: The male is slimmer and grows larger.

Breeding: Unknown

Special care: This fish requires a large aquarium with lots of rockwork, pieces of bogwood, and tree roots for decoration. While vegetable matter will be eaten, it is an omnivore and should be fed catfish tablets, small live foods, and small pieces of fish or crustacea as well.

ANCISTRUS TEMMINCKI
Temminck's Bristlenose
FAMILY: *Loricariidae*

Range: Brazil, Guyana, and Suriname

| 1 | 24 | 5½ in (14cm) | 5½ in (14cm) | 70–77°F (21–25°C) | | | |

Characteristics: A peaceful, algae-eating species that has a flat-bottomed airfoil shape. Bony scutes take the place of scales. The brown body color contrasts with lighter spots that extend into the fins. The snout's upper surface has growths of tentacle-like bristles, and the lips form a sucker-like disk.

Gender: The female has a single row of bristles, while the male has a double row.

Breeding: Pairs spawn hidden away in caves, after which the male guards the eggs until they hatch.

Special care: This fish needs plenty of retreats formed from roots, rocks, plastic pipes, and so on.

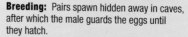

FARLOWELLA GRACILIS
Mottled twig catfish
FAMILY: *Loricariidae*

Range: Columbia

8 in
(20cm)

8 in
(20cm)

75–80°F
(24–27°C)

Characteristics: The body shape is unusual, being long and stick-like, and mimics a twig perfectly. The background body color is light brown, and a darker line runs from the tip of the snout to the caudal peduncle. Some brown speckling is present on the fins and body; the underside is pale; and the disk-like mouth is located beneath the head. The caudal fin is lyre-shaped, with the outer rays extended.

Gender: The male has bristles on the snout.
Breeding: The female lays her eggs on any firm, pre-cleaned surface, and the male guards the eggs.
Special care: This herbivore requires a planted, well-oxygenated environment with some algal growth; it should also be fed vegetable matter.

GLYPTOPERICHTHYS GIBBICEPS
Spotted sailfin pleco; leopard pleco
FAMILY: *Loricariidae*

Range: Brazil, Ecuador, Peru, and Venezuela

23⅝ in
(60cm)

19⅝ in
(50cm)

73–79°F
(23–26°C)

Characteristics: A very large and robust suckermouth catfish that really grows far too large for the average aquarium. The body and fins are reddish-brown, overlaid with large black spots. Both dorsal and caudal fins are large, rounded, and sail-like.
Gender: Unknown
Breeding: These are egg depositors in caves. The male tends the eggs.
Special care: While these fish will eat algae, they prefer almost any other vegetable matter, so additional feeds of pieces of boiled potatoes, peas, and scalded lettuce leaves should be given just after you turn the lights out.

HYPANCISTRUS ZEBRA
Zebra plec
FAMILY: *Loricariidae*

Range: Rio Xingu, Brazil

3   36

6 in   6 in   73–79°F
(15cm)   (15cm)   (23–26°C)

Characteristics: A remarkably colored fish with a pure white body overlaid with jet black lines running from a black vertical band behind the head, right along the body and into the caudal fin. All the other fins have this black and white zebra pattern. Several variations on this color theme are now known from nearby habitats, and there are probably several different species of "zebra plec" in the wild.

Gender: Males have longer odontodes when in breeding condition; otherwise, they are slimmer than females.

Breeding: This is an egg depositor in caves; the males tend the spawn until the eggs hatch.

Special care: While primarily a herbivore, this species will also eat small live or frozen meaty foods.

HYPOSTOMUS PLECOSTOMUS
Suckermouth catfish; common plec; pleco; plecostomus
FAMILY: *Loricariidae*

Range: Northern and Central South America

1   48

17½ in   12 in   68–82°F
(45cm)   (30cm)   (20–28°C)

Characteristics: This peaceful suckermouth is usually active at the beginning and end of the day. Its flat-bottomed body has an airfoil shape, and it is brown in color overlaid with dark spots that continue into the fins. The mouth is underslung, with the lips forming a sucker-like disk to rasp off algae. The dorsal fin is tall and flag-like. The caudal fin is lyre-shaped, the lower lobe longer than the upper.

Gender: Unknown

Breeding: It spawns in caves; the male cares for the eggs.

Special care: Feed additional green foods as a matter of course, especially the adult fish.

PANAQUE NIGROLINEATUS
Royal panaque
FAMILY: *Loricariidae*

Range: South America: Orinoco Basin, Orinoco tributaries; Amazon Basin, southern, middle, and lower Amazon tributaries

17½ in (45cm) 10 in (25cm) 73–79°F (23–26°C)

Characteristics: A remarkable-looking fish with a flat ventral surface, a suckermouth, and a humped body with a large, upright dorsal fin. The body is greenish-yellow overlaid with a network of black lines that continue into the paired fins. The mouth is equipped with teeth designed to rasp away at wood that makes up an important part of its diet.

Gender: Unknown
Breeding: Unknown
Special care: This large catfish is peaceful enough with other fish, although it will be aggressive toward its own kind. Include lots of pieces of bogwood and tree roots in the aquarium, and feed some vegetable matter in its diet.

SCABINANCISTRUS AUREATUS
Sun suckercat
FAMILY: *Loricariidae*

Range: Brazil

15¾ in (40cm) 11¾ in (30cm) 73–86°F (23–30°C)

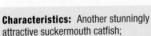

Characteristics: Another stunningly attractive suckermouth catfish; however, this is one that grows too large for most aquaria. The body is black, with white to cream polka dots (fine spots in some specimens). The fins are bright orange for the most part, although they may have the same color as the body close to the fin base.
Gender: The males have odontodes on their pectoral fins.
Breeding: Unknown

Special care: Keep these fish in a well-planted aquarium with some bogwood. Primarily a herbivore, so make sure they are fed additional pieces of cooked potato, thawed frozen peas, and other vegetable matter.

SYNODONTIS NIGRIVENTRIS
Black-spotted upside-down catfish; Congo backswimmer
FAMILY: *Mochokidae*

Range: The Congo

| 1 | 24 | 3½ in (9cm) | 3½ in (9cm) | 71–79°F (22–26°C) | | | |

Characteristics: The body coloration is light brown covered with numerous dark, leopard-like spots and bands. The nearly flat underside is dark colored because the fish spends a lot of its time swimming upside down, so a light belly would be readily spotted by a predator. The eyes are large, and there are three pairs of barbels. The dorsal fin is large, and most fins carry dark blotches.
Gender: The female is fuller.

Breeding: It spawns in caves, where both parents protect the eggs and young.
Special care: It needs a well-planted aquarium with root systems for hideaways, together with some floating plants.

SYNODONTIS SCHOUTEDENI
Vermiculated synodontis
FAMILY: *Mochokidae*

Range: Zaire

| 1 | 48 | 4¾ in (12cm) | 4 in (10cm) | 71–79°F (22–26°C) | | | |

Characteristics: This largely nocturnal catfish is peaceful, hardy, and easy to feed. The body is white, overlaid with a bold pattern of black swirls and squiggles. The colorless fins are highlighted by black rays, and even the barbels are marked in black and white.
Gender: Unknown
Breeding: Unknown

Special care: Provide plenty of plants and driftwood. Water conditions are not critical, but care should be taken to use aged water free of chlorine, to which this catfish seems particularly sensitive. It feeds greedily on a variety of easily available aquarium foods, including flakes, tablets, and frozen or live invertebrates.

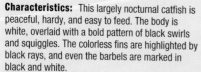

PANGASIUS HYPOPHTHALMUS
Iridescent shark
FAMILY: *Pangasiidae*

Range: Thailand

1   180   39 in   13¾ in   71–79°F
            (1m)   (35cm)   (22–26°C)

Characteristics: This silvery-blue fish with black fins and tail is misidentified as a shark because of its sleek, streamlined appearance and constant swimming. Despite the fact that it spends most of its time on the bottom, like some other catfish it can breathe atmospheric oxygen and will dash to the surface to gulp air.
Gender: The female is plumper.
Breeding: It has never been spawned in the aquarium, but Asian breeders raise the fish successfully in outdoor ponds for food.

Special care: This fish grows far too large for normal hobbyists to keep. It becomes more vegetarian as it ages.

PHRACTOCEPHALUS HEMILIOCEPHALUS
Red-tailed catfish
FAMILY: *Pimelodidae*

Range: Brazil, Guyana, Peru, and Venezuela

8   240   72 in   72 in   70–77°F
            (182cm)   (182cm)   (21–25°C)

Characteristics: This very large catfish has a bright orange/red caudal fin. The dorsal and adipose fins are speckled, dark for most of their areas, shading to red with red edging. The large pectoral, pelvic, and anal fins are also dark, with some red and even white coloring at their edges.

Gender: Unknown
Breeding: Unknown
Special care: This fish grows far too large for a normal hobbyist.

PIMELODUS ALBOFASCIATUS
White-Striped pimelodus
FAMILY: *Pimelodidae*

Range: Guyana, Suriname

| 1 | 48 | 10 in (25cm) | 6 in (15cm) | 70–77°F (21–25°C) | | |

Characteristics: This fish is easily maintained in a roomy aquarium. The body is pale and silvery, with darker blotches forming horizontal bands along its entire length. The blotches, though paler, extend onto the dorsal, adipose, caudal, and anal fins. The pelvic and pectoral fins are colorless, and the latter bear venom glands at the base of the first spine, with which the fish can inflict a painful sting. Use caution when handling this species.

Gender: Unknown
Breeding: Unknown
Special care: This species will swallow anything that will fit into its mouth, and can be fed a wide variety of common aquarium foods.

PSEUDOPLATYSTOMA FASCIATA
Tiger shovelnose catfish
FAMILY: *Pimelodidae*

Range: Venezuela, Peru

| 8 | 180 | 35⅜ in (90cm) | 35⅜ in (90cm) | 71–79°F (22–26°C) | | |

Characteristics: This nocturnal predator is dark-gray in color, shading to silvery white on the belly. A number of equally spaced dark bands cross the body vertically, but do not quite encircle it. The head is very large and broad with a very shallow-sloping forehead; the eyes are set high. There are three long pairs of barbels.

Gender: Unknown
Breeding: Unknown
Special care: This fish grows far too large for a normal hobbyist.

PSEUDOPIMELODUS RANINUS RANINUS
Bumblebee catfish
FAMILY: *Pimelodidae*

Range: Peru, Brazil

4¾ in   4¾ in   70–77°F
(12cm)   (12cm)   (21–25°C)

Characteristics: This is a nocturnal predator, not to be trusted in the company of small fish. Its coloration ranges from dark blue-black to brown with irregular blotches and narrow bands of lighter brown. The ventral surface itself is pinkish. The blunt, flat head has small eyes, a wide mouth, and three pairs of barbels.

Gender: Unknown
Breeding: Unknown
Special care: This fish needs a well-planted aquarium provided with plenty of hideaways and retreats.

SORUBIM LIMA
Shovelnose catfish
FAMILY: *Pimelodidae*

Range: Amazon region

8 in   6 in   71–79°F
(20cm)   (15cm)   (22–26°C)

Characteristics: The somewhat flattened body is white underneath, and dark brown or black above. Below the dorsal fin lies a longitudinal stripe of light brown to white. A dark, mid-body stripe runs the full length of the body, turning sharply downward at the caudal peduncle into the lower lobe of the caudal fin.

Gender: Unknown
Breeding: Unknown
Special care: This is a hardy predator that will eat any fish small enough to be swallowed. During the day the fish spends its time in hiding.

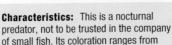

EUTROPIELLUS DEBAUWI
African glass catfish; three-striped glass catfish
FAMILY: *Schilbeidae*

Range: The Congo

3 in
(7.5cm)

3 in
(7.5cm)

71–82°F
(22–28°C)

elongated and translucent, with three black stripes running horizontally. The head is small with relatively large eyes; the mouth is terminal, with three pairs of barbels.

Gender: The male is slimmer.

Breeding: This fish scatters its eggs in fine-leaved plants.

Special care: It needs a well-planted aquarium with some water currents and floating plants.

Characteristics: This sociable fish prefers to be with its own kind and other non-boisterous fishes. It is usually constantly on the move, with its caudal fin sloping downward, but when stationary it waves its tail from side to side. The body is

KRYPTOPTERUS MINOR
Glass catfish
FAMILY: *Siluridae*

Range: Borneo, Java, Sumatra, and Thailand

4 in
(10cm)

3½ in
(9cm)

71–79°F
(22–26°C)

Characteristics: A peaceful species that thrives in a shoal. The elongated body is compressed laterally, it is scale-less and glasslike, so that the backbone and internal organ sac are both visible. The pair of long barbels trails back past the pectoral fins. The anal fin runs the length of the body, but is not joined to the caudal fin. The lower lobe of the tail is slightly larger than the upper.

Gender: The female is plumper.

Breeding: This fish scatters its eggs in fine-leaved plants.

Special care: The aquarium should be well-planted and include floating plants, and some strong currents should be supplied by an efficient filtration system.

Other Egglayers

There are many egglaying fish that cannot be neatly classified. Some are monotypic (a single species within a genus), other families have very few representative species, and there are those that just won't fit into recognized groups. Although diverse in natural habitats and in body shapes and sizes, all make excellent aquarium subjects. Some, because of their size, behavioral characteristics, or needs for special conditions, would be better suited in a single species collection. Some may come from brackish waters, as well as freshwater, and are almost an interim choice on the way to keeping fully-fledged marine fish. Faced with the problems of describing such fish we have arranged them in scientific alphabetical family order.

In the aquarium trade, fish come from a wide variety of habitats. Local conditions, including military coups and political upheavals, can influence the availability of wild-caught fish, as can the weather, season, or even an interruption in air cargo service. Furthermore, fish may come from a variety of water conditions, but a dealer can usually only provide a single set of conditions for his inventory (aside from maintaining freshwater, coldwater, and marine species in separate holding systems). Thus, the actual availability of species varies widely from place to place and dealer to dealer. When considering any species that is not commonly available in your area, consult references to determine if you can provide for its needs.

In this chapter we can only hope that the following collection of varying shapes, sizes, and colors will at least give some indication of the vast range of interesting fish from around the tropical waters of the world that can delight, even in the most modest aquarium.

FEATURED IN THIS SECTION

APTERONOTUS SP.
Unidentified speckled knifefish
FAMILY: *Apteronotidae*

Range: South America

6   36

20 in   12 in   73–83°F
(50cm)   (30cm)   (23–28°C)

Characteristics: This fish is generally nocturnal. All species are drably colored in black, dark brown, or mottled shades of tan. Timid in the aquarium, especially until they become accustomed to life in captivity, knifefish nevertheless can develop into pets owing to their unusual level of intelligence. They can swim equally well backward or forward.

Gender: Unknown
Breeding: Unknown
Special care: Provide a hiding place for the fish to retire into during the daylight hours. The best approach is to keep a single specimen in a tank that is specifically devoted to its needs. It adapts best to slightly acidic, moderately soft water. The tank should be heavily planted.

BEDOTIA GEAYI
Madagascar rainbowfish
FAMILY: *Atherinidae*

Range: Madagascar

3   36

4¼ in   4 in   73–75°F
(11cm)   (10cm)   (23–24°C)

Characteristics: It has an elongated, light greenish-yellow body. A bluish-violet sheen becomes most apparent under sidelit conditions. A dark line runs from the snout to the end of the caudal fin. There are two dorsal fins, the first mostly folded, the base long; the second dorsal and the anal fins are set well back, the male's dark with yellowish-orange streaks and a black-red margin. The caudal fin is slightly spade-shaped and has a yellowish center (crossed by the dark body stripe) edged with black and red.
Gender: The female may be identified by black and white edging in the caudal. The other fins lack color.
Breeding: This fish lays eggs among plants or artificial spawning mops.
Special care: An active, peaceful, shoaling species. It needs plenty of swimming space and generous plantings.

TELMATHERINA LADIGESI
Celebes rainbowfish
FAMILY: *Atherinidae*

Range: Sulawesi

2¾ in (7cm)   3 in (7.5cm)   72–82°F (22–28°C)

Characteristics: This species' coloration varies according to lighting conditions: a light yellow-gold body shades down to a silver belly. An iridescent light blue line runs from midway along the flanks to the end of the caudal peduncle. The large, dark-centered eyes have silvery-blue rims. The first dorsal is small, the second dorsal has black and yellow filaments. The anal fin is deeply forked, and the male's has filamentous extensions. The top and bottom edges of the caudal are yellow with black edging inside.

Gender: The males have elongated rays in the second dorsal and anal fins.

Breeding: This fish lays its eggs among plants.

Special care: It adapts to hard water; some sea salt is beneficial. It prefers a well-planted aquarium.

BADIS BADIS
Badis
FAMILY: *Badidae*

Range: India

2½ in (6.5cm)   2½ in (6.5cm)   72–77°F (22–26°C)

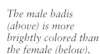

The male badis (above) is more brightly colored than the female (below).

Characteristics: This fish is stocky, the ventral contour is often slightly concave, while the dorsal surface is often arched. The badis is sometimes called the dwarf chameleon fish, as it appears to change color to suit its surroundings. Its body is reddish-brown; in prime specimens this will change to a red and blue speckled pattern with clearly defined scales. The dorsal fin has a long base, it has spiny and soft-rayed parts, and bluish markings.

Gender: The female is less brightly colored.

Breeding: This is a cave spawner, and lays adhesive eggs.

Special care: It needs a well-planted aquarium with plenty of rocky retreats.

GNATHONEMUS PETERSI

Long-nosed elephant fish; Peter's elephant-nose; ubangi mormyrid
FAMILY: *Cyprinidae*

Range: Nigeria, Cameroon, and Zaire

10 in   9 in   72–82°F
(25cm)   (23cm)   (22–28°C)

Characteristics: This fish emits electrical impulses by which it navigates in the dark or in muddy waters. Its body is deep, elongated, and laterally compressed in shape. In color it is dark gray, with two pinkish-white bracket-shaped marks on the flanks. It has a long snout on a large head, with an extended, finger-like lower jaw. The dorsal and anal fins are set very far back on the body; they are narrow and deeply forked. The caudal fin is set on a thin caudal peduncle. The pectoral fins are flipper-like, and the pelvic fins are fairly small.

Gender: Unknown
Breeding: Unknown
Special care: Peaceful but territorial; it needs a thickly planted tank with plenty of hideaways.

BRACHYGOBIUS DORIAE
Bumblebee fish; bumblebee goby
FAMILY: *Gobiidae*

Range: Borneo, Malaysia, Java, and Thailand

2 in (5cm)   1½ in (4cm)   77–86°F (25–30°C)

Characteristics: This fish has a sooty black-blue body with pale yellow bands of differing widths. It has a broad, blunt head, a large mouth, and high-set eyes. The dorsal fins and anal fins have dark bases and yellowish outer margins. The pelvic fins are fused together to form a suction cup. It has no swim bladder to give it buoyancy.

Gender: The female has a fatter body.

Breeding: This is a cave spawner.

Special care: It needs a well-planted tank and the company of its own kind or that of non-boisterous fish; the addition of some sea salt to the water is essential. It thrives in a species tank.

DORMITATOR MACULATUS
Spotted sleeper goby; striped sleeper goby
FAMILY: *Gobiidae*

Range: U.S. to Brazil

10 in (25cm)   6 in (15cm)   70–77°F (20–27°C)

Characteristics: Gobies have fused pectoral fins that enable the fish to hang on to solid substrates. The silvery to olive-green body has numerous dark spots. A blue to blue-green patch often lies just anterior to the gill cover. The paired dorsal fins are marked with spots, each being lighter in color along its upper margin.

Gender: The male has larger, more colorful dorsal and anal fins than the female.

Breeding: This is an open spawner that lays and guards adhesive eggs.

Special care: It needs brackish water; this limits the selection of plants the aquarist can use in the tank.

GYRINOCHEILUS AYMONIERI
Chinese sucking loach; Chinese algae eater
FAMILY: *Gyrinocheilidae*

Range: Thailand

10 in (25cm) 8 in (20cm) 77–86°F (25–30°)

Characteristics: Its elongated body is yellow-gold, complemented by dark-edged scales. A dark band runs from the snout to the caudal peduncle, crossed at regular intervals by dark bars. The fins are generally clear of patterning, although the caudal fin may have some small, dark dots. Its underslung mouth forms a sucking disk for rasping algae. It breathes through special slits in its head.

Special care: It needs a well-planted aquarium with some algal growth, as it requires a lot of green matter in its diet.

Gender: Unknown
Breeding: Unknown

DATNIOIDES MICROLEPIS
Siamese tiger fish
FAMILY: *Lobotidae*

Range: Borneo, Thailand, and Sumatra

16 in (40cm) 12 in (30cm) 72–79°F (22–26°C)

Characteristics: This is an aggressive predator. It has a golden-brown body, a pointed snout, and a narrow caudal peduncle. Vertical dark bars cross the body. A dark-edged, pale stripe runs from the snout, along the forehead to the long-based dorsal fin; the latter is black-edged to the front. The pelvic fins are dark with a creamy front edge; the anal fin is crossed by a body bar. The caudal fin is yellow with a dark bar across its base.

Gender: Unknown
Breeding: Unknown
Special care: This fish needs a spacious, brackish, heavily planted tank. It is best kept in a single species aquarium, as it is not safe with smaller fish.

MASTACEMBELUS ARMATUS
Spiny eel
FAMILY: *Mastacembelidae*

Range: India, Sri Lanka, Thailand, and Sumatra

29½ in (75cm)	29½ in (75cm)	72–82°F (22–28°C)

Characteristics: The body of this fish is a golden yellow-brown, changing to a darker shade underneath. It is marked with a dark brown, blotched band from its pointed snout to the end of the caudal peduncle. There are two rows of oval blotches on the lower half of the body. The snout has a movable portion. The dorsal, anal, and caudal fins form one unit encircling the rear half of the body; in front of the dorsal fin is a row of tiny spines. There are no pelvic fins.

Gender: Unknown

Breeding: Unknown

Special care: This fish needs a well-planted tank, a soft substrate, many hiding places, and the addition of some salt to the water. It should not be kept with small fish: a single species aquarium is best.

MASTACEMBELUS ERYTHROTAENIA
Fire eel
FAMILY: *Mastacembelidae*

Range: Southeast Asia, Borneo, Myanmar, Sumatra, and Thailand

39 in (100cm)	26 in (66cm)	74–82°F (24–28°C)

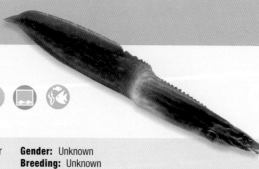

Characteristics: This fish has a deep brown or black body with fiery red lines from the pointed snout to the end of the caudal peduncle. The pectoral fins are similarly marked; the caudal fin is red. These lines may break up from the dorsal fin backward. It has a small head with red markings, which may contain some yellow.

Gender: Unknown
Breeding: Unknown
Special care: It needs plenty of hiding places. It is best kept in a single species aquarium.

IRIATHERINA WERNERI
Threadfin rainbowfish
FAMILY: _Melanotaeniidae_

Range: Papua New Guinea, northern Australia

| 3 | 24 | 2 in (5cm) | 1½ in (4cm) | 72–75°F (22–24°C) | | | |

Characteristics: In shape the body is elongated; in color it is golden brown-silver, with a bluish shine to the dorsal ridge. Some fine, reddish-brown vertical lines cross the body. It has a small head with golden eyes. The first high dorsal fin has a rounded tip; the second dorsal has separated, black thread-like rays. The pelvic fins are also black and thread-like. The anal fin carries black extensions, and the lyre-shaped caudal has extended rays from the top and bottom tips.

Gender: The female has short fins with no extensions.
Breeding: The eggs are laid in bushy plants or artificial mops.
Special care: This is a shoaling species; it needs a well-planted tank, and the company of small, non-boisterous species.

GLOSSOLEPIS INCISUS
Red rainbowfish
FAMILY: _Melanotaeniidae_

Range: Papua New Guinea

| 1 | 36 | 6 in (15cm) | 4¾ in (12cm) | 72–75°F (22–24°C) | | |

Characteristics: It has a deep, red body, a pointed snout, and a drawn-out caudal peduncle. The lower half of the body is often a deeper red, with a silver-white area behind and below the gill cover. The head is small, and the dorsal surface rises very steeply just behind the eyes. There are two dorsal fins, the second being larger, and a long-based anal fin. The fins are red.
Gender: The female is slimmer, with a yellowish body and fins; the male's back is more highly arched.
Breeding: The eggs are laid in bushy plants or in artificial mops.
Special care: This shoaling fish needs plenty of swimming space.

MELANOTAENIA BOESMANI
Boeseman's rainbowfish
FAMILY: *Melanotaeniidae*

Range: Papua New Guinea

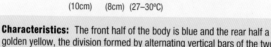

4 in (10cm)   3¼ in (8cm)   81–86°F (27–30°C)

Characteristics: The front half of the body is blue and the rear half a golden yellow, the division formed by alternating vertical bars of the two colors. The paired fins are colorless, while the dorsal, caudal, and anal fins mimic the golden yellow of the body. The dorsal fin is edged in white, and the anal fin in sky blue.

Gender: The female is smaller and less colorful.

Breeding: It spawns into plants or artificial mops.

Special care: A community of different species from this family works best. It is a good jumper, so keep the tank covered.

MELANOTAENIA HERBERTAXELRODI
Axelrod's rainbowfish
FAMILY: *Melanotaeniidae*

Range: Papua New Guinea

3¼ in (8cm)   3¼ in (8cm)   72–80°F (22–27°C)

Characteristics: The body of this fish is a pale golden yellow, with a bright blue horizontal stripe running from the eyes to the caudal peduncle. The paired fins and caudal fin are colorless, the dorsal and anal fins have golden yellow highlights. Brightly metallic scales give it a striking appearance.

Gender: The male is more intensely and deeply colored than the female.

Breeding: It spawns into plants or artificial mops.

Special care: A community of different species from this family can be chosen. It needs a well-planted tank, and hard, slightly alkaline water. It is a good jumper, so the tank should be covered.

MELANOTAENIA LACUSTRIS
Lake Kutubu rainbowfish
FAMILY: *Melanotaeniidae*

Range: Lake Kutubu, Papua New Guinea

4¾ in   4 in   75–80°F
(12cm)   (10cm)   (24–27°C)

Characteristics: The upper half of the body is electric blue; there is a dark blue horizontal band along the lateral line, and the lower half is silvery. The paired fins are colorless; the dorsal, caudal, and anal fins are tinged with blue. The fish's back often shimmers with a greenish iridescence. The head is silvery.
Gender: The females are less colorful than the males.
Breeding: This fish spawns into plants or artificial mops.
Special care: A community of different species from this family can be chosen. However, a tight-fitting cover will be needed for this good jumper.

MELANOTAENIA PRAECOX
Diamond rainbowfish
FAMILY: *Melanotaeniidae*

Range: New Guinea, Irian Jaya

2⅜ in   2⅜ in   77–82°F
(6cm)   (6cm)   (25–28°C)

Characteristics: Its metallic, electric blue body is strikingly offset by the bright red edging to the fins.
Gender: The females, when young, have a blue edging to the yellowish fins.
Breeding: Occurs often as a shoal, among bushy plants, or in spawning mops.
Special care: It is important to allow adequate swimming space, combined with planted thickets to provide security. Some sunlight through the front glass "lights up" fish quite spectacularly, especially if they are kept as a shoal. Of modest proportions, this fish does not need a spacious aquarium in which to thrive.

MELANOTAENIA SPLENDIDA AUSTRALIS
Western rainbowfish
FAMILY: *Melanotaeniidae*

Range: Australia

4¾ in   4 in   70–77°F
(12cm)   (10cm)   (21–25°C)

Characteristics: The yellow body has a horizontal dark stripe running from behind the gill cover to the caudal peduncle. Below this are several zigzag black lines. The dorsal and anal fins are edged in red and the caudal fin is also reddish. Females are less colorful than males. Many fish sold as Melanotaenia maccullochi are in fact this species.

Gender: The males are more brightly colored, with extended dorsal and anal fins.
Breeding: This fish spawns into plants and artificial mops.
Special care: This is a lively, peaceful, schooling species. It is a good jumper. Provide moderately hard, alkaline water. Planted tanks should leave ample swimming room.

MONODACTYLUS ARGENTEUS
Mono; Malaysian or Singapore angel; fingerfish
FAMILY: *Monodactylidae*

Range: East coast of Africa to Indonesia

20 in   12 in   75–82°F
(50cm)   (30cm)   (24–28°C)

Characteristics: This fish has a tall, disc-shaped, laterally compressed silver body. A dark bar passes down the head and through the large eyes, and a thinner line runs down from the front of the dorsal fin, through the base of the pectoral fin to the pelvic fins. The lateral line is highly arched. The dorsal and anal fins are yellowish-orange, with black front edges. The very small pelvic fins and caudal fin are yellow.
Gender: Unknown
Breeding: Unknown
Special care: It needs brackish water with good aeration. It is omnivorous, and will eat all plants. It is best kept in a shoal in an unplanted, roomy, brackish water aquarium.

MONODACTYLUS SEBAE
Fingerfish
FAMILY: *Monodactylidae*

Range: West African coast from Senegal south to Zaire

6 | 72 | 8 in (20cm) | 6 in (15cm) | 75–79°F (25–26°C)

Characteristics: It has a flattened silver body, with elongated dorsal and anal fins. Dark vertical bands run through the eyes, just anterior to the gill cover, down the middle of the body from the tip of the dorsal fin to the tip of the anal fin, and along the rear margins of the body where the upper and lower bands join at the caudal peduncle.

Gender: Unknown

Breeding: Unknown

Special care: This fish needs full-strength sea water in a roomy tank. It preys on smaller fishes. It can be kept in a small school. A very large tank is needed.

MONOCIRRHUS POLYACANTHUS
South American leaf fish
FAMILY: *Nandidae*

Range: Amazon region, Guyana

3 | 36 | 4 in (10cm) | 3½ in (9cm) | 72–77°F (22–25°C)

Characteristics: This fish has an oval, golden brown body, with darker irregular blotches. Its color changes to help it blend in with its surroundings. The very large mouth can be opened out into a funnel shape for taking in food. The caudal fin is often held in a closed position in its characteristic head-down fashion.

Gender: Unknown

Breeding: It lays its eggs on a flat surface.

Special care: This predatory fish swims at all levels of the aquarium. It requires plenty of plants, and it should only be kept with larger fish.

NOTOPTERUS CHITALA
Clown knifefish; featherback
FAMILY: *Notopteridae*

Range: Burma, India, Sumatra, and Thailand

| 35⅜ in | 28 in | 75–82°F |
| (90cm) | (71cm) | (24–28°C) |

Characteristics: It swims using an undulating wave-movement of its long anal fin. Nocturnal, it navigates in total darkness using a self-generated electromagnetic force field. Its body is similar in shape to an aerofoil section, flattened ventrally, with a highly arched dorsal surface. It is silvery gray-brown in color, with irregular-sized, white-rimmed black spots on the flanks below the lateral line. The pelvic fins are rudimentary, or absent altogether.

Gender: Unknown

Breeding: It will spawn on solid substrate, and practices brood care.

Special care: A potentially predatory species needing a large tank with a secure lid.

SCLEROPAGES JARDINI
Gulf Saratoga; northern spotted barramundi
FAMILY: *Osteoglossidae*

Range: Northern tropical Australia

| 35⅜ in | 35⅜ in | 75–86°F |
| (90cm) | (90cm) | (24–30°C) |

Characteristics: In shape this fish's body is elongated and heavily built; in color it is dullish gray, relieved by the gold-yellow rear edges to the scales, and the facial markings on the head and gill covers. It has a large, upturned mouth, a bony tongue, and chin barbels. The dorsal and anal fins are set well back on the body; the pectoral fins are pointed, the caudal fin rounded.

Gender: Unknown

Breeding: Mouth brooder

Special care: This fish will swim at all levels of the aquarium. It requires a great deal of space, and it needs a very secure lid.

PANTODON BUCHHOLZI
Butterflyfish
FAMILY: *Pantodontidae*

Range: Nigeria, Cameroon, and Zaire

1 | 36 | 4 in (10cm) | 4 in (10cm) | 73–86°F (23–30°C)

Characteristics: The boat-shaped blotchy dark brown body has a hint of a horizontal line along the flanks. A dark bar passes diagonally through the eyes. The caudal fin has several extended central rays; the pelvic fins are extremely long. The darkly patterned pectoral fins are very large and resemble butterfly wings when viewed from above.

Gender: The female can be identified because the trailing edge of her anal fin is straight.

Breeding: In this species the eggs rise to the surface.

Special care: It is intolerant of fish that invade its surface-dwelling areas. Keep it with middle- and bottom-dwelling species. It is also predatory toward smaller fish. It is a good jumper, so the tank needs a firm lid.

POLYPTERUS SENEGALUS
Senegal bichir; rope fish
FAMILY: *Polypteridae*

Range: Senegal, Gambia, and Niger

7 | 48 | 12 in (30cm) | 10 in (25cm) | 77–82°F (25–28°C)

Characteristics: It is brown in color, but with colorless fins. The dorsal fin has multiple elements.

Gender: Unknown

Breeding: Unknown

Special care: It is generally peaceful toward fish too large to eat, but commonly will not tolerate another member of its own kind in the same aquarium.

PSEUDOMUGIL FURCATUS
Forktail blue-eye
FAMILY: *Pseudomugilidae*

Range: New Guinea

1 | 24 | 2 in (5cm) | 2 in (5cm) | 73–79°F (23–26°C)

Characteristics: A beautiful, slender little rainbowfish with a lemon-yellow chest and pale yellow body. All the following parts are yellow: the pelvic fins, the outer two-thirds of both dorsal fins, the outer edge of the anal fin, and the top and bottom of the caudal fin. The pectoral fins are large, almost wing-like, and are also bright yellow.

Gender: The male's posterior dorsal fin is larger, and they are much more colorful than the female.

Breeding: This is an egg scatterer, each female producing a couple of eggs a day. These are laid in fine-leaved plants near the surface.

Special care: A great small community fish. It is best kept as a single male to several females, either by themselves or in a small fish community.

SCATOPHAGUS ARGUS
Scat; argus fish
FAMILY: *Scatophagidae*

Range: India to Tahiti, including the Philippines

12 in   10 in   68–82°F
(30cm) (25cm) (22–28°C)

The difference in patterning of these two scats shows just how varied their markings can be.

Characteristics: Its body is tall, and laterally compressed. Its coloration is a mixture of streaky brown and gold, with numerous round dark spots. Two dark lines run up the forehead. A golden streak runs vertically behind the gill cover; there are red markings toward the top of the dorsal surface. The dorsal fin has a spiny front section. The pelvic, pectoral, and anal fins are reddish-brown. The anal fin has a spined front.

Gender: Unknown

Breeding: Unknown

Special care: The scat is a true scavenger and eats anything—including plants. Brackish water is required. It is a lively shoaling species, but peaceful with its tankmates.

TOXOTES JACULATOR
Archerfish
FAMILY: *Toxotidae*

Range: East Africa to Australia

10 in   6¾ in   77–86°F
(25cm) (17cm) (25–30°C)

Characteristics: Its pursed mouth acts as a form of primitive gun barrel, which it uses to shoot down insects. Its silver body has dark blotches on the flanks. It has a dark band along the outer edge of the anal fin, the dorsal fin is marked with black, the caudal fin is clear. It has a long, tapered head, with a protruding lower lip; the eyes are set well forward.

Gender: Unknown

Breeding: Unknown

Special care: It needs ample swimming space with some "above-water" plant roots hanging in the water. Ideally, the aquarium could form part of a paludarium.

Livebearers

There are literally thousands of species of fish in dozens of different unrelated families that are livebearers. These range from guppies right through to great white sharks. Yes, Jaws is a livebearer! The natural habitats of these fish are as diverse as the fish themselves. Delve into the deepest parts of the oceans of the world and you will find livebearers—dive into Lake Baikal in Russia and you will find livebearers; trek deep into caves in Cuba and you will find blind cave livebearers; and the greatest fear every fisherman in the Amazon has is that he will step on a stingray, which has to be one of the most majestic of all the fish in the livebearer world.

Although all these fish are livebearers each family has evolved its own method of reproduction. In guppies, platies, and mollies (all members of the *Poeciliidae* family) the male's fin takes on a rod-like appearance with sexual maturity. It is not a hollow tube; instead the rays are bunched together so a groove is formed down which packets of sperm can be shot. At the end of the gonopodium (what the male's fin is now called) are several hooks that catch hold of the female's vent and make sure the sperm hits its target.

Another amazing adaptation in this family is the ability to store some of these sperm packets for later use. Thus from one mating the female can produce several broods. In this family gestation generally takes about one month, but there are exceptions.

In the *Goodeidae* family the male's anal fin (andropodium) has a notch in it and the front rays are shorter and bunched together. These rays are again used to channel sperm into the female. In this family the babies have long ribbon-like structures that are called trophotaeniae (literally "feeding worms"). These allow the baby to obtain huge amounts of nutrient from its mother, so the babies are born much larger than most *Poeciliids*. They also take longer to develop, and it may be six or even eight weeks between broods.

The secret to breeding these fish successfully is recognizing when to move the gravid (pregnant) female from the main aquarium to a nursery tank. Too soon is far better than too late. At normal aquarium temperatures the gestation period is around 30 days.

FEATURED IN THIS SECTION

CHARACODON AUDAX
Black prince; bold characodon
FAMILY: *Goodeidae*

Range: Mexico

2¼ in 2¼ in 68–75°F
(5.5cm) (5.5cm) (20–24°C)

Characteristics: A torpedo-shaped species, silver-gray on the flanks. The dorsal fin is set well back on the body opposite the anal fin; all the fins are rounded. The alternative common name may reflect the species' aggressive behavior typical between territorially-minded males.
Gender: Males have a hint of pink around the throat, and jet-black fins.
Breeding: Broods born every six to eight weeks. The large fry may number from 4 to 30.
Special care: This generally peaceful fish requires a well-planted aquarium to mimic its natural habitat.

DERMOGENYS PUSILLUS
Wrestling halfbeak; Malayan halfbeak
FAMILY: *Hemirhamphidae*

Range: Indonesia, Java, Sumatra, Malaysia, and Thailand

3¼ in 3¼ in 70–86°F
(8cm) (8cm) (21–30°C)

Characteristics: This fish has a spindly body with a very flat dorsal surface. It is greenish-yellow to gold, with some blue under sidelighting. The lower jaw is extended to about twice the length of the short upper jaw.
Gender: The male's anal fin appears semi-folded rather than rod-like; the female's is fan-shaped.

Breeding: Broods are born every 28 days and number up to 30.
Special care: Males tend to fight, interlocking their jaws for several minutes at a time. This fish tolerates both fresh and brackish waters. If startled, they may dash into the side walls of the tank, injuring their "beaks."

ALFARO CULTRATUS
Knife livebearer
FAMILY: *Poeciliidae*

Range: Costa Rica, Guatemala, Panama, and Nicaragua

4 in   3 in   70–77°F
(10cm) (7.5cm) (21–25°C)

Characteristics: The knife livebearer's body is semi-transparent and elongated with a flat dorsal profile. The ventral contour is keel-like, formed from modified scales. It is silvery green to metallic blue with sidelighting. The dorsal fin is rounded, and set halfway along the body. All the fins are yellowish.

Gender: Males have a modified anal fin (gonopodium), which acts as a means of internally fertilizing the female.
Breeding: Up to 100 fry are born every four to eight weeks.
Special care: A surface feeder that appreciates well-filtered water.

POECILIA (LEBISTES) RETICULATA
Guppy; millionsfish
FAMILY: *Poeciliidae*

Range: Central America, Trinidad, and northern South America

N/a   2½ in   70–77°F
(6.5cm) (21–25°C)

Characteristics: Originally a small fish with just splashes of bright colors on the male's body and fins, the guppy has been transformed by selective breeding into the most brilliantly colored fish with huge finnage. The alternative name is a good indication of this species' willingness to breed.
Gender: The males have more color, and the anal fin is rod-like.
Breeding: Broods of up to 100 young are born every 28 days. Females can store sperm internally, and so produce successive broods of young without re-mating.
Special care: This fish is content in a well-planted aquarium with a collection of fish of similar size.

POECILIA SPHENOPS
Lyretail black Molly
FAMILY: *Poeciliidae*

Range: Man-made cultivar

24 N/a 2½ in (6cm) 73—82°F (23—28°C)

Characteristics: The black Molly is a long-established aquarium favorite, as its jet-black coloration contrasts sharply with the silver, red, and yellow coloring of other fish. In this aquarium-cultivated variety, the caudal fin is in the shape of a lyre.

Gender: The male has a modified rod-like anal fin.

Breeding: Broods of up to 80 fry are born on a monthly cycle. Ideally separate the female in a well-planted aquarium so that she may give birth undisturbed by other fish.

Special care: This fish requires a regular supply of green matter in its diet, and plenty of space for optimum development.

XIPHOPHORUS HELLERI
Common swordtail
FAMILY: *Poeciliidae*

Range: Mexico, Belize, and Guatemala

36 4 in (10cm) 4 in (10cm) 70–77°F (21–25°C)

Characteristics: The body shape of this fish is elongated, the males having a sword-like extension of the caudal fin. The swordtail has been hybridized with platies to produce many varying color strains, plus lyretail and hi-fin forms.

Gender: The males have a rod-like anal fin. The females grow larger, and lack the sword.

Breeding: Broods are born on a monthly cycle, and can number up to 250.

Special care: Although generally peaceful, males may quarrel between themselves.

XIPHOPHORUS MACULATUS
Southern platy; platy
FAMILY: *Poeciliidae*

Range: Mexico, Guatemala, and Belize

2½ in   2½ in   70–77°F
(6cm)   (6.5cm)   (21–25°C)

Characteristics: This species is stocky, with a deep, short caudal peduncle. The platy is now represented in the aquarium by a wide variety of color strains that have been created by hybridization with the common swordtail and the variable platy. Hi-fin, plumetail, and lyretail fin forms exist as well.
Gender: The male's anal fin is modified into a gonopodium.
Breeding: Broods of up to 50 fry are born on a monthly cycle.
Special care: This is a perfect community fish that will thrive in a well-planted aquarium.

Many different color strains of the platy are commercially available.

XIPHOPHORUS VARIATUS
Variable platy; variatus platy
FAMILY: *Poeciliidae*

Range: Mexico

2¾ in   2½ in   72–77°F
(7cm)   (6.5cm)   (22–25°C)

Characteristics: The body shape of this fish is more elongated than in the southern platy. Many color forms exist thanks to hybridization, although even in the wild this is a very variable fish—hence the scientific name. Hi-fin, plumetail, and lyretail forms have also been produced.

Gender: Males have a gonopodium.
Breeding: Broods are born on a monthly cycle and can number over 50. Fry hide near the bottom when they are first born, only later venturing upward. The females can store sperm, so they can have successive broods without a male being present.
Special care: This perfect community fish likes some plant cover.

MARINE FISH

Marine fish demand the same attention (keeping and collection) as endangered species or those whose aquarium acclimatization is known to be problematical, for example as with freshwater fish. A typical case is that of the seahorse. For every fishkeeper who strives (usually unsuccessfully) to keep it there is also a huge demand for it in the curio souvenir trade, and also in the oriental medical trade where it is thought to be endowed with special properties. Throughout this book it has been the intention to keep some conformity so that you become familiar with the pattern of knowledge presented. However, one cannot find a common set of parameters to fit all species under all circumstances, especially when there is the difference between freshwater and saltwater fish to be considered, so some of the symbols take on a slightly different meaning in this section.

Anenomefish and Damselfish

The modestly proportioned members of this family are, without doubt, where every marine aquarist begins his or her collection. The fish have several factors in their favor, which set them apart from the rest.

First, they are hardy, readily available, and relatively inexpensive. Second, because they are of modest sizes, you can accommodate more of them (providing some caution is exercised) in the aquarium and so your collection appears to build up quite quickly. Third—and this applies primarily to the anemonefish—there is the fascination of watching a symbiotic (some say commensal) relationship exist before your very eyes, as the anemonefish conforms to its description and enters into a joint existence with a sea anemone. In recent years, clownfish (as anemonefish are sometimes known) have been commercially bred in increasing numbers. To be sure of getting damselfish off to a good start in your aquarium, it is recommended that you do not buy either the smallest or largest specimens, as the smallest often die off quickly while the largest can be the most difficult to acclimatize to captivity. Being "nitrite-tolerant" fish, they can be introduced into the newly set up aquarium earlier than most other genera and their waste products will supply "food" that biological filtration's nitrifying bacteria can utilize and so build up the filter's effectiveness much faster.

Throughout the group you will find herbivores, omnivores, and planktivores. In nature these fish will be found at different levels of water depth. Hence, planktivores are found near the surface to catch the drifting microscopic foods while the herbivores hang around algae-encrusted outcrops in slightly deeper water. In both clownfish and damselfish breeding takes the form of egg depositing on hard surfaces, and the subsequent guarding and fry care is very reminiscent of that of freshwater cichlids.

FEATURED IN THIS SECTION

Anemonefish

Anemonefish are also known as "clownfish" because of their characteristic waddling action. They have intimate contact with sea anemones within whose tentacles they shelter. The fish develops a mucous covering to its skin, which appears to prevent the stinging cells of the sea anemone from firing due to the presence of something within its tentacles. Some clownfish depend on a sea anemone more than others, however. All anemonefish begin life as males and remain so as long as a female is present in the host anemone. If the female is lost, the dominant male changes to a female. This ensures that a female will always be present in an occupied anemone, the anemones being essential to the survival of the fish in the wild. A natural host anemone has been suggested for most species, but keeping them can be challenging and is not required for success with the fish.

AMPHIPRION AKALLOPISOS
Skunk anemonefish
FAMILY: *Pomacentridae*

Range: Indo-Pacific

    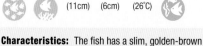

3	24	4¼ in (11cm)	2⅜ in (6cm)	79°F (26°C)

Characteristics: The fish has a slim, golden-brown body. The white line runs along the dorsal surface. The dorsal and caudal fins are white, while the pectoral, pelvic, and anal fins are golden brown.
Gender: Unknown
Breeding: Egg depositor
Special care: Requires high-quality water conditions with low levels of nitrogenous wastes (ammonia, nitrite, nitrate). Coral retreats such as *Heteractis magnifica* or *Stichodactyla mertensii* sea anemones would be appropriate.

AMPHIPRION CLARKII
Clark's anemonefish
FAMILY: *Pomacentridae*

Range: Northern Indo-Pacific from Japan to East Africa

3	36	5 in (12.7cm)	3 in (7.5cm)	79°F (26°C)

Characteristics: The body is dark brown, with bright yellow in front of the eyes. Three vertical white stripes cross the body: one between the eyes and the pectoral fins, another midway along the flanks, and one at the end of the caudal peduncle. The caudal and pectoral fins are yellow, other fins are dark brown. The dorsal fin may have a yellow area at its rear.
Gender: Unknown
Breeding: Egg depositor
Special care: It needs high-quality water conditions with low levels of nitrogenous wastes. Host anemones are *Cryptodendrum*, *Heteractis magnifica*, and *Stichodactyla mertensii*.

AMPHIPRION FRENATUS
Tomato clownfish; bridled clownfish; fire clown
FAMILY: *Pomacentridae*

Range: Central Indo-Pacific to East Africa

3 | 36 | 5½ in (14cm) | 3 in (7.5cm) | 79°F (26°C)

Characteristics: The body is a rich tomato red-brown, with a darker suffusion of color toward the rear end of the gill cover. A dark-edged white vertical bar runs behind the eyes and across the gill covers. Its blunt-shaped head tapers gently at the caudal peduncle. The fins are red-brown and rounded. The dorsal fin is long and spiny.

Gender: Females tend to be slightly larger than the males.

Breeding: Egg depositor

Special care: It needs high-quality water conditions. It is hardy but aggressive. It is not so dependent on the anemone as some others in the genus.

AMPHIPRION MELANOPUS
Black anemonefish
FAMILY: *Pomacentridae*

Range: Indo-Pacific to Oceania

5 | 36 | 5 in (13cm) | 5 in (13cm) | 79°F (26°C)

Characteristics: This is an orange-bodied fish with a vertical, black-edged white band behind the eye. The rear part of the body is darker in adults, becoming almost black. Small juveniles are red, with one to two additional white bars at the mid-body and the base of the tail.

Gender: The female is larger.

Breeding: Egg depositor; the male guards the eggs. It has been reared in captivity.

Special care: This is a very territorial and aggressive species that will attack anything that comes near. Keep it in a species tank with its own anemone, either *Physobrachia douglasi* or *Entacmaea quadricolor*.

AMPHIPRION NIGRIPES
Black-footed clownfish
FAMILY: *Pomacentridae*

Range: Indian Ocean Maldives, Sri Lanka

3	24	4¼ in (11cm)	2⅜ in (6cm)	79°F (26°C)

Characteristics: This shy fish has a yellow body, a vertical white band across its head, and a vertical facial stripe. However, the dorsal surface lacks either a longitudinal stripe, or any other white markings such as are found in many of its near relatives. The pelvic and anal fins are dark brown-black.
Gender: Unknown

Breeding: Egg depositor
Special care: The species requires high-quality water conditions, with low levels of nitrogenous wastes. It is also in need of some coral retreats and, if desired, a *Heteractis* sea anemone.

AMPHIPRION OCELLARIS
Common clownfish
FAMILY: *Pomacentridae*

Range: Central Indo-Pacific to Oceania

3	36	4¼ in (11cm)	2⅜ in (6cm)	79°F (26°C)

Characteristics: *Amphiprion ocellaris* is often confused with the similar-looking *Amphiprion percula*. Its elongated, bright orange body has three black-edged white bands traversing it: the first band follows the outline of the gill cover; the central band runs from below the narrowest part of the dorsal fin to between the pelvic and anal fins; and the last band crosses the rear of the caudal peduncle. All the bright orange fins outlined in black are rounded. The center of the eye is black.
Gender: Unknown
Breeding: Egg depositor
Special care: A peaceful species requiring high-quality water conditions.

AMPHIPRION PERCULA
Percula clown
FAMILY: *Pomacentridae*

Range: Papua New Guinea, Solomon Islands, and Great Barrier Reef

3	36	4¼ in (11cm)	2⅜ in (6cm)	79°F (26°C)

Characteristics: This fish is often mistaken for the *Amphiprion ocellaris*. The white bands of *Amphiprion percula* have much thicker edges.
Gender: Unknown
Breeding: Egg depositor
Special care: High-quality water conditions with low levels of nitrogenous wastes (ammonia, nitrite, nitrate) are required for this fish. It prefers to have some coral retreats, as well as a number of *Heteractis magnifica* or *Stichodactyla gigantea* sea anemones.

AMPHIPRION SANDARACINOS
Salmon clownfish, pink skunk clownfish
FAMILY: *Pomacentridae*

Range: Pacific

8 36

3¼ in (8cm) 1½ in (4cm) 79°F (26°C)

Characteristics: The body and fins are yellow to orange, and there is a white dorsal stripe running from the caudal right over the back to the top of the lip. *Amphiprion akallopisos* looks similar to this species, but the white vertical stripe behind the head is missing.

Gender: The females are larger.

Breeding: Egg depositor; the male guards the eggs.

Special care: This shy, timid fish must have an anemone to feel secure in an aquarium; without this refuge they will be bullied and will lose condition. They are easy to feed, and take all meaty foods. Ideally, keep them in their own aquarium with a host anemone such as *Stoichactis giganteum* or *S. mertensii*.

PREMNAS BIACULEATUS
Maroon clownfish; spine-cheeked clownfish
FAMILY: *Pomacentridae*

Range: Tropical Indo-Pacific

3 36

6¾ in (17cm) 4½ in (11.5cm) 79°F (26°C)

Characteristics: This is more heavily built than other species of clownfish and has a blunt head. Its oval, brown-red body is crossed vertically by three thin white stripes. A distinguishing feature of this species is the pair of large spines below the eyes. The brown-red, rounded fins may have some blacker areas inside their orange edges.

Gender: Unknown

Breeding: Egg depositor

Special care: It may become aggressive if kept as a solitary species; keeping a number of differently sized specimens may help to establish a more peaceful community. Its dependence on the sea anemone is not so strong as others in this family.

Damselfish

Damselfish have a characteristic method of swimming, constantly bobbing up and down as they move between coral branches, as though influenced by variations in water height above their heads. Damselfish do tend to be argumentative and gregarious; this can be mitigated by providing enough hiding places and retreats within the aquarium. Bullies should be removed, and the introduction of one or two larger fish (of other genera) sometimes brings an overall peace to the aquarium. However, don't use very large fish that might look upon your damselfish as a potential meal.

ABUDEFDUF SAXATILIS
Sergeant major
FAMILY: *Pomacentridae*

Range: Indo-Pacific, tropical Atlantic

3	36

6 in (15cm) 4 in (10cm) 79°F (26°C)

Characteristics: Characterized by its deep yellowish-blue color, this fish has a highly arched dorsal and ventral contour across its body that is crossed vertically with five complete dark bands; a sixth band may just be visible at the top and bottom of the caudal peduncle. The anal, pelvic, and pectoral fins are white; the dorsal and caudal fins have some darkish coloration.
Gender: Unknown
Breeding: Egg depositor

Special care: Although peaceful when juvenile, this fish becomes increasingly territorial with age and when spawning. If a number are kept together, they will need a large aquarium and high water quality. Create some coral retreats, and ensure that there is a little algal growth.

CHROMIS CYANEA
Blue chromis; blue reef fish
FAMILY: *Pomacentridae*

Range: Western Atlantic, Caribbean

4¾ in (12cm)   3¼ in (8cm)   79°F (26°C)

Characteristics: Adults and juveniles are bright blue, with jet black on the dorsal surface. The outer margins of the caudal fin are edged in black. The dorsal, anal, and pelvic fins are electric blue, while the pectoral fins are colorless.
Gender: Unknown
Breeding: Egg depositor

Special care: Provide this fish with a roomy tank with perfect water conditions. Keep a group of at least three specimens together. Lack of a continuous supply of suitable foods has led to unnecessary failures with this species.

CHROMIS IOMELAS
Bicolor chromis
FAMILY: *Pomacentridae*

Range: Red Sea

3¼ in (8cm)   3¼ in (8cm)   79°F (26°C)

Characteristics: The head and half of the body are black, as are the first dorsal and the paired fins. The second dorsal, anal, and caudal fins match the yellow rear body color. It is non-aggressive, feeding on plankton in mid-water from the safety of a vast shoal of its own kind.
Gender: Unknown
Breeding: Egg depositor
Special care: A large tank with ample filtration is best. It should be kept in a small school. Vary the diet to ensure adequate nutrition. Invertebrates are ignored. Avoid keeping it with aggressive species, such as triggers or lionfish. Brilliant illumination shows off its coloration to perfection.

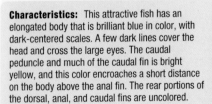

CHROMIS SCOTTI
Purple reef fish
FAMILY: *Pomacentridae*

Range: Western Atlantic, Caribbean

4 in (10cm)   3¼ in (8cm)   79°F (26°C)

Characteristics: Adults are cerulean blue all over; juveniles have a brilliant blue "V" on the snout, and a similarly gaudy crescent above each eye. Both of these features disappear as the fish matures.

Gender: Unknown

Breeding: Many members of the damselfish family have been successfully spawned and reared by aquarists.

Special care: These fish are hardy, but they still need high-quality water with ample filtration. Keeping a small group together will help in successful maintenance.

CHRYSIPTERA PARASEMA
Yellow-tailed damselfish
FAMILY: *Pomacentridae*

Range: Indo-Pacific, Red Sea

2¾ in (7cm)   2 in (5cm)   79°F (26°C)

Characteristics: This attractive fish has an elongated body that is brilliant blue in color, with dark-centered scales. A few dark lines cover the head and cross the large eyes. The caudal peduncle and much of the caudal fin is bright yellow, and this color encroaches a short distance on the body above the anal fin. The rear portions of the dorsal, anal, and caudal fins are uncolored.

This fish is also referred to as *Glyphidodontops hemicyaneus*.

Gender: Unknown

Breeding: Egg depositor

Special care: Ensure high water quality and create some coral retreats. At times this fish can display territorial behavior.

DASCYLLUS ARUANUS
Humbug; white-tailed damselfish; three-striped damselfish
FAMILY: *Pomacentridae*

Range: Western Pacific, Central Indo-Pacific

3¼ in   2 in   79°F
(8cm)   (5cm)   (26°C)

Characteristics: This hardy species has a a stocky, black and white body. It has three black bands running across the body from top to bottom. The pelvic fins are black. The final band includes the rear part of the anal fin, the front half of the caudal peduncle, and the rear of the dorsal fin.
Gender: Unknown
Breeding: Egg depositor
Special care: It can be quarrelsome and territorial, but a roomy aquarium with many retreats should help to keep the number of skirmishes to a minimum. It requires high-quality water conditions.

DASCYLLUS CARNEUS
Cloudy damsel
FAMILY: *Pomacentridae*

Range: Indo-Pacific

2⅜ in   2 in   79°F
(6cm)   (5cm)   (26°C)

Characteristics: This fish has a stocky, deep body, with a steeply rising forehead. The body varies from cream to velvety black-brown, spotted with blue, with a white blotch on the upper part, beneath the dorsal fin. An indistinct black stripe separates the creamy-brown head area (again, spotted with blue) from the main body. Most of the fins are black, with the rear edge of the dorsal fin slightly clear with a blue edge. The caudal fin is white. This fish is sometimes confused with *D. reticulatus* that has less black in the dorsal and anal fins.
Gender: Unknown
Breeding: Egg depositor
Special care: Provide ample hiding places.

DASCYLLUS MELANURUS
Black-tailed humbug
FAMILY: *Pomacentridae*

Range: Western Pacific

3 | 24 | 3¼ in (8cm) | 2⅜ in (6cm) | 79°F (26°C)

Characteristics: Similar in appearance to *D. aruanus*, the white body of this fish is covered by three equally spaced black stripes. The positive identifying feature is that there is a black area on the caudal fin, almost making up a fourth stripe, compared with the plain white caudal fin of *D. aruanus*.
Gender: Unknown
Breeding: Egg depositor

Special care: This fish is never far away from coral heads and any other handy hiding places. The aquarium should be furnished to mimic its natural environment. It is suitable to be kept with a community collection of fish.

DASCYLLUS TRIMACULATUS
Domino damselfish
FAMILY: *Pomacentridae*

Range: Indo-Pacific, Red Sea

3 | 36 | 5½ in (14cm) | 4 in (10cm) | 79°F (26°C)

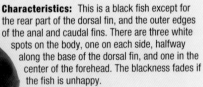

Characteristics: This is a black fish except for the rear part of the dorsal fin, and the outer edges of the anal and caudal fins. There are three white spots on the body, one on each side, halfway along the base of the dorsal fin, and one in the center of the forehead. The blackness fades if the fish is unhappy.
Gender: Unknown
Breeding: Egg depositor
Special care: This boisterous fish is easy to keep. It usually leads the rush for food, even to the extent of snatching it away from others in the process. Maintain high-quality water conditions in the aquarium, with low levels of nitrogenous wastes.

HYPSYPOPS RUBICUNDUS
Garibaldi damselfish
FAMILY: *Pomacentridae*

Range: Pacific coast of California

| 9 | 72 | 10 in (25cm) | 6 in (15cm) | 70°F (21°C) |

Characteristics: The large size, bright orange coloration, and apparent adaptability to captive conditions have combined to result in a constant low level of importation of this fish, despite its protected status in many areas. However, aquarists report that the fish does not survive beyond a few months in a tropical tank.

Gender: Unknown

Breeding: Unknown

Special care: This is a totally inappropriate choice for combining with the other marine species in this book. Aquarists unable to resist its temptation should provide a tank of at least 100 gallons (378 liters). This is definitely not a species for beginners.

MICROSPATHODON CHRYSURUS
Jewel fish; yellow-tailed damsel
FAMILY: *Pomacentridae*

Range: Western Atlantic, Caribbean

| 3 | 48 | 8¼ in (21cm) | 6 in (15cm) | 79°F (26°C) |

Characteristics: Deep and stocky shaped, this fish's body color changes with maturity. The juveniles are dark blue-black with a covering of bright blue spots; the caudal fin is colorless. The dorsal, anal, and pelvic fins are dark blue with a light blue edging. The adult fish loses the body spots, but develops a vivid yellow caudal fin.

Gender: The female goes a deeper color when spawning.

Breeding: Egg depositor

Special care: This fish enjoys retreating to shady coral areas. Provide some algal growth.

POMACENTRUS CAERULEUS
Blue devil
FAMILY: *Pomacentridae*

Range: Indo-Pacific

| 3 | 24 | 3¼ in (8cm) | 2⅜ in (6cm) | 79°F (26°C) | | | |

Characteristics: The elongated body of this fish has only a shallow curvature to the dorsal and ventral contours. The brilliant blue of the body is divided with a black line from the snout crossing the eyes, and each scale has a central mark. A small black blotch appears at the base of the soft portion of the long-based dorsal fin. The caudal fin and the rear-most areas of the dorsal and anal fins are clear.

Gender: Unknown
Breeding: Egg depositor
Special care: Observe the same guidelines for keeping this fish as for other members of this family. Note that this species can often be territorial.

STEGASTES LEUCOSTICTUS
Beau Gregory
FAMILY: *Pomacentridae*

Range: Caribbean

| 3 | 36 | 4¼ in (10cm) | 3¼ in (8cm) | 79°F (26°C) | | |

Characteristics: As a juvenile this fish has a dark blue crown marked with bright blue dots. Below this, the crown breaks into blue dots scattered on the otherwise sulfur-yellow body. The fins are also yellow. When the fish is adult, the bright colors are lost, and it becomes olive brown with a few specks of yellow here and there on the body and fins.
Gender: Unknown
Breeding: Egg depositor
Special care: An aggressive adult may require a small tank to itself. Apart from typical marine-tank conditions, provide it with a rock, coral head, or other structure around which it will establish and defend a territory. Invertebrates are ignored, so they make good tankmates.

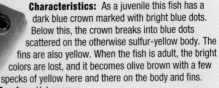

The vivid yellow coloring of this juvenile will fade to dark gray as it matures into adulthood.

STEGASTES PLANIFRONS
Orange damselfish; three-spot damselfish
FAMILY: *Pomacentridae*

Range: Caribbean, western Atlantic

4⅞ in   3 in   79°F
(12.5cm) (7.5cm) (26°C)

Characteristics: Three spots mark this fish's yellow body; one appears just below the dorsal fin, one on the top of the caudal peduncle, and the third at the base of the pectoral fin. The body spots may vary in size with age, getting larger in the adult.

Gender: Unknown

Breeding: Egg depositor

Special care: Set up the aquarium as described for all the fish in this family. This species is rather aggressive (especially when adult) toward others venturing into its territory. Juveniles tend to be more passive.

Angelfish

Recognizing a member of this family is relatively easy due to the characteristic stout, sharp spine that extends backward from the rear of the gill cover. While distributed worldwide throughout tropical seas, the allocation is disproportionate. The majority of species are found in the western Pacific Ocean, with fewer in the Atlantic, and even fewer in the eastern Pacific. Their physical size varies from the small, aquarium-size fish, to those large enough to eat.

In nature, angelfish tend to be independent. Sometimes a pair will be seen together, but you will never see a school of angelfish. This leads to excessive confidence and often translates into aggressiveness toward other fish. In the aquarium it likes to assert itself. Putting an angelfish into a well-established aquarium may lessen its anti-social behavior, but it really depends upon the phyiscal conditions (the size of the aquarium and the number of retreats).

As angelfish feed on invertebrates and seaweeds, living corals and sponges will not survive in their presence. Feeding the more exotic species may be problematic because of the lack of availability of appropriate foods, although manufacturers have now started producing them. A proportion of green matter is important too, so algae should not be discouraged in the aquarium. Should a fish refuse to eat at first, offer it a wide variety of seafood (shellfish, shrimps, etc.) to get it feeding as quickly as possible.

Despite their sturdy proportions, which are reminiscent of freshwater cichlids, angelfish do not share their breeding habits. They are egg scatterers and when the eggs are expelled and fertilized at the water's surface, they drift away on the currents. No parental care is exercised and the spawning pair soon part and go their separate ways. Egg scattering is unlikely to occur in the average-size aquarium because the fish may not have reached full maturity or because there is not enough space.

CENTROPYGE ARGI
Cherub-fish; purple fireball; pygmy angelfish
FAMILY: *Pomacanthidae*

Range: Western Atlantic, Caribbean

3¼ in   3¼ in   79°F
(8cm)   (8cm)   (26°C)

Characteristics: The body color of this fish is deep blue with dark dots, as are the dorsal, pelvic, and anal fins, but these have black streaks radiating outward to a dark margin with an electric blue edging. The caudal fin has lighter blue top and bottom edges, but the rearmost edge lacks the paler shade. The head and throat region includes shades from yellow to golden purple. The yellow-gold eyes are ringed with blue.

Gender: Sexual differences unknown
Breeding: Egg scatterer
Special care: This fish is hardy, requiring a modest-sized aquarium with plenty of algae-covered retreats.

CENTROPYGE AURANTOPS
Flameback dwarf angelfish
FAMILY: *Pomacanthidae*

Range: Caribbean

3¼ in   2 in   79°F
(8cm)   (5cm)   (26°C)

Characteristics: This fish has a dark iridescent blue body. The bright yellow to orange coloration of the face and nape continues along the dorsal surface to just before the caudal peduncle.

Gender: Unknown
Breeding: The fish will form a natural harem, and the aquarist may be treated to almost daily spawning activity, provided they are in prime condition.
Special care: Feed a varied diet, although this species consumes a large amount of filamentous algae, which can be encouraged to grow in the tank.

CENTROPYGE BICOLOR
Bicolor cherub; blue and gold angel; oriole angel
FAMILY: *Pomacanthidae*

Range: Indo-Pacific

6 in   6 in   79°F
(15cm) (15cm) (26°C)

Characteristics: The deep blue rear of this fish is separated from the bright yellow anterior area by a narrow band of white that crosses the body vertically. These colors continue into the dorsal and anal fins, which are caudal yellow with a similar white stripe. A small band of blue crosses the forehead and ends at the eyes. A thin strip of pale blue runs along the edge of the dark-flecked, deep blue anal fin.

Gender: In a group containing a male and several females, a female will change sex to replace the male if he dies or is removed.
Breeding: Egg scatterer
Special care: For general care and breeding information, see *C. argi* above.

CENTROPYGE BISPINOSUS
Coral beauty; dusky angelfish; red and blue angelfish
FAMILY: *Pomacanthidae*

Range: Indo-Pacific

4 in (10cm) 4 in (10cm) 79°F (26°C)

Characteristics: This fish has a deep blue-purple body that is overlaid with a red-gold oval shape. Both of these colors are then further covered by a number of vertical dark bars and speckles. The long-based dorsal, anal, and caudal fins are dark, patterned with blue, with light blue edgings. The pectoral fins are plain yellow, the pelvic fins bright yellow-orange. Young fish are darker but lighten with age—their color also depends on where they were collected.

Gender: Unknown
Breeding: Unknown
Special care: This fish needs a good number of caves and other retreats.

CENTROPYGE EIBLI
Eibl's angelfish
FAMILY: *Pomacanthidae*

Range: Indo-Pacific

6 in (15cm) 4 in (10cm) 79°F (26°C)

Characteristics: Most of this fish's body area is colored gray-gold, and is covered vertically with evenly spaced, wavy lines. These lines are red-gold at the front of the body, but gradually change to gold-black toward the rear, where they match the black rear portion of the long-based dorsal fin, caudal peduncle, and caudal fin. The eyes are ringed with three concentric circles, first gold, then blue, then gold again.

Gender: Unknown
Breeding: Unknown
Special care: This fish eats most foods, and will graze continually.

HOLACANTHUS CILIARIS
Queen angelfish
FAMILY: *Pomacanthidae*

Range: Western Atlantic

4   72

17½ in   12 in   79°F
(45cm)   (30cm)   (26°C)

Characteristics: The whole body of this fish is yellow, outlined with bright blue, apart from the plain yellow caudal fin. The rear edge of the gills and the base of the pectoral fins are bright blue; a small, dark circular patch on the forehead is also ringed with bright blue. The opercular spine is blue. The anal and dorsal fins elongate beyond the caudal fin. Juvenile specimens have a dark blue body crossed by vertical, light blue lines; the snout, pectoral fin area, and caudal fin are yellow-orange. The juveniles are often cleaner than the larger species.
Gender: Unknown
Breeding: Unknown in captivity
Special care: This fish requires plenty of swimming space in well oxygenated water with a strong current, as well as many retreats.

HOLACANTHUS TRICOLOR
Rock beauty
FAMILY: *Pomacanthidae*

Range: Western Atlantic

10   72

12 in   6 in   79°F
(30cm)   (15cm)   (26°C)

Characteristics: The juveniles are yellow-orange with a black spot on the flank; in the youngest specimens, the spot is ringed in bright blue. With maturity the spot enlarges to encompass the entire posterior two-thirds of the body, and most of the dorsal and anal fins. The latter remain edged in yellow; the caudal fin is completely yellow. The lips, in some individuals, are blue.
Gender: Unknown
Breeding: Unknown in captivity
Special care: This fish feeds mostly upon benthic invertebrates, especially sponges. It is possible that dietary specialization limits the ability of this species to adapt to aquarium life.

POMACANTHUS ANNULARIS
Blue ring angelfish
FAMILY: *Pomacanthidae*

Range: Indo-Pacific

4   72   17½ in   12 in   79°F
        (45cm)   (30cm)   (26°C)

Characteristics: Juveniles have alternately thin and thick, equally spaced white lines running vertically downward across the body, and slanting backward into the blue dorsal and anal fins, whose outlines are pale blue. The caudal fin is barely colored, but may have a few pale spots. Adults are golden brown with blue ring markings on the shoulder, and blue lines running diagonally across the body. Two blue lines run backward horizontally above the mouth, terminating at the pectoral fin. The caudal fin is white, with a thin yellow rear edging.

Gender: Unknown
Breeding: Egg scatterer
Special care: This is a territorial fish that grazes on algae, but will accept live and prepared foods.

POMACANTHUS IMPERATOR
Emperor angelfish
FAMILY: *Pomacanthidae*

Range: Indo-Pacific

4   72   16 in   12 in   79°F
        (40cm)   (30cm)   (26°C)

Characteristics: The juveniles are dark blue with concentric white markings on the body behind the gill cover. At the front the lines are almost vertical, with only a slight sweep back in their pattern. The outer edge of the dorsal fin is white, while that of the caudal is colorless. Adults have a plain yellow body crossed diagonally by many blue lines extending into the dorsal fin, which becomes pointed in mature fishes. They have yellow caudal and dark-blue anal fins with lighter blue lines. A dark patch spreads upward from beneath the pectoral fins to separate the main body pattern from a blue-edged plain yellow forehead and cheeks. The eyes are hidden within another dark band, but the mouth area is blue-gray, again edged with light blue.

Gender: Unknown
Breeding: Unknown
Special care: This fish needs plenty of algae-covered retreats. The water must be well oxygenated, and should have a strong current.

POMACANTHUS MACULOSUS

Half-moon angelfish; purple moon angelfish; Red Sea half-moon angelfish; seabride; yellowbar angelfish
FAMILY: *Pomacanthidae*

Range: African coast of Indian Ocean

| 6 | 72 | 20 in (50cm) | 16 in (40cm) | 79°F (26°C) | | | | |

Characteristics: Juveniles have a dark blue body with transverse white lines, but take on the "new moon," crescent-shaped yellow marking of the adult before the white lines fade away with approaching maturity. The adults are purple-gray with some darker speckling. A curved yellow arc appears across the mid-point of the body, extending upward and backward into the dorsal fin, but stopping short of the anal fin. The caudal fin is yellow. The dorsal and anal fins sweep back more with increasing age, and often have extended filaments at their extremities.

Gender: Unknown

Breeding: Unknown

Special care: This terrotorial fish will swim at all levels of the aquarium. For care information, see *P. imperator*.

Left: This fish still has the white markings of juvenility.

POMACANTHUS PARU
French angelfish
FAMILY: *Pomacanthidae*

Range: Western Atlantic

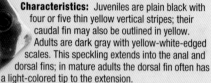

| 6 | 72 | 12 in (30cm) | 10 in (25cm) | 79°F (26°C) | | |

Characteristics: Juveniles are plain black with four or five thin yellow vertical stripes; their caudal fin may also be outlined in yellow. Adults are dark gray with yellow-white-edged scales. This speckling extends into the anal and dorsal fins; in mature adults the dorsal fin often has a light-colored tip to the extension.

Gender: Unknown

Breeding: Unknown

Special care: This fish should be kept in a spacious aquarium with well-oxygenated water that has a strong current and some algal growth.

POMACANTHUS SEMICIRCULATUS
Koran angelfish
FAMILY: *Pomacanthidae*

Range: Indo-Pacific, Red Sea

| 6 | 72 | 15 in (38cm) | 12 in (30cm) | 79°F (26°C) | | |

Characteristics: Juveniles have a dark blue-brown body covered by thin white lines based on a semicircular pattern that radiates from a center on the rear end of the caudal peduncle. The lines gradually become straighter and veer more toward the vertical closer to the head. Adults have a green-brown-blue background with dark spots. From the front edge of the dorsal fin, right around to the beginning of the anal fin, the rear outline of the fish is outlined in light blue, as are the pelvic fins. The gill cover is also outlined like this, as is the opercular spine.

Gender: Unknown

Breeding: Unknown

Special care: Provide plenty of swimming space and algae-covered retreats. Water should be well-oxygenated with a strong current.

Butterflyfish

This stunning family of fish is probably more responsible for the attraction of marine fishkeeping than any other. However, butterflyfish can be both a source of delight and despair to the aquarist. Some are suited to the aquarium, others are not; some are easy to feed, others are exasperatingly difficult. As a general guideline, the more exotically colored species are usually the hardest to keep and the most expensive to buy.

Butterflyfish are found worldwide in tropical waters on coral reefs and near the shore. Their size ranges from 3 in (7.5cm) to 12 in (30cm). All have laterally-compressed, oval-shaped bodies with a pointed snout, ideally suited for flitting in and out of the crevices of coral stands in the search for food.

Taking into account the considerations of providing ample space and numerous retreats, the butterflyfish (if a correct, aquarium-suitable species is chosen) will thrive in captivity. They require clean, fairly agitated, well-oxygenated water in an aquarium that is well lit. Many are intolerant of their own kind and, perhaps more importantly, should not be included in a reef system as they will devour the invertebrate life.

Most of the hardy species will accept foods (fresh or frozen) but those species that feed on coral life in the wild may prove impossible to acclimatize to the aquarium. Similarly to angelfish, butterflyfish may refuse to eat and, again, the answer is to offer a wide variety of foods until they regain their appetite.

Butterflyfish are often seen traveling in pairs on the reef, although gender differences are not usually apparent. Many, however, must select their own partners, and may not tolerate a choice made by the aquarist. Spawning follows the pattern of the angelfish, with the eggs being released and fertilized at the water's surface, usually at dusk. The young often take several months to develop into miniature fish.

FEATURED IN THIS SECTION

CHAETODON ACULEATUS
Atlantic long-nosed butterflyfish
FAMILY: *Chaetodontidae*

Range: Florida, Caribbean

2¾ in (7cm)   2 in (5cm)   79°F (26°C)

Characteristics: This fish has a dark dorsal fin, with some streaks of yellow that continue to the upper half of the body; the lower half is blue-white. The anal and pectoral fins are yellow, with light blue edging. The face is pale, streaked with yellow, and has an extended mouth.
Gender: Unknown
Breeding: Unknown

Special care: Feed small, live invertebrates until the fish readily accepts aquarium foods. Because the fish uses its long snout to probe for invertebrates in recesses of the reef, try pressing various food items into the rough surface of a rock or piece of coral.

CHAETODON AURIGA
Threadfin butterflyfish
FAMILY: *Chaetodontidae*

Range: Indo-Pacific, Red Sea

9 in (23cm)   4⅞ in (12.5cm)   79°F (26°C)

Characteristics: The anterior three-quarters of the body of this fish is white, and the rear quarter yellow, with these colors carried into the fins. There are two overlaid areas of diagonal dark lines, one group rising up from behind the head into the dorsal fin, the other running down at right angles to the first set of lines toward the anal fin. A vertical dark bar crosses the head, passing through the eyes. There is a false eye spot in the upper rear corner of the dorsal fin, and a thread-like extension on the dorsal fin in mature fishes.
Gender: Unknown
Breeding: Unknown
Special care: Feed small invertebrates. Provide a roomy tank with lots of decorations among which the fish can feel secure. Maintain high-quality water conditions.

CHAETODON CAPISTRATUS
Four-eye butterflyfish
FAMILY: *Chaetodontidae*

Range: Western Atlantic, Caribbean

| 10 | 48 | 4¼ in (11cm) | 2⅜ in (6cm) | 79°F (26°C) | | | |

Characteristics: This fish has a pure white body marked with a trace of dark lines that run diagonally above and below the lateral line. It has a black spot ringed in white near the upper part of the caudal peduncle. The snout and pelvic and pectoral fins are yellow, and this color continues to the belly and lower edge of the anal fin.

Gender: Unknown
Breeding: Unknown
Special care: This fish is usually seen in pairs and may benefit from a companion in the aquarium.

CHAETODON DECUSSATUS
Decussate butterflyfish
FAMILY: *Chaetodontidae*

Range: Indo-Malay archipelago

| 5 | 60 | 8 in (20cm) | 4⅞ in (12.5cm) | 79°F (26°C) | |

Characteristics: The pale cream body of this fish is patterned in two areas with dark diagonal lines: the first patch rises up from behind the head to the dorsal region, the other runs down from the first set of lines toward the rear of the anal fin. A vertical bar passes over the eyes. The rear body and long-based anal and dorsal fins are black. The caudal fin is yellow, with a black vertical bar at its mid-point, and a white outer edge. The dark anal fin has two longitudinal yellow lines.
Gender: Unknown
Breeding: Unknown
Special care: See *C. auriga* for care and breeding information.

CHAETODON LUNULA
Racoon butterflyfish
FAMILY: *Chaetodontidae*

Range: Indo-Pacific

| 6 | 60 | 8 in (20cm) | 4⅞ in (12.5cm) | 79°F (26°C) | |

Characteristics: Dark diagonal lines cross the yellow body of this fish upward from the pectoral fins, becoming less distinct as they reach the dark brown upper flanks. A dark saddle, bordered in front by a thin white line and behind by a broad white band, lies across the forehead, masking each eye. In juveniles, the area in front of the eye bar is much paler; they have an eye spot on the rear of the dorsal fin.
Gender: Unknown
Breeding: Unknown
Special care: This is the only nocturnal butterflyfish imported for the aquarium, and it should be offered food straight after dark.

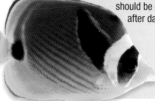

CHAETODON QUADRIMACULATUS
Hawaiian teardrop butterflyfish
FAMILY: *Chaetodontidae*

Range: Hawaiian, Japanese, Micronesian, and Polynesian waters

 10 48

6¼ in (16cm)   4 in (10cm)   79°F (26°C)

Characteristics: This is a deep-bodied fish with a sharply rising forehead. Its coloration is divided into two distinct areas: the dorsal area is dark brown shading to golden yellow midway down the body. Two white patches appear within the brown area below the base of the dorsal fin. The fins are golden reddish-yellow, and the dorsal and anal fins have a blue line along their mid-sections; the base of the dorsal fin is brown, that of the anal fin yellow, and the caudal fin base is red.

Gender: Unknown

Breeding: Unknown

Special care: This fish is very difficult to manage, and is probably best not kept in an aquarium due to its very specialized feeding requirements.

CHAETODON SEDENTARIUS
Reef butterflyfish
FAMILY: *Chaetodontidae*

Range: Florida, Caribbean

 9 48

5¼ in (14cm)   4 in (10cm)   79°F (26°C)

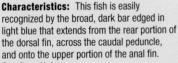

Characteristics: This fish is easily recognized by the broad, dark bar edged in light blue that extends from the rear portion of the dorsal fin, across the caudal peduncle, and onto the upper portion of the anal fin.

Gender: Unknown

Breeding: Unknown

Special care: Many adult individuals will refuse to eat in captivity, and for this reason it is suggested that juveniles are obtained. Specimens about 3 in (8cm) in diameter offer the best chance for acclimatization to aquarium life.

CHAETODON STRIATUS
Banded butterflyfish
FAMILY: *Chaetodontidae*

Range: Tropical Atlantic Ocean

5½ in (14cm)	4 in (10cm)	79°F (26°C)

Characteristics: The body of this fish is white to silver; a dark band passes across the eyes. Two more vertical bands cross the mid-body region—one from the dorsal fin to the anal, and another on the outer portion of the caudal fin; these are complete with blue and pale yellow lines on each side, at the tips of the dorsal and anal fins.

Gender: Unknown
Breeding: Unknown
Special care: Most individuals of this species will refuse to eat in captivity. Try small, live invertebrates until the fish will readily accept aquarium foods.

CHAETODON UNIMACULATUS
Teardrop butterflyfish
FAMILY: *Chaetodontidae*

Range: Red Sea, Indo-Pacific

8 in (20cm)	4⅞ in (12.5cm)	79°F (26°C)

Characteristics: The body is yellow, the anterior part a paler shade, with an obtuse-angled yellow chevron patterning crossing the pale area. Midway along the body there is a large, dark, teardrop marking—though very often in adult fishes this is a circular blob, the rest of the "tear" being smudged or missing altogether.

A vertical bar lies across the head, passing over the eyes, and another passes across the caudal peduncle and is picked up again, this time bordered on each side by a narrow white margin, in the rear edges of the yellow dorsal and anal fins.
Gender: Unknown
Breeding: Unknown
Special care: See *C. auriga* for care information.

CHAETODON VAGABUNDUS
Vagabond butterflyfish
FAMILY: *Chaetodontidae*

Range: Indo-Pacific

5 · 60

9 in
(23cm)

4⅞ in
(12.5cm)

79°F
(26°C)

Characteristics: The pale cream body of this fish is overlaid with diagonal dark lines, one set rising up from behind the head to the dorsal fin, and another running down to the anal fin. A dark bar passes across the head and through the eyes, and another across the caudal peduncle and into the dorsal and anal fins. The caudal fin is yellow with a black bar midway, and a dark outer margin. The dorsal and anal fins have yellow rear portions.

Juveniles have a pale body, with the yellow coloration limited to areas behind the posterior black bar; they have a dark eye spot in the rear of the dorsal fin, but this fades with maturity.

Gender: Unknown
Breeding: Unknown
Special care: None

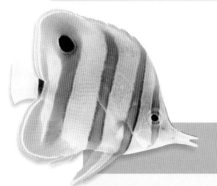

CHELMON ROSTRATUS
Copperband butterflyfish
FAMILY: *Chaetodontidae*

Range: Indo-Pacific, Red Sea

7 · 48

8 in
(20cm)

4⅞ in
(12.5cm)

79°F
(26°C)

Characteristics: The body of this fish is plain silver, with four black-edged deep orange bands that cross the body vertically; the first band passes over the eyes, the fourth carries a dark, white-ringed eye spot. A fifth band crosses the rear parts of the dorsal and anal fins and the caudal peduncle, in front of a white-edged black vertical band. The bands in juvenile fish are more intensely colored.

Gender: Unknown
Breeding: Unknown
Special care: Initially, this fish needs small, live foods, but it will adapt to other foods. It eats aptasia.

FORCIPIGER LONGIROSTRIS
Long-nosed butterflyfish; forcepsfish
FAMILY: *Chaetodontidae*

Range: Indo-Pacific

8¾ in
(22cm)

4¼ in
(12.5cm)

79°F
(26°C)

Characteristics: This fish has a bright yellow body, but the top half of the head, including the top jaw, from the gill cover forward, is jet black. The lower half of the head, lower jaw, and throat region is silver. The rear edge of both the dorsal fin and the anal fin is light blue, as is the extreme edge of the caudal peduncle, and the anal fin is also marked with a black eye spot in the upper corner nearest to the body.

Gender: Unknown

Breeding: Unknown

Special care: It feeds on small invertebrates, but will adapt to commercial foods in captivity.

HENIOCHUS ACUMINATUS
Wimplefish
FAMILY: *Chaetodontidae*

Range: Indo-Pacific, Red Sea

10 in
(25cm)

6 in
(15cm)

79°F
(26°C)

Characteristics: The body form of this fish is deep, almost disc-like, with a high flowing dorsal fin in mature fish. The body is white, with two vertical black bands, one just behind the operculum, and the other toward the rear of the body; these bands run into the dorsal and the anal fins. A short black band runs from eye to eye over the head. The caudal and the rear half of the dorsal fin are yellow.

Gender: Unknown

Breeding: Unknown

Special care: For care information, see *C. auriga*.

Surgeonfish and Tangs

Fish in this family have oval-shaped bodies, steep sloping foreheads, and some extremely bizarre facial decoration. Another physical characteristic that most share is the presence of one, or sometimes two, sharp spines on each side of the caudal peduncle. It takes little imagination to appreciate what damage these "scalpels" can do to anything that they come into contact with (including the aquarist's hand or net) when held erect from the side of the fish and moved like a razor-sharp scythe as it flexes its body.

A further common feature of these fish is that they are mostly herbivores, content to graze endlessly over lush macro-algae. A hungry school can lay bare any green outcrop in a very short space of time. A notable exception among the members of this family is the popular hippo tang, which lacks the scalpel at the base of the tail, and feeds mostly on plankton rather than plant matter. These fish are safe with invertebrates. Most species are found in all tropical seas around reefs where the light encourages green growth.
Breeding occurs at the water's surface, with the fertilized eggs being swept away to develop naturally.

These active, constantly-browsing fish require well-oxygenated water and an efficient filtration system to deal with the constantly-produced waste. Although these fish may school in the wild, they do like to find less crowded areas in which to seek refuge every now and then. In the aquarium this isn't really possible and very often they will resent fellow surgeons intruding into their swimming space. However, given a large enough aquarium and with the presence of some other non-surgeonfish species to distract their attention, small numbers can successfully be kept together.

FEATURED IN THIS SECTION

ACANTHURUS CAERULEUS
Atlantic blue tang; blue surgeonfish
FAMILY: *Acanthuridae*

Range: Florida, Bahamas, and Caribbean

15 in	8 in	79°F
(38cm)	(20cm)	(26°C)

Characteristics: The juveniles are bright yellow, with the dorsal and anal fins edged in bright blue. As the fish ages, the blue on the fins expands until only the tail remains yellow, until finally the entire body is dark blue, marked with wavy lines of electric blue.
Gender: Unknown
Breeding: Pelagic egg spawner

Special care: All surgeonfish can deliver a nasty cut with the scalpel-like modified scale that lies in a groove on the caudal peduncle; therefore exercise caution when handling, especially large specimens. Young fish can be domineering, but this lessens with maturity. Given a roomy tank, this is a hardy and adaptable species. Its diet is largely vegetarian.

ACANTHURUS GLAUCOPAREIUS
Gold-rim tang
FAMILY: *Acanthuridae*

Range: Pacific Ocean; sometimes found in the eastern Indian Ocean

8 in	4 in	79°F
(20cm)	(10cm)	(26°C)

Characteristics: The mouth is at the end of the snout, for easy algal browsing. In color its rich brown body shades to bright yellow on the caudal peduncle. There is a large white area stretching from the mouth to the eye, and a small yellow area at the base of the pectoral fin. A yellow line runs along the base of the dorsal and anal fins, and extends into the caudal peduncle.
Gender: Unknown
Breeding: Unknown
Special care: This fish needs a spacious aquarium, as it swims at all levels. It likes plenty of macroalgal growth.

ACANTHURUS LEUCOSTERNON
Powder blue surgeon
FAMILY: *Acanthuridae*

Range: Indo-Pacific

9 in (23cm) 4⅞ in (12.5cm) 79°F (26°C)

Characteristics: The head and gills are dark blue-black, with a white line running beneath the lower lip. The throat region is white, shading into the light blue body. The center of the eye is dark with a pale surround. The dorsal fin is bright yellow, and the anal fin is white, both fins having a light edging. The bright yellow scalpel bridges the blue and yellow areas at the front of the caudal peduncle.
Gender: Unknown
Breeding: It spawns pelagic eggs that drift away.
Special care: It is quarrelsome, so keep only one in the aquarium. It is an active fish that needs plenty of swimming room and luxuriant algal growth.

NASO LITERATUS
Lipstick tang; smooth-head unicornfish; Japanese Tang
FAMILY: *Acanthuridae*

Range: Indo-Pacific

12 in (30cm) 6⅞ in (17.5cm) 79°F (26°C)

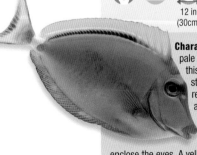

Characteristics: The pale gray-brown body of this fish is very sleekly streamlined. It has red-orange lips set against a yellow-edged, dark brown area that runs up the forehead to enclose the eyes. A yellow patch separates the eyes from another dark brown band (with body edging in light blue) along the base of the dorsal fin. The crescent-shaped caudal fin is light colored, but with a dark top, bottom, and rear edges. The top and bottom few rays of the caudal fin are formed into long filaments. There are scalpels on each side of the caudal peduncle, set in yellow patches.
Gender: Unknown
Breeding: Unknown
Special care: This fish needs a spacious aquarium. Do not feed only on green algae, or it will not thrive.

PARACANTHURUS HEPATUS
Hippo tang; yellow-tail blue tang; regal tang
FAMILY: *Acanthuridae*

Range: Indo-Pacific, East Africa and mid-Pacific

12¼ in (31cm) 6 in (15cm) 79°F (26°C)

Characteristics: This tang has a deep royal blue body with distinctive black markings, and a bright yellow triangular area in the center of the tail. It carries hidden scalpels on the caudal peduncle.
Gender: Unknown
Breeding: Unknown
Special care: Unlike other surgeons, its diet consists largely of plankton and other animal matter, with roughly one third consisting of microalgae. More than one specimen can be kept if the tank is roomy and there are numerous retreats.

ZEBRASOMA DESJARDINII
Sailfin tang, Desjardin's sailfin tang, western sailfin tang
FAMILY: *Acanthuridae*

Range: Indian Ocean: Red Sea to the Maldives

16 in (40cm) 16 in (40cm) 79°F (26°C)

Characteristics: This oval-bodied fish has tall dorsal and anal fins that make it look almost discus-like in shape. As a juvenile the fins are even taller, and the body is cream-colored with brown vertical stripes. These stripes change to spots on the ventral region, throat, and head. The body and fins also develop faint yellow undulating lines.
Gender: Unknown
Breeding: Pelagic spawner
Special care: Feed algae daily, and otherwise at least three times daily. It needs some vegetable matter in its diet. It will not tolerate other members of its genus in the aquarium, except as its partner in a pair.

ZEBRASOMA FLAVESCENS
Yellow tang
FAMILY: *Acanthuridae*

Range: Pacific Ocean

| 8 in (20cm) | 3 in (7.5cm) | 79°F (26°C) |

Characteristics: An oval bright yellow body is surrounded by fins that give this fish a disc-shape appearance. It has a relatively long snout, with a steeply sloping forehead and high-set eyes. The white scalpels on the caudal peduncle bring contrasting relief. The dorsal fin is very long-based, reaching the short caudal peduncle; the anal fin is large. All the fins are bright yellow.

Gender: Unknown

Breeding: Unknown

Special care: This herbivorous fish will spend most of its time at the middle and lower levels of the aquarium. It requires adequate swimming space, and plenty of macroalgal growth on which to feed.

ZEBRASOMA XANTHURUM
Purple sailfin tang
FAMILY: *Acanthuridae*

Range: Indo-Pacific, Red Sea

| 8¾ in (22cm) | 6 in (15cm) | 79°F (26°C) |

Characteristics: The body profile of this fish is oval, but it appears disc-shaped by virtue of the stiffly held surrounding fins. Its deep blue-purple body is marked with darker, purple-red dots and lines concentrated mainly on the head and front portion of the body. A dark line edges the gill cover. It has a steep forehead, and the eyes are ringed in red.

Gender: Unknown

Breeding: Unknown

Special care: Although territorially minded and probably best kept as a single specimen, some reports suggest that keeping a shoal might be possible. It requires plenty of green foods—algae-coated aquarium decorations provide an ideal grazing ground.

Triggerfish and Filefish

Oblong or lozenge-shaped bodies, very sharp teeth, and bizarre markings are among the physical features of members of this family. However, the most distinctive characteristic that these fish have is what gives them their common name. The name triggerfish is very descriptive—the "trigger" is part of the mechanism that locks the dorsal fin into an upright position. This is either to prevent the fish from being swallowed by a predator, or to help wedge it in a crevice from which it cannot be moved, until it releases the trigger to lower the fin. When purchasing a triggerfish, don't refuse to buy it on the grounds that its pelvic fins have broken off, as it doesn't have any.

Found in shallow tropical waters of the Indo-Pacific and Atlantic Oceans, triggerfish are both solitary and territorial which, in terms of aquarium culture, means that they need space if quarrels are to be avoided between similar species. As well as needing space, they also require retreats and places to rummage in. Make sure the aquarium decorations are fixed firmly in place as these fish will attempt (and usually succeed) in rearranging the substrate and other "fixtures and fittings" if they get a chance. They will assume that anything is good to eat and will attempt to chew at it, so their inclusion in a mixed fish and invertebrate collection is not a good idea. Because triggerfish are not fussy feeders this makes feeding unproblematic, but take care their sharp teeth don't have a chance to get a taste of you when maintaining their aquarium.

Their relations, filefish, differ in that they are unable to lock the first dorsal spine into an upright position. They have extremely rough skin and are known by the alternative popular name of "leather-jackets."

FEATURED IN THIS SECTION

BALISTOIDES CONSPICILLUM
Clown trigger
FAMILY: *Balistidae*

Range: Tropical Indo-Pacific

20 in (50cm)   4⅞ in (12.5cm)   79°F (26°C)

Characteristics: This trigger is dark brown-black in color, with round white spots of varying sizes. A yellow saddle area surrounds the base of the flat first dorsal fin; a small saddle tops the small caudal peduncle. A black patch crosses the forehead, and the eyes are separated from the snout by a white band and encircled by a dark black ring. It has a small mouth, with a wide yellow lipstick band edged in light blue/white. In the adults the caudal fin is often black with a white central area.

Gender: Unknown

Breeding: Egg depositer

Special care: This fish tends to become aggressive, and requires plenty of well-anchored retreats. It needs a tank on its own, or with other large fish.

XANTHICHTHYS RINGENS
Sargassum triggerfish
FAMILY: *Balistidae*

Range: Brazil to Bermuda

8 in (20cm)   6 in (15cm)   78°F (26°C)

Characteristics: This trigger has a gray-blue body flecked with red-brown dots, in parallel rows from the back of the head to the caudal peduncle. The bases of the dorsal and anal fins, and the foldable first dorsal fin, are reddish brown. The margins of the caudal fin are red-orange. Three blue streaks appear across the cheeks. The pelvic fins are mere stumps.

Gender: Unknown

Breeding: Egg depositer

Special care: Once established in an aquarium, this trigger may not be receptive to new introductions.

MONACANTHUS CILIARIS
Fringed filefish
FAMILY: *Monacanthidae*

Range: Indo-Pacific

8 in (20cm)   6 in (15cm)   78°F (26°C)

Characteristics: The first spines of the dorsal and anal fins can be erected so the fish can lodge itself tightly in a crevice when danger threatens. Its body varies in color from tan to green, with lighter spots and blotches. Swimming slowly along, it uses its tiny mouth to grab benthic invertebrates. There is a noticeable hump at the anterior base of the dorsal fin, and this is a reliable identification characteristic for a species that is highly variable in coloration.

Gender: Unknown

Breeding: Unknown

Special care: It is important to provide perfect water conditions. A habitat tank featuring sea grasses and a sandy bottom would make this species feel more at home than a traditional reef tank.

MONACANTHUS SETIFER
Pygmy filefish
FAMILY: *Monacanthidae*

Range: Indo-Pacific

4 in
(10cm)

3¼ in
(8cm)

79°F
(26°C)

Characteristics: This fish has a pale yellow to cream body, with a pattern of dashes and blotches that give the impression of stripes. This provides near-perfect camouflage, as it hides in masses of floating seaweed, or hovers just above rocks encrusted with algae and invertebrates. Swimming slowly, it uses its tiny mouth to pluck food from recesses in its surroundings.
Gender: Unknown
Breeding: Unknown
Special care: Provide perfect water conditions, and plenty of rocks with algae and invertebrates. Feed small, live invertebrates until the fish is properly acclimatized to aquarium foods.

PERVAGOR MELANOCEPHALUS
Red-tailed filefish; lace-finned leatherjacket
FAMILY: *Monacanthidae*

Range: Indo-Pacific

4 in
(10cm)

3 in
(7.5cm)

78°F
(26°C)

Characteristics: This shy, peaceful fish has a long snout and a short caudal peduncle. The front half of the fish is purple, shading through brown to a bright yellow at the caudal fin. It has a steep forehead and red-rimmed eyes. It has two dorsal fins; the pelvic fins are very rudimentary, but it has a movable pelvic spine. The yellow, fan-shaped caudal fin is streaked with brown-red radial stripes, and is blue-edged.
Gender: Unknown
Breeding: Unknown
Special care: The aquarium must be furnished with numerous retreats for this secretive fish.

Wrasses

If asked to put a name to a member of the Labridae family, a fishkeeper would probably answer, "cleaner wrasse" but there are other fish that are included in this family that, at first glance, seem to be "outsiders." The family contains over 50 genera, represented by over 500 species, so some of them must, by the law of averages, be different. Factor in the differences between juveniles and adults, males and females, and the fact that the fish often change sex, and you have an indication as to what an interesting family of fish this is.

Wrasses are found worldwide in shallow waters and vary greatly in size. They are inveterate eaters and forage around coral rubble for food, darting in and out of caves. The cleaner wrasse offers a cleaning service to all fish that visit its "service station," usually a definite area on the coral reef. It picks off parasites from the visiting fish's skin, even from inside the mouth and gills of larger specimens. While very welcome, this service has important ramifications for members of this genus; Labroides do this in order to get food and are dependent on other fish bringing it to them. Removing cleaner fish from the reef results in other species of fish ceasing to visit, as they know that its services will no longer be available. This dependency between species is a vital part of coral reef life and denuding the reef of cleaner fish is to be discouraged. One also has to consider what the cleaner wrasse might feed on once the parasites have been cleaned from its tankmates.

Some wrasses burrow into the substrate at night. To ensure that you provide suitable "sleeping accommodation" for these species, the substrate should be sandy and some inches deep. Wrasses are territorial, which means that considerable thought has to be given as to their tankmates, but they are quite hardy. Don't always assume that the sight of a wrasse "flashing" off the substrate is a sign of skin irritation—they sometimes adopt this tactic to uncover food. Look carefully at how wrasses swim—they hardly use their caudal fins at all; all of the movement is generated with the pectoral fins, which allows the fish to glide through the water.

FEATURED IN THIS SECTION

BODIANUS PULCHELLUS
Cuban hogfish; spotfin
FAMILY: *Labridae*

Range: Carribean, tropical west Atlantic

4   36

8 in (20cm)   5 in (13cm)   79°F (26°C)

Characteristics: Adults have a reddy-brown body becoming yellow behind the dorsal fin. A dark bar separates the two colors. A dark spot on the tip of the pectoral fins accounts for the fish's alternative name. It has a red-rimmed eye. Juveniles are yellow, with a dark mark on the front of the dorsal fin, and red lines running through the eyes.
Gender: Unknown
Breeding: Unknown
Special care: This fish needs an efficient filtration system as it is a greedy feeder.

BODIANUS RUFUS
Spanish hogfish
FAMILY: *Labridae*

Range: Carribean

4   36

16 in (40cm)   8 in (20cm)   36 in (90cm)

Characteristics: This fish has a stockily built body, a tapering snout, and a fairly long caudal peduncle. The basic overall body coloration is bright yellow, but the upper back patch is blue-brown in juveniles and red in adults. In shallow water it retains the blue shade, whereas deep-water fishes are red and yellow. All the fins are yellow, with the exception of the dorsal fin. Filamentous extensions are found on the dorsal and anal fins of adult fish.
Gender: Unknown
Breeding: Unknown
Special care: Young specimens make good aquarium subjects and may act as "cleaners" to other fish.

CIRRHILABRUS LEUTEOVITTATUS
Yellowbar fairy wrasse
FAMILY: *Labridae*

Range: Indo-Pacific

7   36

4¾ in (12cm)   4¾ in (12cm)   79°F (26°C)

Characteristics: The males are burgundy red, with a bright yellow streak from the caudal peduncle almost to the gill cover. The dorsal and anal fins are edged in yellow and decorated with blue lines.
Gender: Females are greenish and purple, with a double row of red spots.
Breeding: Unknown

Special care: Although this fish will not harm reef invertebrates, it does best in dim light. Give three small feedings daily, consisting of meaty seafoods of appropriate size for its small mouth. Keep only one male and several females in the same tank.

CORIS GAIMARDI
Clown wrasse, yellowtail coris
FAMILY: *Labridae*

Range: Indo-Pacific

16 in (40cm)   15 in (36cm)   79°F (26°C)

Characteristics: As a juvenile this is a bright orange fish with a series of five white patches edged in black dorsally. The caudal peduncle also has a white crescent edged in black toward the body. As an adult the colors change, and the fish becomes a dark bluish color in the body, with a yellow to pinkish head and throat region, red dorsal and anal fins, and a bright yellow tail. The patterning varies between individuals. There are two geographic color morphs.

Gender: Dominant males may display a green mid-body bar.
Breeding: Unknown
Special care: This species feeds mainly on mollusks, shrimps, hermit crabs, and other meaty foods. It can become aggressive with age. It likes a deep substrate to retire into at night.

GOMPHOSUS COERULEUS
Birdmouth wrasse
FAMILY: *Labridae*

Range: Indo-Pacific

11 in (28cm)   6 in (15cm)   79°F (26°C)

Characteristics: This wrasse has a deep mid-section to its body, and a much extended snout. Body coloration varies considerably from juvenile to adult, and also between the sexes. Adult males are a plain, dark blue-green. The jaws resemble a bird-like beak in shape. The dorsal and anal fins are green, the pectoral fins purple. The caudal fin is green, with darker outer rays, and it may become lyre-shaped with age.
Gender: Adult males are plain dark blue-green; females and juveniles are brown with red speckles.
Breeding: Unknown
Special care: This is a very active species. It needs an efficient filtration system and some rubble on a soft substrate.

HALICHOERES BIVITTATUS
Slippery Dick
FAMILY: *Labridae*

Range: North Carolina to Brazil

8¾ in (22cm)	6 in (15cm)	79°F (26°C)

Characteristics: Juveniles have longitudinal stripes in tan, red-brown, white, gold, and white, from the dorsal to the ventral side. Adults are a gaudy mix of sea-foam green, yellow, purple, and turquoise. The intermediate stages are complex in coloration also, making identification confusing.
Gender: Unknown

Breeding: Unknown
Special care: Provide good water conditions. Do not trust this wrasse, or any other, with any fish or crustacean small enough to eat.

HALICHOERES GARNOTI
Yellowhead wrasse
FAMILY: *Labridae*

Range: Florida, Carribean

8 in (20cm)	6 in (15cm)	79°F (26°C)

Characteristics: Juveniles are bright yellow-orange in color, with a striking electric blue line down the mid-line of each side of the body. A thin black edging separates the blue from a ruddy orange that extends toward the back and belly. Intermediate-phase adults are dark turquoise, with a stunning bright yellow band replacing the blue band of the juvenile. Adults are even gaudier, with a bright yellow head and yellow anterior body; otherwise the body is black, highlighted toward the rear in fluorescent green. There is a purple stripe along the anal fin.
Gender: Unknown
Breeding: Unknown
Special care: This fish needs a roomy tank. Filtration must be adequate to maintain reef-tank water conditions.

HALICHOERES MACULIPINNA
Clown wrasse
FAMILY: *Labridae*

Range: Western Atlantic: North Carolina, U.S., and Bermuda to Brazil

6 in (15cm)   4 in (10cm)   79°F (26°C)

Characteristics: The juvenile has a dark brown upper body, and a pearly white belly. A bright yellow band begins on the snout, and extends along the dorsal surface to the caudal peduncle. The dorsal fin and the tip of the snout are brick red. It matures to a bright blue phase, with a broad yellow stripe running from beneath the eye to the tail. The dorsal fin has a dark eye-spot on the side, and before the anal fin.

Gender: Unknown

Breeding: Unknown

Special care: Provide perfect water conditions. This wrasse may bury itself in the substrate, and so it needs a layer of sand several inches deep on the bottom of the aquarium.

HALICHOERES RADIATUS
Puddingwife
FAMILY: *Labridae*

Range: Caribbean, western Atlantic

17¾ in (45cm)   10 in (25cm)   79°F (26°C)

Characteristics: The yellow-orange body of this fish is marked with a ladder pattern of electric blue from the lateral line to the dorsal fin. In the juvenile, a dark eye-spot, lighter in the center and outlined in pale blue, extends from the dorsal fin down the back. Adults become blue-green. Intermediate specimens are golden, and develop blue lines on the face, paired fins, and caudal fin. The juvenile eye-spot expands to form a dark area flanked by white blotches on the dorsal fin and back.

Gender: Unknown

Breeding: Unknown

Special care: Provide ample filtration.

HEMIPTERONOTUS MARTINICENSIS
Rosy razorfish
FAMILY: *Labridae*

Range: Atlantic, Caribbean

6 in   4 in   79°F
(15cm)   (10cm)   (26°C)

Characteristics: The cheeks and gill covers of this fish are pale greenish-yellow, with a blue line. An area of deep blue surrounds the eye, which is coral red. The body color is a mixture of pastels, blue, and yellow. This fish will dive into the sand to escape danger.
Gender: Unknown
Breeding: Unknown

Special care: Provide a sandy substrate several inches deep or the fish may injure itself trying to escape perceived harm. It is easily fed, and harmless to anything it cannot eat; it is, however, fussy. It can be maintained with stinging invertebrates, such as the *Condylactis* anemone that shares its sea-grass habitat.

LIENARDELLA FASCIATA
Harlequin tuskfish
FAMILY: *Labridae*

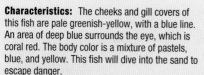

Range: Western Pacific

12 in   7 in   79°F
(30cm)   (18cm)   (26°C)

Characteristics: This fish has a heavily built body with a steeply rising forehead and arched dorsal surface. Its gray body is crossed by vertical, bright red, blue-edged bands. The dorsal and anal fins are bright red, the pelvic and caudal fins have red edges, and the pectoral fins are yellow with a red base. The eyes are small and high set, and the mouth is filled with bright blue teeth.
Gender: Unknown
Breeding: Unknown
Special care: Provide a roomy aquarium with an efficient filtration system.

PSEUDOCHEILINUS HEXATAENIA
Neon wrasse; six-line wrasse
FAMILY: *Labridae*

Range: Indo-Pacific

2¾ in   2 in   79°F
(7cm)   (5cm)   (26°C)

Characteristics: The body of this fish is mauve, marked on the flanks with alternating horizontal bars of golden yellow and blue.
Gender: Unknown
Breeding: Unknown
Special care: It is important to provide numerous hiding places into which this wrasse can retire if it feels threatened. It is the ideal reef fish. However, it may fight with other fish with similar markings.

PSEUDOCHEILINUS OCTOTAENIA
Eight-lined wrasse
FAMILY: *Labridae*

Range: Indo-Pacific

5 in   5 in   79°F
(13cm)   (13cm)   (26°C)

Characteristics: This wrasse is aggressive, and likely to feed on some types of invertebrate. It is pale orange in color, with red horizontal stripes. The dorsal, caudal, and anal fins are translucent orange, and the paired fins are colorless.

Gender: Unknown
Breeding: Unknown
Special care: This is an excitable species, and a jumper, so special attention must be taken to keep the tank covered and to avoid stressing it unnecessarily.

THALASSOMA BIFASCIATUM
Bluehead wrasse
FAMILY: *Labridae*

Range: Atlantic, Caribbean

| 1 | 36 | 6 in (15cm) | 4 in (10cm) | 79°F (26°C) |

Characteristics: The head of the adult male is bright blue, with a collar of alternating black and white bands immediately behind. The streamlined body is green, with black marks accenting the fins and tail. Juveniles are bright yellow, with a black spot on the anterior portion of the dorsal fin.
Gender: Unknown

Breeding: This species has been successfully propagated in captivity, but commercial specimens are all collected from the sea.
Special care: This fish needs reef-tank water quality, plenty of swimming room, and regular feeding. It will not harm corals, anemones, or other invertebrates that do not form part of its diet.

THALASSOMA KLUNZINGERI
Klunzinger's wrasse
FAMILY: *Labridae*

Range: Red Sea

| 3 | 48 | 6 in (15cm) | 6 in (15cm) | 79°F (26°C) |

Characteristics: The torpedo-shaped body of this fish is pale turquoise, with a white stripe outlined in orange on each flank. The face is patterned with lines in orange and blue. The fins are largely colorless. It likes to sleep among rocks.
Gender: Unknown
Breeding: Unknown
Special care: Wrasses are generally carnivorous and predatory. This species easily reaches its natural size in a roomy tank with typical marine water quality parameters and a regular maintenance schedule. Do not keep it with any smaller, mobile organisms that it might consider as food.

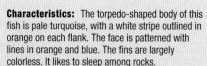

THALASSOMA LUCASANUM
Rainbow wrasse; paddlefin wrasse
FAMILY: *Labridae*

Range: Indian Ocean to Solomon Islands in Pacific; Philippines

| 3 | 36 | 6 in (15cm) | 6 in (15cm) | 79°F (26°C) |

Characteristics: The male has a turquoise head, with a bright yellow collar, pink body, and blue tail. It swims with a rowing motion of the pectoral fins.
Gender: The female is dark brown, with white on the head, yellow on the back, a yellow stripe running from the mouth to the caudal peduncle, and a red stripe on the posterior flank that extends to the lower element of the caudal fin.
Breeding: Unknown
Special care: Provide the usual care and a varied diet with frozen or fresh seafoods, chopped into pieces appropriate for the size of the fish's mouth.

THALASSOMA LUNARE
Moon wrasse; green parrot wrasse; lyretail wrasse
FAMILY: *Labridae*

Range: Indo-Pacific

| 4 | 48 | 10 in (25cm) | 4⅞ in (12.5cm) | 79°F (26°C) | | | | |

Characteristics: Adults have green body coloration, with purple-dotted scales making a reticulated pattern. The smoothly contoured head is marked with purple and green streaks. The long-based dorsal and anal fins are relatively narrow and have red, yellow, and blue lines along their margins. The center of the pectoral fins is purple; the center of the caudal fin is bright yellow, with red and blue top and bottom edges. Juvenile fishes have dark blotches on their dorsal and caudal fins.

Gender: Unknown

Breeding: Unknown

Special care: This is an active species. Choose tankmates that will not be disturbed by its increasing activity. The tank should have ample filtration.

THALASSOMA QUINQUEVITTATUM
Red and green wrasse
FAMILY: *Labridae*

Range: Indo-Pacific: East Africa to Hawaiian, Marquesas, and Tuamotu Islands, north to Ryukyu Islands; throughout Micronesia

| 3 | 36 | 6 in (15cm) | 6 in (15cm) | 79°F (26°C) | | | |

Characteristics: This fish has an olive-green body, fading to white on the belly. A coral-red line runs along the base of the dorsal fin, and another, broken into dashes by a series of white patches, decorates the mid-line of the body.

Gender: Unknown

Breeding: Pelagic spawner

Special care: Do not keep this wrasse with any smaller, mobile organisms that it might consider as food, and select moderately aggressive, larger tankmates. Normal marine water quality and regular maintenance are all that is necessary. Feed a varied diet of meaty seafoods.

Blennies and Gobies

Because these species are often confused with each other—an understandable occurrence given that they both inhabit the same part of the aquarium and have similarly shaped bodies and swimming actions—we have grouped these fish together, while pointing out the differences where they exist. These fish are bottom-dwelling species and, to a certain extent, share a similar cylindrical body shape, with the eyes set up fairly high toward the front of a steeply-rising forehead.

These fish often make efficient use of the substrate by making burrows and generally hiding themselves among the rubble. At times they do become territorial and skirmishes with tankmates can occur. These fish are excellent jumpers for bottom-dwelling species, so keep the aquarium cover firmly in place. However, maintaining blennies and gobies successfully in the aquarium is fairly easy for the aquarist, particularly as feeding presents few problems. They have an appetite for almost anything small enough to swallow.

Despite their diminutive forms, these two families have much to offer. Because these fish are of modest size, they can be accommodated in a medium-size aquarium. They do not need much swimming space as they confine their activities to the substrate level, with only one or two gobies venturing into midwater.

Despite the fact that they do not strictly belong to either the Blenniidae or Gobiidae families, for convenience, fish such as fire gobies (*Microdesmidae*) have been included in this chapter, as they are often spoken of within these groups as far as aquarium-keeping is concerned.

FEATURED IN THIS SECTION

Blennies

In spite of their limited area of activity, blennies soon become the characters of the aquarium, with their constant bustling ways, and the sudden dash for cover as anything passes overhead. Blennies can be recognized quite easily from their bottom-sharing neighbors, the gobies—blennies have a single dorsal fin and separated pelvic fins that, unlike other fish, emerge on the body ahead of the pectoral fins. They often sport curly eyebrow-like growths (called *cirri*) on their heads. Body coloration is cryptic, making for excellent camouflage among their surroundings. Blennies are egg depositors (usually in hiding places such as pipes or caves), and exercise parental care of their young.

ACANTHEMBLEMARIA ASPERA
Roughhead blenny
FAMILY: *Blenniidae*

Range: Indo-Pacific

1½ in
(4cm)

1½ in
(4cm)

79°F
(26°C)

Characteristics: The common name for this fish comes from the collection of spines and densely branched *cirri* on its head. Coloration varies from yellow to tan and various combinations of brown and gray that allow the blenny to blend into its surroundings. It lives on coral reefs, where it seeks out a hole in the coral rock made by a burrowing worm or mollusk; from this secure haven it peers out, darting to snatch food and returning instantly to the hole.

Gender: Unknown

Breeding: Egg depositors

Special care: It is important to provide perfect water conditions and rocks with suitable holes. Also, feed small, live invertebrates, or other plankton substitutes.

ECSENIUS BICOLOR
Two-colored blenny
FAMILY: *Blenniidae*

Range: Indo-Pacific

4 in
(10cm)

2½ in
(6.5cm)

79°F
(26°C)

Characteristics: This fish has a laterally compressed, elongated body with a blunt head and a tapering rear section; in color the body is brown-purple, shading to yellow-orange at the rear. The spawning male becomes red with white bars; after spawning the male is often dark blue with pale blotches on the flanks. The long-based, brown-purple dorsal fin nearly joins up with the spade-shaped caudal fin; the anal fin is long. The caudal and anal fins have body-colored edges.

Gender: The female is light brown and orange-yellow.

Breeding: Egg depositor; displays considerable parental care.

Special care: It needs a modest-sized aquarium, with a rubble-type substrate with some open areas of sand. It is particularly important to provide plenty of retreats. This blenny is best kept in a species aquarium.

MEIACANTHUS SMITHII
Smith's sawtail blenny
FAMILY: *Blenniidae*

Range: Indian and Pacific Oceans

5 | 36

8 in (20cm) | 6 in (15cm) | 79°F (26°C)

Characteristics: The delicate gray body of this fish shades to a paler hue on the ventral surface. A dark stripe runs from the eyes diagonally to the front of the dorsal fin. It has a blunt head, with the eyes set well forward. The long-based dorsal fin is bordered by light blue and white on the outside edge; the anal fin and rounded caudal fin are blue. Lookalike *Plagiotremus sp.* lacks the stripe from the eyes to the dorsal fin, and the dark stripe on the dorsal fin has white edges.

Gender: Unknown
Breeding: Egg depositor; displays parental care.
Special care: This fish needs a modest-sized aquarium, with rubble-type substrate, open, sandy areas, and some hidey holes.

OPHIOBLENNIUS ATLANTICUS
Redlip blenny
FAMILY: *Blenniidae*

Range: Western Atlantic

3 | 24

4¾ in (12cm) | 3 in (7.5cm) | 79°F (26°C)

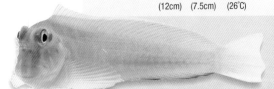

Characteristics: This territorial species has high-set eyes on an almost vertical forehead, giving it a commanding view of its surroundings; it has a red-lipped terminal mouth. The front half of the thickset but tapering body is black-brown, fading to a delicate blue-gray; it varies in color from dark to very pale. The dorsal fin runs the length of the dorsal surface, but the anal fin is only half length. The small caudal fin fans out from the caudal peduncle.

Gender: Unknown
Breeding: Egg depositor; provides parental care for its young.
Special care: It does best in a modest-sized aquarium, with rubble-type substrate, and some open areas of sand. It is important to provide rocky retreats.

Gobies

Gobies and their related species total over 2,000. Species are found in all manner of waters—salt, brackish, and freshwater. Gobies have two separate dorsal fins, and their pelvic fins are fused together to form a suction disc, by means of which the fish can anchor itself in position. There are no lateral line system openings along the flanks, but such a sensory system is present, with the opening pores appearing on the head. It is the arrangement of these pores that may be the main distinguishing feature among the various species in this large family. Vertebrae counts and adult coloration patterns are also often used to sort out the lookalikes. Gobies deposit their eggs under a stone or a similar hiding place, and these are guarded by the male.

AMBLYELEOTRIS GUTTATA
Spotted prawn goby
FAMILY: *Gobiidae*

Range: Philippines, Samoa, northwest Australia, and Great Barrier Reef

3 | 24 | 3½ in (9cm) | 2½ in (6.5cm) | 79°F (26°C)

Characteristics: The body and fins are covered with a sprinkling of bright red spots. Two dark triangular areas spread upward from the ventral surface, one on either side of the pelvic fins. The eyes are set high on the head and are marked with four dark quadrants. The caudal fin is spear-shaped.
Gender: Unknown
Breeding: Egg depositor
Special care: Provide a rubble-type substrate and some open areas of sand; rocky caves and pieces of plastic pipe will supply retreats.

GOBIOSOMA MULTIFASCIATUM
Green-banded goby
FAMILY: *Gobiidae*

Range: Western Atlantic

| 1½ in (4cm) | 1¼ in (3cm) | 79°F (26°C) |

Characteristics: Numerous light green bands encircle the dark green body. Two red stripes run from the snout, each crossing an eye above the pectoral fins. The underside of the head is white. All the fish's fins are pale green. Lookalike species *Ginsbergellus novemlineatus* has a bluish-black body marked with blue rings.

Gender: Unknown

Breeding: Egg depositor

Special care: Provide a modest-sized aquarium with a rubble-type substrate and some open areas of sand. Rocks and caves will provide retreats.

GOBIOSOMA OCEANOPS
Neon goby; cleaner goby
FAMILY: *Gobiidae*

Range: Western Atlantic

| 1½ in (4cm) | 1¼ in (3cm) | 79°F (26°C) |

Characteristics: The dark body is trimmed with two parallel electric blue lines running along the dorsal surface from snout to caudal fin. It is the position and variance in pattern in these lines (particularly over the head) that helps distinguish this fish from other species of *Gobiosoma*.

Gender: At breeding time the male's genital papilla is pointed, and the female's blunter.

Breeding: This goby is an egg depositor. It is frequently bred in aquariums.

Special care: This fish needs a modest-sized aquarium with plenty of rubble. It offers some degree of "cleaning service" to other fish. Although peaceful, the neon goby may be more interesting in an aquarium of its own.

VALENCIENNEA STRIGATA
Blue-streak goby; blue cheek goby
FAMILY: *Gobiidae*

Range: Indo-Pacific

5	24	7 in (18cm)	3 in (7.5cm)	79°F (26°C)

Characteristics: The basic body color of this species is steely blue. The most striking feature, however, is the bright yellow area of the snout, lower face, and gill cover that is topped by an electric blue line. There is a faint covering of red lines on the body and fins.
Gender: Unknown

Breeding: Its eggs are laid freshwater cichlid-fashion; they are guarded by the male.
Special care: Provide a modest-sized aquarium with a rubble-type substrate, and some open areas of sand; rocks, and caves will supply retreats.

NEMATELEOTRIS DECORA
Purple firefish
FAMILY: *Microdesmidae*

Range: Central Indo-Pacific

3	36	3½ in (9cm)	2⅜ in (6cm)	79°F (26°C)

Characteristics: The front half of the body is silvery-cream, with a violet area to the top of the head and along the dorsal surface; the rear half of the body is brownish-gray. The first few rays of the extended first dorsal fin are black, violet, and red just like the long-based second dorsal fin, the anal fin, and the lyre-patterned caudal fin. The small, unfused pelvic fins are patterned in a similar way.

Gender: Unknown
Breeding: Unknown
Special care: This fish does best in a modest-sized aquarium with rubble-type substrate. Several can be kept together if enough retreats are provided. A shoal makes a spectacular display.

NEMATELEOTRIS MAGNIFICA
Firefish; magnificent hover goby
FAMILY: *Microdesmidae*

Range: Indo-Pacific

2¾ in   2 in   79°F
(7cm)   (5cm)   (26°C)

Characteristics: The front half of the body is silvery-cream with a yellow area to the top of the head and along the dorsal surface; the rear half is brownish-gray shading to red, then to very dark crimson. The small head has large bluish eyes set well forward. The first few extended rays of the first dorsal fin are yellow with a red front edge; the long-based second dorsal and anal fins have a yellow base with a dark red outer margin marked with a dark blue or brown line. The pelvic fins are elongated and whitish yellow.

Gender: Unknown

Breeding: Unknown

Special care: See *N. decora* for care information. Both of these species are equally interesting aquarium subjects.

PTERELEOTRIS ZEBRA
Chinese zebra goby
FAMILY: *Microdesmidae*

Range: Indo-Pacific

4 in   4 in   79°F
(10cm)   (10cm)   (26°C)

Characteristics: This very elongated fish has a greenish body and approximately 20 vertical salmon-pink bars. The lower half of the eye has a broad, blue-edged, dark red to purple area. The pectoral fin base is adorned with an orange-red bar broadly bordered with bright blue. The posterior dorsal fin has a longitudinal row of blue spots.

Gender: Unknown

Breeding: Unknown

Special care: A schooling fish that should be kept in a group. It is a great escapologist, so keep the aquarium well covered.

Boxfish, Cowfish, and Pufferfish

Few other fish have more sophisticated means of defense than those in this group, for they use almost every trick in the book to stay safe from harm. Bony plates (effectively an outside skeleton), cryptic camouflage, sharp spines, means of at least doubling their size, and the ability to exude toxins are all put to good use. Members of this group are found in most tropical areas of the Atlantic, Indian, and Pacific Oceans.

Boxfish are the "armored tanks" of the fish world, with fins sited at almost all the corners of their oblong bodies. Cowfish have "horns" on the head. Coloration is sometimes brilliant and bizarre, causing some confusion over species identification—this was eventually resolved when it was discovered that the color patterning was different between the sexes of the same species. Many attractive juveniles grow up to be less appealing and dull-colored adults. Handle these fish with extreme care, as any kind of stress will trigger the release of a toxin that kills everything, including the originator.

Pufferfish use inflation tactics to thwart predators; inflating their bodies not only makes the attacker question the practicability of swallowing the pufferfish, but also the presence of erectile spines over the body is another most effective deterrent. Should these deterrents not prove sufficient, the puffer's toxic flesh may kill the predator. Pufferfish have sharp teeth that are simply two bony plates on each jaw; these can sever equipment cables and crush heaters just as effortlessly as shelled invertebrates.

Because of their toxin-producing reaction in the face of possible adversity, these fish should not be kept in a "busy" aquarium of active fish that might stress them, and certainly not in a reef tank or with invertebrates.

FEATURED IN THIS SECTION

CHILOMYCTERUS SCHOEPFI
Spiny boxfish; striped burrfish
FAMILY: *Diodontidae*

Range: Caribbean

12 in (30cm) 6 in (15cm) 79°F (26°C)

Characteristics: The body is yellow, with undulating dark lines and yellow-ringed dark spots; the underside is white. Its body is covered in short spines that are held erect. The teeth are fused together to form two large teeth. It inflates when threatened.
Gender: Unknown
Breeding: Unknown
Special care: This fish needs excellent water quality, maintained by frequent water changes and efficient filtration. Provide plenty of retreats. It should not be kept with small fishes, particularly as males tend to quarrel among themselves.

DIODON HOLOCANTHUS
Long-spined porcupinefish
FAMILY: *Diodontidae*

Range: All warm seas

20 in (50cm) 6 in (15cm) 79°F (26°C)

Characteristics: This fish has a golden brown body, with a paler underside; it has several widely spaced, dark dots all over the body. It has large pectoral fins and a rounded caudal fin. The dorsal and anal fins are set well back and the pelvic fins are absent. It has a terminally placed mouth with fused teeth.
Gender: Unknown
Breeding: Unknown
Special care: This fish should not be kept in an aquarium with invertebrates. Excellent water quality should be maintained.

LACTORIA CORNUTA
Long-horned cowfish
FAMILY: *Ostraciidae*

Range: Indo-Pacific

5 | 36 | 20 in (50cm) | 3 in (7.5cm) | 79°F (26°C)

Characteristics: This fish has a tapering, box-shaped body covered by a series of bony plates. The caudal peduncle emerges from the back of the "box." It has a blue, dotted yellow body. There are two horn-like growths at the top corners of the head and at the bottom rear corners; also a down-turned mouth. The dorsal fin is set well back, and the small anal fin between the two rear "horns." The caudal fin is also small, and there are no pelvic fins.

Gender: Unknown
Breeding: Unknown
Special care: It is advisable to transport this fish separately from others as it releases poison into the water when it is frightened. It needs excellent water quality, frequent water changes, and efficient filtration.

OSTRACION MELEAGRIS
Blue-spotted boxfish
FAMILY: *Ostraciidae*

Range: Indo-Pacific

7 | 36 | 8 in (20cm) | 4⅞ in (12.5cm) | 79°F (26°C)

Coloration differs between the male (above) and female (below) blue-spotted boxfish.

Characteristics: This fish's body is elongated and box-shaped. The males have a black dorsal surface covered with white spots, separated from the lower part of the body by a thin yellow line. The lower flanks are violet with yellow dots. The dorsal and anal fins are yellowish, and the caudal fin is violet with black spots and a yellow rear edge. The male's eyes are dark, surrounded by yellow.
Gender: The females are black all over with a covering of white dots; the eyes are dark with a white-spotted surround.
Breeding: Unknown
Special Care: Provide a peaceful aquarium with non-boisterous tankmates. Ensure that water quality is maintained.

AROTHRON NIGROPUNCTATUS
Black-spotted puffer; dog-face puffer
FAMILY: *Tetraodontidae*

Range: Indo-Pacific

13 in (33cm) 10 in (25cm) 79°F (26°C)

Characteristics: The coloration of this fish is variable; the overall pigmentation is usually blue-gray or brownish, while in some individuals the entire body is black, gold, or orange. There are varying numbers of black and yellow spots. The face is commonly darker, with white below the eyes and on the snout, and the tip of the snout is black.

Gender: Unknown

Breeding: Unknown

Special care: This species may be shy, and might refuse to eat at first. It is a community dweller, and more than one specimen can be housed in the same tank, unlike some members of the genus.

CANTHIGASTER AMBOINENSIS
Ambon Toby
FAMILY: *Tetraodontidae*

Range: Indo-Pacific

6 in (15cm) 6 in (15cm) 79°F (26°C)

Characteristics: This fish is gray to brownish in color, overlaid with bluish-white dots on the flank and caudal peduncle, and darker dots and scrawls on the face and gill covers. The paired fins are colorless. Dorsal, caudal, and anal fins are dark, often trimmed in a pale blue.

Gender: Unknown

Breeding: Unknown

Special care: Provide a large tank with ample filtration. Reef conditions suit most puffer species. Chop foods into suitable-size pieces for the puffer's tiny mouth. Sessile invertebrates are ignored. Avoid keeping puffers with aggressive species.

CANTHIGASTER CORONATA
Crowned Toby; three-barred Toby
FAMILY: *Tetraodontidae*

Range: Indo-Pacific

5 in (13cm) 5 in (13cm) 79°F (26°C)

Characteristics: The crowned Toby is white with three dark brown saddles, each outlined in yellow-orange dots. Yellow and blue lines radiate from each eye, above which is the dark brown "crown." There are blue-green and yellow spots on the tail and caudal peduncle, and a yellow stripe on the cheek.

Gender: Unknown

Breeding: Unknown

Special care: Provide food that is sufficiently small for the fish's mouth. Avoid keeping it with aggressive species, such as triggers or lionfish. The brilliant illumination required for living corals shows off its coloration to perfection.

CANTHIGASTER EPILAMPRA
Yellow-tailed Toby
FAMILY: *Tetraodontidae*

Range: Indo-Pacific

3 | 24

4 in (10cm) | 4 in (10cm) | 79°F (26°C)

Characteristics: This is a sharp-nosed puffer mottled in gray, black, and white, with a distinctive bright yellow caudal fin. The paired fins are colorless, while the dorsal and anal fins sometimes continue the coloration of the body.
Gender: Unknown
Breeding: Unknown

Special care: Provide a roomy tank, and feed a varied diet of meaty seafood, chopped into small pieces. Dim lighting is appreciated, not the brilliant illumination of a reef tank. Surgeonfish or larger angelfish make good tankmates. Likely predators should be avoided.

CANTHIGASTER MARGARITATUS
Sharp-nosed puffer; ocellated pufferfish; peacock-eyed pufferfish; diamond-flecked pufferfish
FAMILY: *Tetraodontidae*

Range: Indo-Pacific

3 | 24

4 in (10cm) | 2 in (8cm) | 79°F (26°C)

Characteristics: The elongated body of this puffer is relatively deep in the mid-section; it is golden brown in color with a paler ventral surface. The upper surface is covered with dark-edged, bluish-white lines. The lower flanks are covered with dark-edged white spots that extend into the caudal fin. There is a large, white-edged dark spot situated at the base of the set-back dorsal fin. The forehead has a pronounced bulge. The mouth is small and terminally situated. The pelvic fins are absent. This puffer only partially inflates when stressed or threatened.
Gender: Unknown
Breeding: Unknown
Special care: This fish needs excellent water quality maintained by frequent water changes and efficient filtration. It can be territorial, but is generally peaceful.

CANTHIGASTER VALENTINI
Black-saddled puffer
FAMILY: *Tetraodontidae*

Range: Indo-Pacific

3 | 30

3.2 in (8cm) | 1.2 in (3cm) | 79°F (26°C)

Characteristics: This puffer has a white body with two black, wedged-shaped markings extending down from the dorsal surface. A saddle marking crosses the eyes, and another covers the top of the caudal peduncle; pale areas of the body are covered with yellow-brown spots. It has a blue-lined, bulged forehead with gold-rimmed eyes, and a small, terminally situated mouth. All its fins are yellowish in color. The pelvic fins are absent.
Gender: Unknown
Breeding: Unknown
Special care: This fish is generally peaceful, though it can be territorial. Snails (from a freshwater aquarium) are appreciated as food—its strong jaws soon crack open the shells. It needs excellent water quality maintained by frequent water changes and efficient filtration.

Eels

An eel of generous (if not terrifying) proportions holds a certain morbid fascination. At once, they can be both very attractive and intimidating, but many are not practical for the average-size home aquarium. Found in all tropical seas, there are around 200 species belonging to the family Muraenidae, with sizes ranging from a few inches to around 10 ft (3m), although most recognized aquarium specimens are a manageable 2–3 ft (61–91cm).

As a cursory acquaintance with eels will show, most of their time is spent in rocky retreats with just their head protruding. They usually have a regularly gaping mouth that betrays their presence. A spacious but rockily-landscaped aquarium is therefore mandatory, with plentiful filtration and well-oxygenated water—the gaping mouth is a respiratory action, not necessarily an invitation for food.

Moray eels are carnivores and a distinction between their preferred foods can be gauged by their teeth: sharp, needle-like teeth are handy for tearing off pieces of fish, while larger teeth are more likely to be used for crushing invertebrates. Because of their appetites, regular partial water changes are necessary.

The cryptic patterning on many species makes them hard to spot in the constantly changing light patterns on the coral reef. Most have poor eyesight but possess an exceptional sense of smell, which is extremely helpful to them, as many morays are more active at night than during the day. Similarly to other marine fishes, some moray eels are not suited to aquarium care, either because of their eventual adult size, death through self-imposed starvation, or simply because they climb out of the aquarium. Handling moray eels is difficult and not without danger. A bite from their often bacteria-infected teeth can bring illness, so always wear strong gloves.

Snake eels (of the Opichthidae family), so closely resemble a reptile that they have been mistaken for sea snakes.

FEATURED IN THIS SECTION

ECHIDNA CATENATA
Chain moray
FAMILY: *Muraenidae*

Range: Western Atlantic waters from Florida to Brazil, including Ascension Islands

30 in (78cm)	23⅝ in (60cm)	26°F (79°C)

Characteristics: Eels have an elongated, snake-like body, lacking pectoral and pelvic fins. The dorsal, caudal, and anal fins are fused to form a continuous ribbon around the posterior of the body. These are nocturnal predators. The dark brown body is patterned in scrawls of pale cream to bright yellow that bear a slight resemblance to chains.

Gender: Unknown
Breeding: Unknown
Special care: Eels need good water conditions and plenty of hiding places. Do not keep an eel with mobile creatures that are small enough for it to swallow.

ECHIDNA POLYZONA
Girdled moray
FAMILY: *Muraenidae*

Range: Red Sea, Indian, and Pacific Oceans

30 in (78cm)	23⅝ in (60cm)	79°F (26°C)

Characteristics: The body shape of this eel is typical of the family, and it has a blunt snout with a relatively small head. The body is patterned with alternate bands of black and white. The dorsal and anal fins both extend around the fish to include the caudal fin. The dorsal fin runs almost the length of the body, and the anal fin for about one-third. This fish is peaceful unless disturbed.

Gender: Unknown
Breeding: It is an egg scatterer.
Special care: This fish likes pots or pipes in which to hide. It is only suitable for a community of very large fishes. It needs a tight-fitting cover to its tank.

GYMNOTHORAX MILIARIS
Goldentail moray
FAMILY: *Muraenidae*

Range: Caribbean islands, less so in Florida

| | | 23⅝ in (60cm) | 17¾ in (45cm) | 79°F (26°C) | |

Characteristics: Yellow spots varying in size cover the dark brown body of this eel. The tip of the tail is bright golden yellow, and there is a golden ring encircling the eyes. This moray has little fear of humans, and may bite if provoked.
Gender: Unknown
Breeding: Unknown
Special care: Provide good water conditions and plenty of rocks with hiding places. Never trust a large moray with any mobile creature small enough for it to swallow.

MYRICHTHYS OCELLATUS
Gold-spotted snake eel
FAMILY: *Ophichthyidae*

Range: Indo-Pacific

45¼ in (115cm) 35⅜ in (90cm) 79°F (26°C)

Characteristics: This fish lacks paired fins, and the dorsal, anal, and caudal fins combine to form a continuous band around the elongated body. The downward-pointing snout often extends over the mouth. It is tan-colored, sometimes yellowish green, with bright golden-yellow spots surrounded by a diffuse area of dark pigment.
Gender: Unknown
Breeding: Unknown
Special care: Provide good marine-tank water conditions and plenty of rocks with hiding places. Keep the tank tightly covered.

Groupers and Basslets

While the larger members of the Serranidae and Grammidae families might be regarded as "status symbols" for the larger aquarium, there are modest-sized species that are quite charming and suitable for most home aquariums.

Groupers are wide-ranging in their distribution, as they can be found worldwide in all tropical seas. While they give the appearance of the "bully on the block," they are more likely to be found resting undercover and prowling around the bottom of coral stands. Therefore, the aquarium should be suitably furnished to accommodate this particular habit.

It is not unexpected that such fish don't get on well together within the close confines of the aquarium and it is usual to keep a single specimen in each aquarium. However, there are exceptions, and while the smaller basslets may not be taxonomically tied to the same family tree, they could be regarded as miniature, or scaled down, counterparts of their larger relative.

These brilliantly colored fish include the rather delicate Anthias, the almost impossibly-colored dottybacks (*Pseudochromis*), and grammas. Many are very territorial and benefit from being kept in a one-species collection in a separate aquarium. A further bonus of these particular fish is that many advances have been made in captive breeding.

Members of both of these families of fish require the very best of conditions; the larger, hearty-eating species need good filtration while the smaller fish are suitable for reef systems.

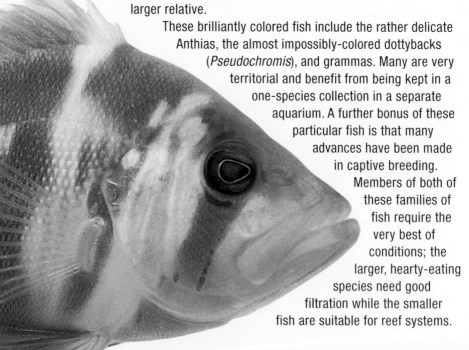

FEATURED IN THIS SECTION

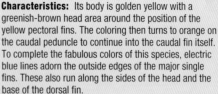

GRAMMA LORETO
Royal gramma
FAMILY: *Grammidae*

Range: Western Atlantic

3.2 in | 2 in | 79°F
(8cm) | (5cm) | (26°C)

Characteristics: A bi-colored fish, the front half brilliant cerise, the rear half an equally brilliant yellow. A dark bar, bordered below by gold, slants down through the eyes to the mouth. A dark spot appears in the front rays of the long-based dorsal fin.
Gender: The male is larger.
Breeding: Paternal mouth brooder

Special care: The aquarium or reef tank should be furnished with many rocky retreats. This fish is generally peaceful, but it may guard its chosen bolt-hole against other fish. It is aggressive against its own kind.

GRAMMA MELACARA
Black-cap gramma
FAMILY: *Grammidae*

Range: Caribbean

4 in | 3 in | 79°F
(10cm) | (7.5cm) | (26°C)

Characteristics: The striking coloration comprises a beautiful violet-purple that covers the whole body and is topped off by a black "cap" that runs through the eyes, over the head, and into the top edge of the dorsal fin.
Gender: Unknown
Breeding: This fish is a nest builder, and the male is responsible for guarding the eggs.
Special care: It needs lots of caves and rocky retreats in which to make a home. It is an excellent subject for reef tanks, where invertebrates will not be bothered by it. This fish is generally peaceful, but it may be a little territorial to members of its own kind.

PSEUDOCHROMIS ALDEBARENSIS
Neon dottyback; Persian dottyback
FAMILY: *Pseudochromidae*

Range: Persian Gulf

2¾ in | 2 in | 79°F
(7cm) | (5cm) | (26°C)

Characteristics: Its body is golden yellow with a greenish-brown head area around the position of the yellow pectoral fins. The coloring then turns to orange on the caudal peduncle to continue into the caudal fin itself. To complete the fabulous colors of this species, electric blue lines adorn the outside edges of the major single fins. These also run along the sides of the head and the base of the dorsal fin.
Gender: The male is larger.
Breeding: The male guards a ball of fertilized eggs.
Special care: The aquarium (or reef tank) should be furnished with plenty of hiding places for this cave-loving species.

CHROMILEPTIS ALTIVELIS
Polka-dot grouper; humped rock-cod; barramundi cod; kerapu sonoh; pantherfish
FAMILY: *Serranidae*

Range: Indian Ocean around East Indies, Philippines, and Queensland coast

| 1 | 96 | 20 in (50cm) | 12 in (30cm) | 79°F (26°C) | | | | | | |

Characteristics: The body is white, and covered with numerous black spots; these become even more numerous, but reduce in individual size, with increasing age. All the fins are white, and are marked with dark spots. The long-based dorsal fin has an obvious "step" halfway along at the beginning of the softer-rayed rear section. The anal fin is rounded, the caudal fin paddle-shaped, and the pectoral fins are large.

Gender: Unknown

Breeding: Egg scatterer

Special care: Provide plenty of hiding places and as much space as you can give it.

EPINEPHALUS SP.
Grouper
FAMILY: *Serranidae*

Range: Tropical oceans

| 2 | 120 | 3⅜ ft (1m) | 23⅝ in (60cm) | 79°F (26°C) | | | |

Characteristics: Because groupers can rapidly and dramatically change both their coloration and color pattern, they can be enormously confusing and difficult for the aquarist to identify. Groupers are intelligent and learn to recognize the aquarist.

Gender: The males are usually larger.

Breeding: These fish usually start life as females and become males in later life. Some species are hermaphrodite.

Special care: Provide good water conditions and a suitable lair among rocks. Feed with live and frozen foods of such size as is determined by the size of the specimen. Groupers usually feed on any other fish or mobile invertebrate that is small enough to swallow.

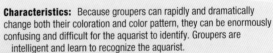

EPINEPHALUS MORIO
Red grouper
FAMILY: *Serranidae*

Range: Atlantic region, from Massachusetts to Brazil

| 1 | 120 | 36¼ in (92cm) | 23⅗ in (60cm) | 79°F (26°C) | | |

Characteristics: The body is a uniform golden to tan color, with a scattering of white spots. The fins are usually dark gray. Like all groupers, its coloration is variable, and can be altered by the fish at will. It lies in ambush, swallowing whole small fishes and similar mobile prey.

Gender: Unknown
Breeding: Unknown
Special care: Given its rather drab coloration, prodigious appetite, and retiring habits, this is not a suitable fish for any but the largest marine tank.

HYPOPLECTRUS INDIGO
Indigo hamlet
FAMILY: *Serranidae*

Range: Caribbean

| 3 | 36 | 4 in (10cm) | 3¼ in (8cm) | 36 in (90cm) | |

Characteristics: This beautiful sea bass is blue, with a series of vertical white bars that begin behind the eyes. The dorsal, caudal, and anal fins are light blue, the pelvic fins are dark blue, and the pectoral fins are white or colorless.
Gender: Unknown
Breeding: Unknown
Special care: Provide perfect water conditions and plenty of rocks. Hamlets usually accept a wide range of aquarium foods. Corals and other reef invertebrates, not sought by the fish for food, are usually left alone.

EPINEPHALUS UNDULATOSTRIATUS
Maori grouper
FAMILY: *Serranidae*

Range: Great Barrier Reef and New South Wales areas of Australia

| 4 | 96 | 24 in (61cm) | 12 in (30cm) | 79°F (26°C) | |

Characteristics: The reddish-brown markings that cover the entire body and the fins often line up to give an undulating, striated patterning: hence the accurate specific name. The fins have yellow outer margins.
Gender: Unknown
Breeding: Unknown
Special care: This large grouper is obviously more suited to public aquariums where it can roam the spacious tanks to its heart's content; however, it can be kept in a home aquarium as long as it is given the space and proper care that it requires.

RYPTICUS MACULATUS
Whitespotted soapfish
FAMILY: *Serranidae*

Range: Rhode Island to Palm Beach

| 3 | 48 | 8 in (20cm) | 6 in (15cm) | 79°F (26°C) | | | |

Characteristics: The common name comes from its ability to secrete, when threatened, a toxic substance resembling soapsuds. In color the body is a medium brown, often with a pale area on the snout, and pale stripes on the cheeks. White spots, often outlined in black, appear on the body. The fins are lighter brown in color.
Gender: Unknown
Breeding: Unknown

Special care: Provide plenty of rocks and caves to hide in. Feed small frozen fish, live shrimp, or other seafoods. Be aware that it may also eat any mobile tankmate small enough to swallow. Expect it to spend most of its time in hiding.

VARIOLA LOUTI
Lyretail grouper; coronation grouper
FAMILY: *Serranidae*

Range: Indo-Pacific

| 1 | 96 | 35 in (89cm) | 29½ in (75cm) | 79°F (26°C) | | | |

Characteristics: The body is pale yellow on the belly, dark brown to black along the mid-line, and orange on top. Blue polka dots overlay most of the upper three-quarters of the body. The tail fin and dorsal fin carry some blue and reddish pigments, while the remaining fins are colorless.
Gender: As with most groupers, younger individuals are female, and mature ones are male.

Breeding: Unknown
Special care: This colorful grouper selects a suitable hiding place among rocks, where it lies in ambush for small fish or crustaceans. It is hardy and long-lived, but provide plenty of filtration to cope with its prodigious appetite.

Other Marine Species

Not all marine fish fit conveniently into the major groups previously described. This has nothing to do with their popularity (or otherwise), but simply that some families do not contain so many individual genera or species. Compared to the previous genera, which, by their very orderliness, may appear quite conventional, each species in this section brings its own particular attraction.

The disparity of body shapes, color patterns, exaggerated finnage, and even living styles all contribute something extra to the marine fishkeeper's enjoyment. From highly colored sedentary species to exotically finned drifters, you will surely find your own particular favorite here. One problem area for those interested in keeping marine fish is breeding, because so little is known for certain of their reproductive behavior, either in captivity or in the wild. Details have been included where possible.

FEATURED IN THIS SECTION

APOGON MACULATUS
Flamefish
FAMILY: *Apogonidae*

Range: Western Atlantic

4¼ in   3¼ in   79°F
(11cm)   (8cm)   (26°C)

Characteristics: The body is bright scarlet, with a single dark spot at the base of the second dorsal fin. The eyes are black, and have two white horizontal lines running through them. This fish is nocturnal, only coming out into open water at night to feed on small invertebrates and fish fry.
Gender: Unknown
Breeding: Unknown

Special care: Remember to feed this fish after the tank lights go out. Good water conditions, non-aggressive tankmates, and a diet of meaty seafoods of appropriate size suit it best. Do not trust it with small fish or shrimps that it can swallow. Corals, however, are ignored.

PTERAPOGON KAUDERNI
Banggai cardinalfish; Borneo or highfin cardinal
FAMILY: *Apogonidae*

Range: Pacific, but very limited range

4⅞ in   2½ in   79°F
(12.5cm)   (6.5cm)   (26°C)

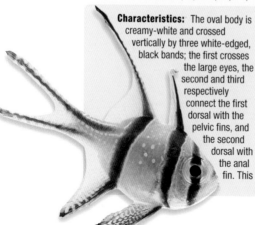

Characteristics: The oval body is creamy-white and crossed vertically by three white-edged, black bands; the first crosses the large eyes, the second and third respectively connect the first dorsal with the pelvic fins, and the second dorsal with the anal fin. This perky species swims with its dorsal fins permanently erect.
Gender: The males are larger.
Breeding: This is a paternal mouth brooder, with the young growing large enough to feed on brine shrimp while in the parent's mouth.
Special care: Aquarists should obtain only hatchery-produced specimens; these are becoming more widely available.

SPHAERAMIA NEMATOPTERA
Pajama cardinalfish
FAMILY: *Apogonidae*

Range: Indo-Pacific

4 | 36 | 3¼ in (8cm) | 2½ in (6.5cm) | 79°F (26°C)

Characteristics: This fish has a stocky body with a relatively long caudal peduncle. Its ground color is purplish-gray; behind a dividing line between the two separate dorsal fins, the body is covered with equally spaced, large red-brown spots. From beneath the first dorsal fin a dark band runs vertically down to the pelvic fins; ahead of this band the large, yellowish head is unpatterned, but the large, red eyes have a dark center. The caudal fin has rounded lobes.

Gender: The males are larger.

Breeding: This is a paternal mouth-brooder.

Special care: This shy species hides during the day, emerging at dusk to feed.

PTEROSYNCHIROPUS SPLENDIDUS
Mandarin fish
FAMILY: *Callionymidae*

Range: Pacific

6 | 36 | 2½ in (6cm) | 2 in (5cm) | 79°F (26°C)

Characteristics: The body color is green, with a pattern of wide, scribbled, dark-edged, blue-colored lines, bars, and dots that extend into the fins. The eyes are gold, and there are some black and light blue lines marking the head and face. The area immediately beneath the eyes is pale and separated from the rest of the body coloration by a horizontal dark line that runs back to the gill cover, which is covered with prominent gold spots.

Gender: In some fishes the first dorsal fin has an elongated first spine; this is probably an indication of the male.

Breeding: Unknown

Special care: This species feeds exclusively on small live foods, and should only be housed in a mature reef tank where these foods have become established. It needs plenty of hiding places.

CENTRISCUS SP.
Shrimpfish
FAMILY: *Centriscidae*

Range: Worldwide

8 | 36 | 6 in (15cm) | 4 in (10cm) | 79°F (26°C)

Characteristics: The body of this fish is elongated, and covered with bony plates, rather than scales. The soft dorsal, caudal, and anal fins are located underneath, and anterior to the spinous dorsal fin. Most specimens are pale, with a single, dark, horizontal stripe. All shrimpfish swim in a head-down position, usually among the spines of a sea urchin or the branches of an acroporid coral.

Gender: Unknown

Breeding: Unknown

Special care: Provide perfect water conditions and plenty of rocks, together with the appropriate host (urchin or coral) with which the fish associates. Feed small, live invertebrates or a similar plankton substitute.

AMBLYCIRRHITES PINOS
Redspotted hawkfish
FAMILY: *Cirrhitidae*

Range: Western Atlantic

2   36

4 in   3¼ in   79°F
(10cm)   (8cm)   (26°C)

Characteristics: This species is pale, with dark vertical bars alternately narrow and wide along the body, ending at the caudal peduncle. The entire body is overlaid with tiny red dots. The fins are white to colorless, and the dorsal fin spines are tipped with "tassels." These fish perch on a rock, and dart out to snatch the small invertebrates that form the basis of their diet.

Gender: Unknown
Breeding: Unknown
Special care: Provide plenty of rocks with algae and invertebrates. Corals and other reef invertebrates are left alone; only small shrimps or worms are at risk.

CIRRHITES FASCIATUS
Red-barred hawkfish
FAMILY: *Cirrhitidae*

Range: Indo-Pacific

3   36

4 in   4 in   79°F
(10cm)   (10cm)   (26°C)

Characteristics: The body is white, with a pattern of red lines on the face. Beginning at the gill cover, five vertical red bars mark the body, ending on the caudal peduncle. The paired fins are pale to colorless, with red rays on the dorsal fin, and the "fringe" at the tips of the first dorsal spines red. There is some red on the pectorals and the caudal fin as well.
Gender: Unknown
Breeding: Unknown
Special care: While these fish pose no threat to corals or other sessile invertebrates, they cannot be trusted with small shrimps or fish small enough for them to eat.

NEOCIRRHITES ARMATUS
Flame hawkfish
FAMILY: *Cirrhitidae*

Range: Indo-Pacific

4   36

3½ in   2½ in   79°F
(9cm)   (6.5cm)   (26°C)

Characteristics: The highly arched body of this fish is bright scarlet, with only a dark margin appearing along the bottom of the long-based dorsal fin. The dark eyes are set high up on the steeply sloping forehead. All the fins are scarlet in color.
Gender: Unknown
Breeding: It is thought that this fish is an egg scatterer, spawning after dusk.
Special care: Although it has a generally peaceful demeanor, the inclusion of other hawkfish species in the same aquarium may lead to quarrels, and small fish and small invertebrates may be at risk.

OXYCIRRHITES TYPUS
Long-nosed hawkfish
FAMILY: *Cirrhitidae*

Range: Indo-Pacific

| | | 4⅞ in (12.5cm) | 4 in (10cm) | 79ºF (26ºC) | |

Characteristics: This fish's elongated body is marked with a bright red square pattern over a white background. It has the most amazingly long snout. The dorsal fin is spiky, and usually held erect. All its fins are whitish, speckled with red.
Gender: This fish will form pairs, which stay together.
Breeding: This is an egg depositor.

Special care: Not an accomplished swimmer, this species sits on a convenient piece of coral or rock on the seabed waiting for food to pass by. Although generally peaceful, it is not wise to keep this hawkfish with small fish.

CHAETODIPTERUS FABER
Atlantic spadefish
FAMILY: *Ephippidae*

Range: Massachusetts to Brazil, and Caribbean

| | | 3¼ ft (1m) | 27½ in (70cm) | 79ºF (26ºC) | |

Characteristics: The silvery body is marked by a series of five or six vertical bars, one of which extends to the leading edges of the dorsal and anal fins. The shape of its body is almost like an elongated disc. It is considered a desirable sport fish.
Gender: Unknown
Breeding: Unknown
Special care: Provide good water conditions and a large tank. The fish hunts its food in open water, and has a voracious appetite. Several specimens can be kept together, as it is usually found in small aggregations. Small fish, live shrimps, and various other foods should be offered.

ANISOTREMUS VIRGINICUS
Porkfish
FAMILY: *Haemulidae*

Range: Caribbean

| | | 14 in (36cm) | 8 in (20cm) | 79ºF (26ºC) | |

Characteristics: The body is white, with lemon yellow coloring on the head and back. The dorsal fin is yellow, as are the pelvics. There is a single black dot on the caudal peduncle, and a pair of horizontal black lines runs from the eyes to the tail. In adults, the fins are all yellow, a black bar runs vertically through the eyes, and another bar marks the rear margin of the gill cover.
Gender: Unknown
Breeding: Unknown
Special care: This fish is sometimes found in large schools over reefs. Small fish, shrimps, and worms are likely to be eaten, but corals will be ignored.

HOLOCENTRUS CORUSCUS
Reef squirrelfish
FAMILY: *Holocentridae*

Range: Florida, Caribbean

5 in	4 in	79°F
(13cm)	(10cm)	(26°C)

Characteristics: The body is red, with white lines running lengthwise from the gill cover to the caudal peduncle. There is a black blotch on the first three or four dorsal fin spines, and each spine of the otherwise bright red dorsal fin is tipped in pure white. The paired fins are colorless. The large eyes indicate that the fish is a nocturnal predator.

Gender: Unknown
Breeding: Unknown
Special care: Provide a suitable cave for the fish to spend the day. It will eat all foods including tankmates small enough to fit in its mouth.

HOLOCENTRUS RUFUS
Longspine squirrelfish
FAMILY: *Holocentridae*

Range: Western Atlantic

10 in	6 in	79°F
(25cm)	(15cm)	(26°C)

Characteristics: This fish's body is red with vague white lines running lengthwise from the gill cover to the caudal peduncle. This species can be recognized by the particularly elongated dorsal fin spines, each tipped with a pure white triangle. The pectoral fins are edged in white as well. Its large eyes help in capturing prey at night.
Gender: Unknown
Breeding: Unknown
Special care: Provide typical marine water conditions and a suitable place for the fish to spend the day.

MYRIPRISTIS BARBONICUS
Squirrelfish
FAMILY: *Holocentridae*

Range: Indian and Pacific Oceans

| 4 | 72 | 12 in (30cm) | 4 in (10cm) | 79°F (26°C) | | | |

Characteristics: The body is pale pink with red markings along the dorsal and ventral surfaces. The scales are dark-edged. A dark vertical area appears behind the rear edge of the gill cover. There are two dorsal fins, and the anal fin is small and set well back on the body. The pelvic fins are red and white, and the caudal fin is pinkish with red markings at the top and bottom edges.

Gender: Unknown
Breeding: Unknown
Special care: The tank should have plenty of retreats and coral outcrops. This fish is active at night and will eat small fish and crustaceans.

OGOCEPHALUS NASUTUS
Shortnose batfish
FAMILY: *Ogocephalidae*

Range: Gulf of Mexico to Brazil

| 5 | 5 | 12 in (30cm) | 8 in (20cm) | 79°F (26°C) | |

Characteristics: Sometimes called the "walking" batfish because of the stout, paired fins that elevate the fish above the bottom, these fish are for the hobbyist with a taste for the unusual. Relying on camouflage coloration, which is usually a blotched mixture of gray and chalk, it lies in wait, ready to lunge forward when a small fish or shrimp approaches, swallowing its prey whole.
Gender: Unknown
Breeding: Unknown
Special care: An ambush predator that may learn to accept non-living foods, if offered by a patient aquarist.

OPISTHOGNATHUS AURIFRONS
Yellow-faced jawfish
FAMILY: *Opisthognathidae*

Range: Western tropical Atlantic

| 4 | 36 | 4 in (10cm) | 3 in (7.5cm) | 79°F (26°C) | | |

Characteristics: This fish has a very elongated body with a prominent, broad head; it is pale creamy gray, with the front part of the head a bright yellow; toward the rear of the body there is a bluish overcast. The eyes have a tear-shaped pupil, giving the fish a sad expression. The mouth is relatively large; the single and pelvic fins are pastel blue.
Gender: Unknown
Breeding: This is a paternal mouth brooder.
Special care: A shy species that resides in a burrow built in the substrate (which should be deep enough to accommodate the burrow), with only its yellow head protruding. It is most suited to a reef tank or a species aquarium.

PLATAX ORBICULARIS
Batfish
FAMILY: *Platacidae*

Range: Indo-Pacific

7 | 96 | 22.4 in (57cm) | 4 in (10cm) | 79°F (26°C)

Characteristics: Juveniles have a very tall body that fills out to form a disc shape with adulthood. The body is reddish-brown in young specimens, with a darker stripe toward the head, but the stripe may fade with increasing age. Its forehead rises very steeply from the snout, and the dark-centered red eyes are set high. The dark dorsal and anal fins are very long-based and tall, almost encircling the body. The pelvic fins are also long.
Gender: Unknown
Breeding: Unknown
Special care: A constantly hungry species, the batfish grows quickly in the aquarium and so needs ample space and deep water.

EQUETUS ACUMINATUS
High hat; cubbyu
FAMILY: *Sciaenidae*

Range: Carribean

8 | 60 | 10 in (25cm) | 6 in (15cm) | 79°F (26°C)

Characteristics: As a juvenile the body is white, with three longitudinal black stripes, and a remarkably long, white dorsal fin with a black spot about halfway along its outer edge. The stripes extend to the caudal fin, and the paired fins are also striped in black and white. In adults the dorsal fin becomes shorter, and the body and fins gradually become a dark gray color, retaining the stripes only on the sides.
Gender: Unknown
Breeding: Unknown
Special care: It is important to provide hiding places for this shy, secretive species. Feed small, live invertebrates, as the fish often find it difficult to acclimatize to typical aquarium foods.

EQUETUS LANCEOLATUS
Jacknife fish
FAMILY: *Scianeidae*

Range: Western Atlantic

8 | 60 | 9 in (23cm) | 6 in (15cm) | 79°F (26°C)

Characteristics: The body is pure white, with a black bar through the eye, another across the posterior edge of the gill cover, and a dramatic, sickle-shaped one that extends from the lower element of the caudal fin to the tip of the dorsal. Juveniles are yellow, rather than white, but they never lack the black bars.
Gender: Unknown
Breeding: Unknown
Special care: This is a nocturnal fish that needs caves to hide in. It may find it difficult to acclimatize to aquarium conditions.

PTEROIS RADIATA
White-fin lionfish
FAMILY: *Scorpaenidae*

Range: Red Sea, Indo-Pacific

9¾ in (24cm)   4⅞ in (12.5cm)   79°F (26°C)

Characteristics: The body is reddish-brown and crossed by narrow white lines that branch out at their top ends and extend into the extended front spiny rays of the dorsal fin and into horny extensions above the eyes; the lower ends extend into the pelvic and pectoral fins. The extended pectoral fins have the first white-edged rays lacking tissue between them.

Gender: Unknown
Breeding: Unknown
Special care: This is a peaceful ambush predator that can be weaned on to dead foods; however, it should never be trusted with smaller fish or shrimps. The spines are venomous, and this fish should be handled extremely carefully.

PTEROIS VOLITANS
Lionfish
FAMILY: *Scorpaenidae*

Range: Red Sea, Indian, and Pacific Oceans

15 in (38cm)   8 in (20cm)   79°F (26°C)

Characteristics: The body is white; it is crossed vertically by alternating narrow and thick deep brown-red bars. The similarly colored eyes are well camouflaged. There is a pair of "horns" on the head. Its mouth is very large and may have extra barbel-like growths. The first rays of the dorsal fin are colored in alternate stripes of white and brown-red, and are spiny and very poisonous. The pelvic fins are similarly structured and colored.
Gender: Unknown
Breeding: Unknown
Special care: Handle with extreme caution, because the venom in the fin rays is just short of being lethal; if you are affected, seek medical help. This species needs plenty of retreats, and suitable amounts of living or dead meaty foods.

SIGANUS VULPINUS
Foxface, badgerfish
FAMILY: *Siganidae*

Range: Western Pacific

2 | 48

9⅜ in
(24cm)

7 in
(18cm)

79°F
(26°C)

Characteristics: A very distinctive-looking fish with a narrow pointed face and snout. The body and fins are yellow except for the head, which has a black patch running from the front of the dorsal fin down to the mouth. Behind this is a white area overlaid with a black chest patch that fades toward the top of the white patch.

Gender: Unknown

Breeding: Unknown

Special care: It is aggressive toward its own kind, but peaceful with other fish. Make sure you feed plenty of vegetable matter in the diet. Take care when handling this fish, as it has venomous spines in the dorsal and anal fins capable of inflicting painful stings.

When alarmed or frightened, the foxfaced fish will erect its anal and dorsal spines as a defense mechanism.

SPHYRAENA BARRACUDA
Barracuda
FAMILY: *Sphyraenidae*

Range: Atlantic region, from Massachusetts to Brazil

9 | 144

6⅝ ft
(2m)

6⅝ ft
(2m)

79°F
(26°C)

Characteristics: Famous for being a supposed danger to humans, an actual unprovoked attack by this fish has never been recorded. It is a large, silvery fish with a torpedo-like shape, great agility, and long, sharp teeth. The body is usually, but not always, marked with black blotches.

Gender: Unknown

Breeding: Unknown

Special care: It feeds exclusively on other fish, and the powerful jaws and canine teeth of a large specimen are capable of severing a human hand at the wrist. This fish is definitely not a suitable choice for any but the most specialized aquarium, tended by an expert aquarist.

HIPPOCAMPUS ERECTUS
Giant Atlantic seahorse
FAMILY: *Syngnathidae*

Range: Tropical Atlantic

9 | 36 | 6 in (15cm) | 6 in (15cm) | 79°F (26°C)

Characteristics: Seahorses need no introduction. Despite their strange appearance they are still fish, just ones that have turned themselves around so their stomach points forward and the dorsal fin provides its propulsion. Its coloring is quite variable, but usually consists of mottled brown or dark gray.
Gender: The male has a pouch on his stomach.
Breeding: Female seahorses become pregnant after an elaborate courtship ritual, and mate for life.

Special care: It needs suitable décor that mimics its sea-grass habitat, and an abundant supply of the living foods it lives on, including small crustaceans and fish larvae. Seahorses are best kept as mated pairs in their own aquarium.

PRIONOTUS OPHYRAS
Sea robin
FAMILY: *Trigilidae*

Range: North Carolina to the Caribbean

5 | 36 | 6 in (15cm) | 4 in (10cm) | 79°F (26°C)

Characteristics: This remarkable fish actually "walks" on the elongated spines of its ventral fins. Divers have also observed them using their fin spines to overturn rubble in search of food. They are generally mottled gray or reddish-brown, to match the bottom over which they forage. They move slowly and deliberately through the vegetation, feeding on small invertebrates.
Gender: Unknown
Breeding: Unknown

Special care: Provide décor that mimics the sea-grass habitat, either with artificial or living plants; and also a bottom of sand, shell fragments, and coral pieces. Feed with small live shrimps, clamworms, and chopped shellfish, shrimp, or fish meat, once accustomed to captivity.

Glossary

ACIDIC Referring to a solution with a pH less than 7.

ADIPOSE FIN Small extra fin between the main dorsal and caudal fins of some fish.

AERATION Process of adding extra air into the aquarium water.

AEROBIC Requiring oxygen.

AIRPUMP A small electrically-driven vibrating diaphragm device used to pump air into the aquarium.

AIRSTONE Device for splitting the air flow from the airpump into small bubbles.

ALGAE Tiny, unicellular plants that may coat aquatic plants or cause a green cloudiness in the water.

ALKALINE Referring to a solution with a pH greater than 7.

ANAL FIN Single vertical fin beneath the rear of the body.

ANABANTID Family of fish with an auxiliary breathing organ that enables them to utilize atmospheric air.

ANAEROBIC Not requiring oxygen.

BARBELS Elongate "whiskers" around the mouth of some fish having a sensory function.

BIOLOGICAL FILTRATION Water-purifying method that uses bacteria to remove dissolved toxic substances.

BRACKISH Mixture of fresh and saltwater; estuarine conditions.

BRINE SHRIMP *Artemia salina*, shrimp whose eggs can be hatched to make excellent first food for fry.

CARBON Filtration medium that absorbs dissolved material from the water.

CAUDAL FIN Fin at the rear of the body.

CAUDAL PEDUNCLE Rear part of the body, just in front of the caudal fin.

CHROMATOPHORES Color cells.

COLDWATER Generally refers to fish kept under ambient temperatures, without additional heating, i.e., goldfish.

CONDITIONING Separating the sexes and feeding with high-quality foods prior to spawning.

COVER GLASS Sheet of plastic or glass on top of the tank to protect lighting equipment from spray damage and to prevent fish from jumping out.

DEMERSAL Heavier than water.

DIFFUSER See Airstone.

DORSAL (fin) Usually a single fin (some species have two) on the top surface of the fish.

EGGLAYER Fish whose eggs are fertilized and hatched externally.

FAMILY Group containing several genera. See Genus.

FANCY GOLDFISH Aquarium-developed strains or varieties from *Carassius auratus*.

FILTER Device for removing suspended or dissolved wastes from aquarium water.

FILTER MEDIUM Any material used as a trapping, straining, absorptive, or bacterial-colonizing device in a filter system.

FINS External paddle-shaped growths, either single or paired, extending from the body of a fish.

FOAM FRACTIONATION Definition of protein-skimming process. See Protein Skimmer.

FRY Recently hatched fish that have not absorbed the yolk sac.

GENUS A group of related species within a family.

GILLS Organ by which fish extract dissolved oxygen from the water.

GONOPODIUM Modified anal fin of male livebearing fish.

GRAVEL NET Plastic netting buried horizontally in the substrate to prevent fish from digging.

GRAVID Describing female livebearer when carrying young, i.e., pregnant.

GUANIN Crystals of urea deposited beneath the skin providing an iridescent sheen.

HAND-STRIPPING The manual removal of eggs from a female, and milt from a male fish. Practiced in the breeding of fancy goldfish and certain marine species.

HARDNESS Condition of water due to dissolved salts.

HOOD Lid of aquarium containing lighting equipment.

LATERAL LINE Row of pierced scales along flanks giving access to nervous system that detects vibrations in the surrounding water.

LENGTH Measured from the snout to end of caudal peduncle, excluding caudal fin.

LIVEBEARER Fish whose eggs are fertilized and developed internally within the body of the parent, either with or without nourishment from parent.

MARINE Pertaining to the sea; saltwater.

MEDIUM Any material used to filter or treat water.

MILT Fertilizing fluid of male fish.

MOUTHBROODER Incubation of externally fertilized eggs occurs within one parent's throat cavity.

NITROBACTER Nitrifying bacteria turning nitrite into nitrate.

NITROSOMONAS Nitrifying bacteria turning ammonia-based compounds into nitrite.

OPERCULUM Gill cover.

OSMOREGULATION Method by which a fish regulates, or balances, its internal salt content against that of the surrounding water.

OVIPAROUS See Egglayer.

OVIPOSITOR Tube for depositing eggs, extended at breeding times by the female of egg-depositing fish.

OVOVIVIPAROUS Livebearing with no nourishment gained from parent. See Livebearer.

OZONE Triatomic oxygen used in water purification.

PECTORALS Paired fins, one on each side of the body, posterior to the gills.

PELAGIC Lighter than water; used in reference to drifting fertilized eggs after spawning.

PELVIC Paired fins, just ahead of the anal fin.

pH Measure, on a logarithmic scale, of acidity or alkalinity of a solution.

PHARYNGEAL TEETH Teeth in the throat of cyprinid species.

PHOTOSYNTHESIS Process by which, under illumination, green plants utilize carbon dioxide and nutrients to build sugars and starches, and give off surplus oxygen.

POWER FILTER Filtration equipment powered by electric impeller.

POWERHEAD Electric impeller fitted to top of return tube from undergravel filtration systems.

PROTEIN SKIMMER Device to remove dissolved organic substances from the water in marine aquariums.

QUARANTINE Period of isolation for new fish to prevent the introduction of disease into the aquarium.

RAYS Tissue-supporting bones in fins.

REFLECTOR See Hood.

SALT Sodium chloride or, in marine systems, synthetic salt mix used to make artificial sea water.

SCALES Small platelets covering the fish's skin.

SCUTES Bony plates (in the place of scales) covering the fish's skin, especially in some catfish.

SHOAL Large number of a single species of fish swimming together.

SINGLE-TAILS Goldfish that have only a single anal and caudal fin.

SOFT Condition of water due to lack of dissolved salts.

SPAWNING The reproductive action of fish.

SPAWNING TANK A separate aquarium for housing a breeding pair (or shoal) of adult fish.

SPECIES Groups of actually (or potentially) interbreeding individuals that do not interbreed with members of other, similar groups.

SPECIFIC GRAVITY (S.G.) Ratio of densities between salt and freshwater. Used to determine the strength of synthetic sea water in marine systems.

STRAIN Aquarium-developed variant, e.g., longer-finned than, or differently colored from, a natural species.

SUBSTRATE Material covering the aquarium tank floor.

SWIM BLADDER Internal organ that provides neutral buoyancy.

TUBERCLES Small white pimples seen on the head and/or gill covers of many male coldwater cyprinids when spawning.

TWIN-TAILS Goldfish that have divided anal and caudal fins.

ULTRA-VIOLET (U.V.) LAMPS Special lamps for disinfecting water.

UNDERGRAVEL FILTRATION See Biological Filtration.

VENTRAL Pertaining to the underside of the body; may be used in the plural form to refer to ventral fins.

VIVIPAROUS Livebearing with nourishment gained from parent. See Livebearer.

Index of Scientific Names

Index of Common Names

Key to care symbols

This handy pull-out key can be used as a quick reference
to check the fish care symbols in this book.

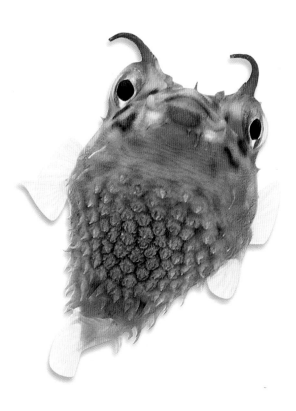

Credits

Quarto would like to thank and acknowledge the following for supplying pictures reproduced in this book:

Key: l left, r right, c center, t top, b bottom

page 10br Soames Summerhays / Natural Visions
page 11 Ian Took / Natural Visions
page 16cl and bl Heather Angel / Natural Visions
page 40b Derek Lambert

All other photographs and illustrations are the copyright of Quarto Publishing plc. While every effort has been made to credit contributors, Quarto would like to apologize should there have been any omissions or errors.

The publisher would like to thank the following aquariums for allowing us to photograph their fish:

Miami Aquatics
6830 Simms Street
Hollywood
Florida 33024
USA

Ornamental Fish Distributors Inc.
3802 NW 32nd Avenue
Miami
Florida 33142
USA

The Goldfish Bowl
118-120, Magdalen Road
Oxford OX4 1RQ
United Kingdom
www.thegoldfishbowl.co.uk
www.photomax.org.uk.

Z-Fish International Inc
7405 41st, Number 2
Miami
Florida 33166
USA